MW00795915

War and Diplomacy in Kashmir
1947–48

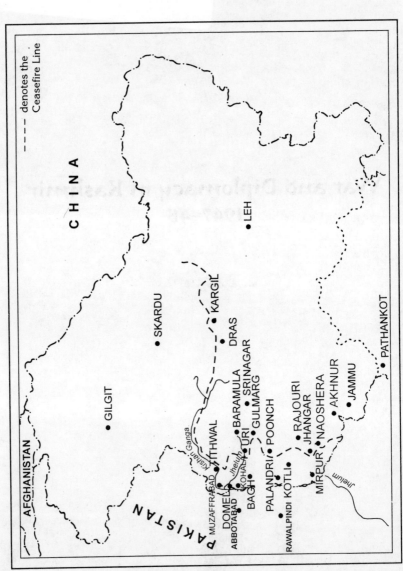

Sketch Map of Jammu & Kashmir

- - - - denotes the
Ceasefire Line

CHINA

AFGHANISTAN

PAKISTAN

GILGIT

SKARDU

KARGIL

DRAS

LEH

MUZAFFRABAD

ABBOTABAD

DOMEL

TITHWAL

BARAMULA

SRINAGAR

GULMARG

KOHALA URI

BAGH

PALANDRI

RAWALPINDI

KOTLI

MIRPUR

POONCH

RAJOURI

JHANGAR

NAOSHERA

AKHNUR

JAMMU

PATHANKOT

Ganga

Kishan

Jhelum

Jhelum

In Memory of My Father

In Memory of My Father

Contents

Contents

1
Introduction

The conflict which broke out between India and Pakistan in 1947 was unique in the annals of modern warfare: it was a war in which both the opposing armies were led by nationals of a third country. British generals commanded the armies of the newly independent states of India and Pakistan. In India, moreover, the Defence Committee of the Cabinet was chaired by Lord Mountbatten, not Prime Minister Nehru. Thus the course and outcome of the Indo–Pakistan conflict cannot be explained simply in terms of the political objectives and military capabilities of the antagonists. A crucial determinant was the role of the British officers at the helm of the two armies and, in the case of India, the British Governor-General, Lord Mountbatten.

While it was unique in this one respect, the first Indo–Pakistan war was also a typical third world conflict from a broader perspective. External factors tend to play a major part in wars between medium or small states. Their dependence on major powers for military supplies, economic assistance and diplomatic support makes these states vulnerable to external pressures. Thus the positions taken by the great powers can influence the duration, intensity and even the outcome of such conflicts. The Kashmir war of 1947–48 is one such example. For both India and Pakistan, Britain was the leading overseas partner in trade, industry and finance. Both countries turned to Britain for military equipment, spares and oil supplies. The war was unique only in the extent to which the two new states were vulnerable to British influence on account of the presence of British officers at the

seniormost levels of their armed forces. These officers were in a position to directly influence the course of the war through the advice
they tendered to their respective governments and the manner in
which they implemented—or ignored—government directives.

India and Pakistan emerged as independent states in a world dominated by two-and-a-half great powers. Two ascendant great powers—the United States and the Soviet Union—strove to consolidate
their respective positions in a war-devastated Europe. Britain, a great
power in rapid decline, no longer possessed the resources required
to play a global role. In March 1947, she handed over to Washington
the task of securing Greece and Turkey against a communist take-
over and she was soon to bow out of her Palestine mandate. Nevertheless, Britain still enjoyed the prestige of a great power. She saw
herself as a true partner of the United States—equal in status and
influence if no longer in actual power. She still ruled over a vast
empire and her American ally continued to defer to her the leading
role in South Asia and the Middle East. It was only in the next decade
that the United States would supplant Britain as the dominant power
in the Indian Ocean area. At the time of India's independence, Washington was content to follow the British lead in the region.

Britain was thus exceptionally well situated to influence the course
of events in the first Indo–Pakistan war. She was largely responsible
for shaping the attitude of the Western powers and, thus, the international context of the conflict. Moreover, her voice could not be ignored
by belligerents depending upon her for military and oil supplies. Above
all, British officers in India and Pakistan were in a unique position to
directly shape military events. Yet, curiously, the role of the British
government and Britons holding high office in India and Pakistan has
received little attention. Moreover, the military and diplomatic developments of 1947–48 have been studied in isolation from each other,
ignoring their interlinkages. As a result, basic questions concerning
the war are still shrouded in mystery: Why did India not carry the war
into Pakistan, as she was to do in 1965? Why did she take the Kashmir
issue to the United Nations? Why was no serious effort made to clear
Pakistani forces from the western areas of Poonch and Mirpur? Why
did India accept a ceasefire when she clearly had military superiority?

India in Imperial Strategy

A study of Britain's policy regarding the Kashmir war must begin with
an examination of her strategic interests in the subcontinent. For two

centuries, the Indian Empire was both the object and the instrument of British strategy in the Indian Ocean. The defence of India was secured by a twofold policy. In the first place, Britain controlled the entry points into the Indian Ocean through a ring of naval bases. Port Said and Aden guarded the entrance through the Red Sea, the Cape route was controlled through the base at Simonstown in South Africa, while bases in Singapore and Fremantle guarded the entrance from the Pacific.

The second element of Britain's imperial policy was to prevent any land-based great power from securing an outlet into the Indian Ocean. The object, in other words, was to prevent the outflanking of British sea-power. In the nineteenth century, Britain viewed the Turkish Empire in Arabia and the kingdoms of Iran and Afghanistan as a buffer against Russia's expansion to the shores of the Indian Ocean. Upto World War I, Britain sought to preserve the integrity of the Ottoman Empire in Asia in the belief that its collapse might advance Russian interests.

The defence of the Indian Empire was thus organised on a regional basis through a policy which effectively converted the Indian Ocean into a 'British lake'. It is equally true that it was the Indian Empire which made it possible to implement this policy. With its central situation in the Indian Ocean, India was the focal point of sea and, later, air communications in the region. It was a great supply and storage centre. Above all, the Indian army was the instrument of British control over the littoral countries. Indian military units were permanently garrisoned at Aden, Singapore and Hong Kong. At various times, Indian troops were sent overseas to protect British imperial interests in East and North Africa, Sudan, the Gulf, Malaya and even China. When the regional defence system was breached by Japan in World War II, the Indian Army—grown to a strength of over 2 million—played a major role in the allied counter-offensive which finally drove out the Japanese from Southeast Asia. On the day of the Japanese surrender, Indian personnel accounted for over 80 per cent of the Commonwealth and Empire forces in the Southeast Asia theatre.

Thus the entire edifice of British imperial strategy was built up around the Indian Empire. The defence of India was a major consideration in imperial expansion and, conversely, the protection of this expanded empire and of the imperial lines of communications with Australasia was secured through the military manpower, bases and resources provided by India. Right upto World War II, British military planners were apt to describe India as the 'keystone in the arch of Imperial defence'.

This strategic picture began to change even before the end of British rule in India and Pakistan. The changes resulted mainly from two factors: oil and air power. The invention of the internal combustion engine and the discovery of petroleum deposits in Iran in 1908 steadily raised the importance of the Gulf region. Territories which were originally brought under British rule or influence in order to secure India's maritime flanks, now came to acquire a strategic importance in their own right. By 1947, the defence of the Middle Eastern oil-fields and the sea-lanes from the Gulf was seen as vitally important for Western defence. Simultaneously, the growing importance of air power exposed the limitations of a sea-based strategy of imperial domination. A dramatic demonstration of air power was provided when the Japanese airforce attacked and sank the much-vaunted battleships, the *Prince of Wales* and the *Repulse*, off the coast of Singapore in December 1941. These new realities combined to shift the strategic focus northwards from peninsular India to the Gulf and its neighbourhood.

With the approach of Indian independence, British defence planners took a new look at the strategic picture. In July 1946, the Viceroy, Field Marshal Wavell, forwarded to London an appreciation prepared by the British Indian Chiefs of Staff Committee.[1] The paper dwelt on the importance of India as a military base, her 'almost inexhaustible supply of manpower', and her rapidly growing industrial capacity. Its most significant feature, however, was the re-assessment of India's geo-strategic value. This reflected a notable shift of emphasis from the naval to the air factor. It noted that shore-based aircraft and guided missiles were making it increasingly difficult to protect shipping in narrow waters such as the Mediterranean. 'In effect our L. of C. [Lines of Communication] will gradually be pushed Southwards and we shall come to rely on the Cape route to the East much more than on the Mediterranean.' The diminished importance of the Suez route meant that 'from a Naval point of view a hostile India within the next few years would not seriously affect our position'.

The service chiefs observed that, unlike maritime communications, the 'Imperial Air Communications between the U.K. and Australia and the Far East must of necessity pass through India', given the existing range of aircraft. It was possible to develop a string of island bases (such as the Seychelles, Diego Garcia and the Cocos Islands) as a subsidiary route for long range aircraft operating from East Africa or 'Arabia', but few existing types of aircraft had the required range and it would be many years before fighter aircraft could use such routes. India was, therefore, an essential link for the Imperial Strategic Air Reserves.

It was also essential that the Soviet Union be denied air bases in India. 'If India was dominated by Russia with powerful air forces it is likely that we should have to abandon our command of the Persian Gulf and the Northern Indian Ocean routes', making it impossible to ensure the uninterrupted flow of vitally important oil supplies.

The paper thus highlighted the threat to British interests which might be posed if an independent India were to come under Russian domination or influence. The strategically important oil supplies from the Gulf region would be at jeopardy and air communications with Malaya, Australia and New Zealand would also be disrupted.

A parallel exercise undertaken in London produced similar conclusions, but the UK Chiefs of Staff placed even greater emphasis on the air factor. They pointed out that, apart from India's resources and growing industrial capacity, 'her territory provides important bases for offensive air action and for the support of our forces in the Indian Ocean and neighbouring areas'. Britain would 'require the right to move formations and units, particularly air units, into India at short notice, in case of threatened international emergency'. Thus while the service chiefs in India pointed to the importance of denying the Soviet Union the use of Indian air bases, the UK Chiefs of Staff underlined the importance of securing access to these bases for offensive operations in the context of Middle Eastern defence.

The UK Chiefs of Staff pushed the analysis to a further conclusion. They emphasised the need to ensure that British officers should continue to serve in the Indian armed forces after independence.

If the [Indian] demand for withdrawal were extended to include all British personnel including those in the service of the Indian government, the fulfillment of any of our strategic requirements would be improbable. It is in our view essential that the Indian Government should be persuaded to accept the assistance of the necessary number of British personnel.[2]

There was general agreement in London about the vital importance of securing British strategic interests in India either through a continuing Commonwealth link or by negotiating a defence treaty, though Nehru's foreign policy pronouncements gave rise to deep pessimism about the prospects of securing the Congress party's co-operation. The India Office advised: 'We think it unlikely that India will wish to remain within the Commonwealth, at any rate as at present constituted.'[3] Nevertheless, on 13 March 1947, at a meeting of the India and Burma Committee of the Cabinet, at which Mountbatten was present, it was agreed that the 'Viceroy should encourage any moves that might be initiated by Indian leaders in favour of the continuation of India within the British Commonwealth'.[4] Attlee's formal instructions to the Viceroy-designate also addressed the problem in the following words:

> You will point out the need for continued collaboration in the security of the Indian Ocean for which provision might be made in an agreement between the two countries. At a suitable date His Majesty's Government would be ready to send military and other experts to India to assist in discussing the terms of such an agreement.[5]

The Pakistan Factor

The military analyses carried out till the time of Mountbatten's departure for India were based on the assumption that India would remain united, at least in the sphere of defence. The deep misgivings in Whitehall over India's willingness to cooperate in a scheme of Commonwealth defence were related to the position of Congress leaders. As for the Muslim League, it was assumed from the outset that a future Pakistan, if it came into existence, would seek an alliance with Britain. As early as October 1946, the India Office advised the Chiefs of Staff Committee that 'if India were to split up into two or more parts, the Muslim areas and the States would probably be anxious to remain in the Commonwealth—if, in such circumstances, we were willing to have them.'[6] In the same vein, the Permanent Under Secretary at the Foreign Office speculated:

> If India falls apart we may, I suppose, expect the Moslems to try and enlist British support by offering us all sorts of military and political facilities, to commit ourselves to what would be in effect the defence of one Indian State against another?[7]

Again, in January 1947, Lord Pethick-Lawrence, the Secretary of State for India, observed that the Muslim League would be guided by expediency and might be influenced by defence considerations in favour of a tie with the British Commonwealth.[8]

On assuming the Viceroyalty, Mountbatten lost no time in exploring the views of Congress and Muslim League leaders on the related issues of a Commonwealth link and retention of the services of British officers in the armed forces. Within a day of assuming office, he sought to impress on Nehru the need to retain British officers in order to prevent a breakdown of law and order. Nehru was unimpressed; he said that India wished to retain friendly ties with Britain but she could not stay on in the Commonwealth.[9] The Muslim League, as the British had anticipated, was most anxious to retain both connections. Liaquat Ali Khan informed the new Viceroy that Pakistan would want to remain in the Commonwealth and would require British officers for her armed forces.[10] Jinnah, pressing the Viceroy to accept his demand for Pakistan, said: 'I do not wish to make any improper suggestion to you, but you must realise that the new Pakistan is almost certain to ask for dominion status within the Empire.'[11]

The Viceroy, who had not yet given up hope of preserving Indian unity, gave no encouragement to the Muslim League leaders. He told Liaquat that he was not prepared to even discuss the question of any part of India remaining within the Empire unless the suggestion came jointly from all parties. The astute Jinnah was not taken in. He subsequently pointed out to Mountbatten: 'You cannot kick us out; there is no precedence for forcing parts of the Empire to leave against their will.' He added that he had been assured by Churchill that the British people would never stand for the forcible expulsion of Pakistan from the Empire.[12]

The responses of the Congress and Muslim League leaders gave rise to a question of vital importance. If Pakistan alone wished to retain the Commonwealth link, should she be allowed to do so? There was a sharp difference of views on this question in the Viceregal Lodge itself. Mountbatten was opposed to accepting an application from only one of the two states. To do so would be to 'back up one part of India against the other, which might involve the United Kingdom in war'. General Ismay, his Chief of Staff, held the contrary view. He felt it would be impossible on both moral and material grounds to eject Pakistan from the Commonwealth. British strategy required the use of bases in the subcontinent. Moreover, relations with the 'whole Mussulman bloc' had to be considered. As for the possibility of a 'civil war', he felt that one way to avoid it would be through 'British backing, if not of the whole, of one part of India'. He suggested that this could be ensured through air power alone.[13]

On Attlee's instructions, the UK Chiefs of Staff met in May 1947 to formulate a strategic appreciation of the situation which would arise if one of the post-partition states desired to remain in the Common-wealth while the rest of India decided to leave. The service chiefs were unanimous in their view that an application should be accepted both on moral and material grounds. Marshal of the RAF, Lord Tedder, pointed to the great importance of air base facilities in 'N.W. India'. Field Marshal Lord Montgomery argued that it would be a tremendous asset if 'Pakistan, particularly the North West', re-mained within the Commonwealth. The bases, airfields and ports in 'North West India' would be invaluable for Commonwealth defence. Admiral Cunningham maintained that if Pakistan's application were rejected, it would shatter Britain's relations with the 'whole Moslem world' to the detriment of her strategic position in the Middle East and North Africa as well as the Indian subcontinent. This dubious view of Middle Eastern politics was shared by Tedder, who referred ominously to the 'repercussions throughout the entire Middle East' if Pakistan were to be ejected from the Commonwealth.[14]

Defence Minister Alexander presented the other side of the picture. He pointed out that if Jinnah's application was accepted, Britain would lay herself open to the charge that she had acted in bad faith, that she never had any real intention of leaving India and that, in order to obtain her strategic requirements, had manoeuvred the coun-try into partition. Ismay, who was present at the meeting, explained the Viceroy's views. Mountbatten felt it would be disastrous to allow Pakistan to stay on in the Commonwealth by herself. This might cause the involvement of Britain in a war between 'Hindustan' and Pakistan and incur the permanent hostility of the former. Ismay, how-ever, added that in his own opinion Indo–British relations would suf-fer no permanent damage if Pakistan were allowed to remain in the Commonwealth. He predicted that 'though Hindustan would be loud in denunciation of our bad faith at first, they would not ... be perma-nently hostile to the British Commonwealth, or seek to ally them-selves with any other great power'. The Chiefs of Staff came to the conclusion that:

*From the strategic point of view there were overwhelming argu-
ments in favour of West Pakistan remaining within the Commonwealth, namely, that we should obtain important strategic facilities, the port of Karachi, air bases and the support of Moslem
manpower in the future; be able to ensure the continued integrity
of Afghanistan; and be able to increase our prestige and improve
our position throughout the Moslem world. Whilst the acceptance of Pakistan only into the Commonwealth would involve a
commitment for its support against Hindustan, the danger would
be small, and it was doubtful if Pakistan ... would ask for more
than the support of British Officers in executive and advisory
positions.*[15]

In June, an agreement was reached between the British authorities, the Congress and the Muslim League on a plan for the transfer
of power to two independent states, India and Pakistan, both of
which would initially have dominion status. Pakistan was now a reality
and British defence planners embarked on a final pre-independence
review of their strategic requirements. In July, the UK Chiefs of Staff
reiterated that the 'main and overriding consideration should be to
retain both India and Pakistan within the British Commonwealth or at
any rate ensure that they will cooperate [militarily] with us'. They
emphasised the importance of bases in the subcontinent, pointing
specifically to the 'use of strategic airfields, primarily in Pakistan, in
the event of a major war'. The Chiefs of Staff concluded that, while
the ideal outcome would be to secure the cooperation of both India
and Pakistan, 'on the other hand, the area of Pakistan is strategically
the most important in the continent of India and the majority of our
strategic requirements could be met, though with considerably
greater difficulty, by an agreement with Pakistan alone'.[16]

Thus by August 1947, the British authorities had determined that
their strategic interests in the subcontinent lay primarily in Pakistan,
though hopes of a defence treaty with India as well had not yet been
given up. The decisive consideration was the proximity of air bases in
West Pakistan to the Gulf region. This was buttressed by the view,
however inaccurate, that Britain's relations with the 'whole Mussulman bloc' would be jeopardised in the absence of close ties with
Pakistan. The traditional perception of a Russian threat via Afghanistan was an added factor, as was the availability of Pakistan's naval
bases and military manpower. A defence treaty with India would be a

valuable bonus but it was not absolutely essential for imperial strategy.

The growing role of strategic airpower and the vital importance of Middle Eastern oil had transformed British policy in Asia. For over a century, British policy in the Gulf had largely been shaped by the strategic interests of her Indian Empire. This was no longer the case by the time India and Pakistan took their place as independent states in the comity of nations. By 1947, the tables had been turned—Britain's strategic interests in the Gulf and Middle East had become a major factor in her South Asia policy.

The 'Stand Down' Instructions

British military planners, as we saw earlier, attached great importance to the continued presence of British officers in the armed forces of India and Pakistan. Apart from the direct influence which could thus be exercised over the two newly independent states, it was believed that the retention of British officers in the executive and engineering branches was necessary to ensure serviceability of the bases and facilities which Britain might require in the event of a war. The lengths to which London was prepared to go in order to ensure retention of British officers is illustrated by the case of *H.M.S. Achilles*, which, under the new name of *INS Delhi*, was to become the pride of the navy of independent India. On Mountbatten's suggestion, it was decided to transfer this modern cruiser to India as it would ensure a continuing dependence on the services of British naval officers![17]

If Pakistan welcomed British officers with open arms, their reception in India was less effusive. Nehru planned for complete nationalisation of the armed forces by June 1948—the date originally envisaged for the transfer of power. However, the partition agreement provided the service chiefs with an unanswerable argument for holding up progress. They maintained that 'it was quite impossible to both reconstitute the Armed Forces and to proceed with rapid nationalisation at the same time'.[18] Nehru reluctantly accepted a delay but he continued to press for early nationalisation. 'It is incongruous for the army of a free country not to have its own officers in the highest ranks', he wrote to Mountbatten in July 1947.[19]

The continued presence of British officers in the armed forces of the two dominions posed a potential problem. British defence planners had formed the clear-eyed assessment that hostilities could well break out between the two new dominions. With the approach of independence and partition, Field Marshal Auchinleck, the Commander-in-Chief of the British Indian army, grew concerned about this possibility. He raised the question with Mountbatten in July 1947. Auchinleck proposed that if hostilities broke out between the two dominions, or if one of them took coercive action against a princely state like Travancore, British officers should not be allowed to take an active part in operations.[20]

The Viceroy was in full agreement. He knew, however, that Congress leaders, already impatient over the pace of nationalisation, would react strongly to the idea that they could not count on the unconditional loyalty of British officers in their army. He thus chose to put the position across in an allusive way. On 29 July 1947, at a meeting of the Provisional Joint Defence Council attended by Jinnah, Liaquat Ali Khan and Sardar Patel, the Viceroy referred to General Rees' force which had been tasked to put down communal disturbances. Mountbatten emphasised that there were British officers in practically every unit of the force and they were the best safeguard not only against attempts to subvert the troops but also in restraining the troops of the two dominions from fighting against each other, since under no circumstances could British officers be ranged on opposite sides.[21]

The implication was that in a tense situation between India and Pakistan, British officers in the two armies would use their influence to avert an outbreak of hostilities and, in the event of their failing to do so, they would be withdrawn from both armies. Judging from later events, it would appear that neither Patel nor Jinnah fully understood the Viceroy's hint. Nevertheless, immediately after the transfer of power, orders were issued by Auchinleck to British officers requiring them to 'Stand Down' in the event of a conflict between the two dominions.[22]

11
Junagadh—A Curtain Raiser

The 'Stand Down' instructions were first tested in the princely state of Junagadh. Belonging to the group of Kathiawar states, Junagadh was surrounded by neighbours who had acceded to India. Junagadh itself was a territorial patchwork quilt: enclaves belonging to neighbours were located within its borders and Junagadh, in turn, owned enclaves within the territories of other states. The position was further complicated by the claims of the Nawab of Junagadh to the overlordship of Babariawad and Mangrol, both of whose rulers were soon to accede to India. The Nawab of Junagadh was one of the most colourful eccentrics among the Indian princes. Famous for his devotion to his 800 pet dogs, he is said to have employed an equal number of manservants to cater to their canine needs!

On 15 August 1947, the Nawab unexpectedly announced that he had decided to accede to Pakistan. The offer elicited no immediate response from Pakistan. On 21 August, V.P. Menon, the Secretary to the States Ministry, wrote to the Pakistan High Commissioner asking for an indication of Karachi's policy. Menon pointed out that Junagadh was not geographically contiguous to Pakistan. Moreover, a large majority of its population was non-Muslim. Menon therefore emphasised the need for consulting the views of the people in regard to accession.[1] A reminder was sent after a fortnight but that, too, drew no response. On 12 September, Nehru proposed sending a telegram to Pakistan to convey India's readiness to accept the verdict of the people of Junagadh on the question of accession to either India or

Pakistan. Since Lord Ismay, Mountbatten's Chief of Staff, was flying to Karachi, it was decided to send the message through him. Karachi refused to take cognisance of the telegram on the grounds that it bore no number or signature to show that its issue had been authorised! However, on 13 September—nearly a month after the Nawab made his offer—Pakistan finally informed India that she had accepted Junagadh's accession.

This precipitated a tense situation in the Kathiawar area. A mass protest movement rapidly gathered strength among the inhabitants of Junagadh and neighbouring states. The rulers of the other Kathiawar states joined in condemning the Nawab's accession to Pakistan. The Indian government came under strong public pressure to save the situation.

Feelings ran so high that Mountbatten feared his ministers would take recourse to armed action in Junagadh. Though India refused to accept the validity of the Nawab's accession to Pakistan, Mountbatten himself regarded it as legally valid even if politically and morally indefensible.[2] In this view, armed action in Junagadh would amount to an act of war against Pakistan. General Ismay drew Mountbatten's attention to the singular delicacy of his constitutional position. Ismay urged that the Governor-General had a right not only to be informed but also to be consulted on measures which might lead to armed conflict. At the same time,

> for the Governor-General of a British Dominion to acquiesce in action which may lead to war with another British Dominion is completely unprecedented, and I should have thought that this was a matter in which the instructions of His Majesty The King should be sought.[3]

In other words, Ismay advised Mountbatten to play an active role in shaping defence policy, while withholding consent (in the absence of instructions from London) from any decision which might result in a military conflict.

The Indian cabinet met on 17 September to decide on a course of action in Junagadh. Mountbatten sent for Nehru and Sardar Patel in advance of the meeting in order to dissuade them from military action which, he believed, was imminent. Ismay, on his return from Karachi, propagated the view that Pakistan's aim in Junagadh was to lure India into a trap: Karachi was deliberately teasing India into taking precipitate military action which would incur international dis-opprobrium.[4] Mountbatten seized on this argument to dissuade the Indian leaders from armed action. 'With all the force of persuasion possible,' he reported to the King, 'I advised Pandit Nehru and Sardar Patel to take no decision which the world could interpret as putting India in the wrong and Pakistan in the right, and that all the resources of negotiation should first be exhausted.'[5] To the Governor-General's great relief, both the Indian leaders broadly agreed that the prevailing situation did not call for offensive military action.

The Cabinet met later in the day and decided that troops from the forces of states which had acceded to India should be suitably posted around Junagadh but should not occupy Junagadh territory. Second, economic measures—such as discontinuance of fuel supplies—might be adopted to put pressure on Junagadh. Finally, it was decided to send Menon to Junagadh to reason with the state authorities and persuade them to accept the proposal for a reference to the people.[6] In other words, India continued to seek a peaceful resolution of the issue, while building up pressure on the Junagadh authorities.

Mountbatten explained his own role to the King in the following words[7]:

> My chief concern was to prevent the Government of India from committing itself on the Junagadh issue to an act of war against what was now Pakistan territory. My own position was singularly difficult.... For the Governor-General of a Dominion to have acquiesced in action which might lead to a war with another Dominion would have been completely unprecedented.
>
> But at the same time I was aware that my own physical presence as Governor-General of India was the best insurance against an actual outbreak of war with Pakistan. To have compromised my position too far over the preliminary threat of war would have undermined my final position. I was therefore anxious to make it clear to my Government that I was not necessarily opposed to their taking all necessary precautions, military and otherwise, to safeguard their own legitimate interest.[8]

V.P. Menon's visit to Junagadh proved to be unfruitful. The Nawab declined to meet him, pleading illness. Menon had a discussion with the Dewan, Sir Shah Nawaz Bhutto, who agreed that the vast majority of the population of Junagadh wanted to join India. He said that he personally favoured holding a referendum but added that he could not commit the Junagadh government in this matter. Menon realised that further conversation would be a waste of time and terminated the exchange with a warning that the Nawab's dynasty would come to an end if the people decided to take the law into their own hands.

Though it failed to produce progress on Junagadh, Menon's trip had an important result in Mangrol. During his meeting with Menon on 18 September, the Sheikh of Mangrol announced his decision to accede to India and signed the Instrument of Accession. The accession was duly accepted by the Governor-General. Shortly afterwards, the Nawab sought to revoke his accession but this was held to be unlawful. The net result of the episode was that Mangrol joined Babariawad as territories claimed by both India and Junagadh—by the former on the basis of the acts of accession and by the latter on the grounds of the Nawab's claims of overlordship vis-à-vis the rulers of these territories.

Tension rose sharply when the Nawab decided to exercise his claims by sending some of his troops into Babariawad. This was a major escalation in view of the state's accession to India. Sardar Patel maintained that the Nawab's move amounted to an act of aggression against India and called for a strong response. Nehru, however, urged that the constitutional position regarding the status of Babariawad and Mangrol should be fully clarified before any military action was taken. He thought that the opinion of constitutional lawyers should be obtained and communicated to the Junagadh authorities. Only if Junagadh still refused to withdraw its troops from Babariawad and Mangrol should recourse be taken to military action.

A compromise emerged in a meeting between Mountbatten, Nehru and Patel on 22 September 1947. The government decided that the army and navy chiefs should prepare an appreciation of an operation designed to occupy Babariawad, including preparations to go to the assistance of Mangrol. The armed forces were also instructed to be prepared to occupy Junagadh itself if—but only if—the Nawab took further offensive action. A telegram was sent to the Dewan of Junagadh pointing out the constitutional position of Babariawad and Mangrol and demanding the immediate withdrawal of Junagadh troops from Babariawad.[9] Two days later, the Indian government decided to deploy a brigade to Kathiawar for the protection of the states which had acceded to India.

Thus, despite the Nawab's provocation in Babariawad, India held back from military retaliation in Junagadh and even from sending her forces into territories which she regarded as her own. Contingency plans were ordered in case it was decided to adopt a military option but for the present, the main thrust of India's policy was to persuade Junagadh to withdraw from Babariawad, respect Mangrol's accession and accept a referendum to decide her own accession to India or Pakistan.

Hopes for a diplomatic resolution, however, soon suffered a setback. On 25 September, Junagadh responded to India's appeal by refusing to withdraw her troops from Babariawad. On the same day, Pakistan turned down India's proposal for a referendum, stating that this was a matter between the Nawab and his subjects. Meanwhile, Mountbatten had informally consulted a leading British constitutional lawyer who was familiar with the position of Mangrol. The opinion of this authority was that Mangrol's accession to India was valid and there could be no legal objection to sending Indian troops to Mangrol.

A Warning from the Service Chiefs

While Indian ministers were pondering over how to react to Junagadh's intransigence over Babariawad, the service chiefs pressed them to stop the troop movements ordered earlier. The chiefs conveyed that they could play no role in an inter-dominion war. On 27 September, General Sir Rob Lockhart, Admiral Hall and Air Commodore Mukherjee (on behalf of Air Marshal Elmhirst) submitted a joint memorandum to the Defence Minister, Sardar Baldev Singh, expressing concern over the possible results of the military measures being planned to protect Mangrol and Babariawad. They pointed to the 'very real danger' of a clash with Junagadh forces, especially in Babariawad where Junagadh police had been posted. If India took military action in Kathiawad, Pakistan might come to Junagadh's assistance. The service chiefs reiterated General Lockhart's view that the 'Indian Army for a variety of reasons was in no position successfully to conduct large scale operations.' Moreover, 'it was essential with the extremely critical situation in the East Punjab and Delhi ... that nothing should be done which might lead to further demands for troops in other parts of India.'

The service chiefs went on to draw attention to the position of British officers, including themselves, serving with the Indian armed

forces. 'These officers,' they pointed out, 'belong to the British fighting services and it would be impossible for any of them to take part in
a war between the dominions or to be the instrument of planning or
conveying orders to others should the operations now contemplated
lead to such a war, or appear likely to do so.' They concluded by urging that the 'movement of Armed Forces for the projected operations
be stopped and that the dispute regarding Junagadh be settled by
negotiations.'[10]

The Cabinet reacted sharply to this invasion of the political domain
by the military. Sardar Patel was outraged by what he regarded as the
disloyalty of the British officers. Nehru conveyed to Mountbatten the
Cabinet's view that in effect the service chiefs had made an 'announcement that they could not carry out Government's policy in case they
didn't agree with it.'[11] Mountbatten warded off a crisis by sending for
General Lockhart and persuading him to withdraw the letter. After
securing the consent of his two colleagues, Lockhart wrote to the
Prime Minister expressing distress that their joint memorandum had
been

> so phrased as to convey the impression that we, your Military
> Advisers, were attempting to trespass outside our proper sphere.
> We have no doubt on re-reading our letter, that it lends itself to
> misinterpretation, but assure you that nothing was further from
> our intention.

He withdrew the offending letter but added that the

> point we were anxious to make was that at the present time all
> the British officers serving in India, whether at Supreme Head-
> quarters or in the Armed Forces of India or Pakistan, are on a sin-
> gle list. We feel it incumbent on us to represent this.[12]

The apology tendered by the service chiefs did not alter the fact
that British officers were prohibited, by orders, from taking part in an
inter-dominion war. On the very next day after the service chiefs withdrew their letter, the Stand Down instructions were reiterated in a
secret message from Field Marshal Auchinleck to all senior British
commanders in the Indian and Pakistani armed forces. The Supreme
Commander for India and Pakistan[13] issued the following orders:

> On receipt of the Code Word 'STAND DOWN' the following order
> will be immediately put into force:

> *Owing to the immediate risk/outbreak of open conflict be-*
> *tween the armed forces of India and Pakistan, all British officers*
> *and other ranks HOWEVER employed and of WHATEVER rank*
> *shall cease forthwith to take any further part in the command or*
> *administration of the Armed Forces of India and Pakistan. You*
> *will take immediate action to this effect, and nothing is to be*
> *allowed to impede it.*[14]

By withdrawing their joint letter, the service chiefs averted a crisis but the incident shook the confidence of India's leaders in their topmost military commanders. Patel's bitter comment to Mountbatten was that senior British officers owed loyalty to and took orders from Auchinleck rather than the Indian government.[15]

Nehru offered his Cabinet colleagues a perceptive analysis of the role of British officers in the event of a conflict between India and Pakistan. Whether the United Kingdom would, in such an event, withdraw these officers from one or both dominions would depend on her foreign policy in relation to the war. If British officers were to be withdrawn from only one of the two dominions, it would be tantamount to the United Kingdom joining the war on the other side. The British government could take the step only if it clearly defined one party as the aggressor. That country would, presumably, withdraw from the Commonwealth. Alternatively, Nehru concluded, British officers would have to be withdrawn from both armies.[16] Such was the assessment of Prime Minister Nehru on 15 October—a week before the tribal invasion of Kashmir.

The incident produced another important result. Ostensibly in order to prevent the recurrence of similar incidents, Mountbatten proposed constituting a Defence Committee of the Cabinet.[17] The proposal was accepted by the Indian government and the Governor-General contrived to obtain the chairmanship of the newly-established committee on the basis of his military experience. The full political and constitutional implications of this arrangement seemed to have eluded the Indian government. A vitally important Cabinet committee was headed not by the Prime Minister but by the Governor-General, who thereby acquired a major role in the executive branch of the state. Mountbatten was to stretch his new powers to their fullest extent during the Kashmir operations, working tirelessly behind the scenes to restrain Indian defence initiatives. But in order to secure this larger objective he often had to accept compromises. Moreover, since he now became an active participant in decision-making, he could no longer dissociate himself in public from his government's policies. This created a lasting misperception of his role, in both Pakistan and India.

Resolution of the Junagadh Problem

At the end of September, the Indian government decided that a show of force in Kathiawar had become unavoidable. Sardar Patel pointed out that by sending its armed personnel into Babariawad, Junagadh had committed an act of war against India. The princely states which had acceded to India had a right to expect that India would protect them against aggression. A weak posture would undermine India's standing with the princely states and would have repercussions in Hyderabad, where the Nizam was holding out against accession.

In an effort to head him off from this course of action, Mountbatten suggested lodging a complaint to the United Nations against Junagadh's act of aggression. Both Patel and Nehru rejected the proposal. Patel observed that possession was nine-tenths of the law and he would in no circumstances lower India's position by going to any court as a plaintiff. The Governor-General asked him whether he was prepared to take the risk of an armed clash in Kathiawar leading to war with Pakistan. The Deputy Prime Minister was unmoved. He said he was ready to take the risk which was, however, very slight since Pakistan was in no position to wage war. Patel made it clear that he would hand in his resignation if a firm line was not taken in Babariawad and Mangrol. As a compromise, however, Patel, agreed that Indian forces need not immediately enter these territories provided the position was reviewed a little later. The Governor-General recorded, 'I reluctantly agreed to a strong show of force provided no part of Junagadh territory and neither Mangrol nor Babariawad were invaded.'[18]

Nehru provided a judicious summing up. On the one hand, there was the need for speedy and effective action to protect Babariawad. India was honour bound to give the state the protection it had undertaken to provide. If this were not done, India's prestige would suffer; her position in Hyderabad would probably be affected; and Pakistan might be encouraged to commit other acts of aggression. On the other hand, India should avoid being drawn into a war or an unfavourable position in the United Nations. 'Any war with Pakistan would undoubtedly end in the defeat and ruin of Pakistan provided no other nations are dragged in. At the same time it may well mean the ruin of India also for a considerable time.' Nehru was particularly concerned about the very grave consequences for the communal situation in the subcontinent at a time when massive refugee flows were taking place. For non-Muslims in West Punjab, war 'means putting a million or two million people in peril of their lives. This also means putting a far greater number of Muslims in India in peril of their lives.... With war being declared people's minds will be still further inflamed and it might be impossible for the Government of India to protect Muslims all over India.'

With these factors in mind, the Prime Minister proposed to send Indian forces from Bombay to Porbander to await further orders; to deploy Indian troops on the borders of Babariawad; and to deploy forces of other Kathiawar states to guard the frontiers with Junagadh. Indian forces should refrain from crossing the Junagadh border or, until further orders, from entering Babariawad or Mangrol. Future action would depend on further developments.

The policy ... will keep the initiative in our hands, will exercise a strangling pressure on Junagadh State, will make people in Kathiawar and elsewhere realise we are actively dealing with the situation, and at the same time avoid an armed conflict leading to war.[19]

Nehru took an important new initiative in his search for a peaceful solution. In the case of Junagadh, India had already proposed that the question of accession should be decided by a reference to the people. On 30 September, the Prime Minister proposed in the newly constituted Defence Committee that the same principle be accepted in all cases where accession was disputed. 'Wherever there is a dispute in regard to any territory,' he suggested, 'the matter should be decided by a referendum or plebiscite of the people concerned. We shall accept the result of this referendum whatever it may be as it is our desire that a decision should be made in accordance with the wishes of the people concerned.'[20] The implications of this proposal for Kashmir and Hyderabad were obvious.

The new initiative was immediately conveyed to Pakistan. Liaquat happened to be in New Delhi on 30 September for a meeting of the Joint Defence Council and Mountbatten engineered a conversation between him and Nehru. After the inevitable agreement over Juna-gadh, Nehru declared that the will of the people should be ascer-tained in all difficult cases. India would always be willing to abide by a decision obtained by a general election, plebiscite or referendum conducted in a fair and impartial manner. Mountbatten intervened to emphasise that this policy would apply not only to Junagadh but also any other state. 'Mr. Liaquat Ali Khan's eyes sparkled,' Mountbatten later recorded, adding that he was, no doubt, thinking of Kashmir.[21]

Significantly, however, Liaquat made no response to Mountbatten's offer. Was this because Pakistan feared she would lose a referendum in Kashmir? Was Jinnah unwilling to close his options in Hyderabad? Definitive answers to these questions will only be available when the Pakistani archives are opened. Whatever the reasons, Pakistan chose to ignore the offer of settling all cases of disputed accession by a ref-erence to the will of the people. She chose to insist on the ruler's pre-rogatives in the case of Junagadh and Hyderabad while, in the case of Kashmir, she made secret preparations to obtain a decision by the force of arms.

Even as the Nehru–Liaquat talks were in progress, the Nawab of Junagadh continued on his reckless course. On 1 October, he occu-pied Mangrol, thus repeating his earlier provocation in Babariawad. India's reaction was notable for its restraint. On 4 October, the Chiefs of Staff were directed to instruct Brigadier Gurdial Singh, the Com-mander of the newly constituted Kathiawar Defence Force, to pre-pare a plan for the occupation of Babariawad and Mangrol, in case this should be ordered.[22] This amounted to little more than a reitera-tion of the previous decision of 22 September concerning contin-gency plans for Babariawad, Mangrol and Junagadh. India continued to observe a self-imposed restraint against entering what she consid-ered to be her own territories by virtue of the accession of Baba-riawad and Mangrol.

India still hoped for an amicable settlement. On 5 October, a press communiqué was issued explaining the circumstances which had compelled India to send a detachment of troops to Kathiawar. It emphasised that the troops had strict instructions not to enter Junagadh and it reiterated India's offer to abide by the results of a plebiscite. Nehru drew Liaquat's attention to the communiqué and expressed the hope that Pakistan would instruct the Nawab of Junagadh to withdraw his troops from Babariawad and Mangrol.

The Pakistan premier responded with a proposal that independent legal opinion might be sought on the question whether Babariawad and Mangrol were free to accede to either dominion notwithstanding Junagadh's claim to sovereignty over them. Nehru pointed out in his reply that the Pakistani proposal avoided the main question, namely Junagadh itself.[23] Hopes rose when Mountbatten reported after a meeting with Liaquat on 16 October that the latter was agreeable to a plebiscite in Junagadh, but these hopes were squashed when Liaquat responded a few days later that there was an apparent misunderstanding.

By 21 October, New Delhi's patience over Babariawad and Mangrol ran out. These territories had languished for weeks under Junagadh occupation while India sought an amicable solution. Her offers of a referendum had been met with evasion. At a meeting of the Defence Committee on 21 October, Patel pressed for immediate action. Delay on the government's part, he stated, had created a general impression of weakness which could have an unfortunate effect on Hyderabad, in the context of ongoing negotiations. Accounts were given of the oppression and terror let loose on the inhabitants of Babariawad and Mangrol. The Committee strongly supported Patel's view that action must not be further delayed. Mountbatten reported to the King:

> eventually I came to the conclusion that I could not, short of threatening to resign myself, stay the hands of my Ministers any longer, and would have to accept with a good grace their unanimous decision that Indian troops should be sent to occupy Babariawad and Mangrol, particularly and firstly the former.[24]

Plans for taking over the two states were finalised and approved on 25 October 1947.

The Governor-General attempted one last stand. At the next meeting of the Defence Committee, Mountbatten urged that the intended action in Babariawad and Mangrol should be carried out by the Central Reserve Police, not the army. He pointed out that the police force was adequate for the purpose and that world opinion might react negatively to the employment of regular troops. Patel agreed that the Central Reserve Police was adequate for the task but he insisted on using the army, doubtless recalling Lockhart's earlier reluctance to carry out the government's directives. The Committee noted that there might be more opposition if a relatively weak force like the police were employed for the purpose. Ministers also held that it would make little difference in terms of international opinion whether the operations were entrusted to the police or the army. The Defence Committee therefore decided to employ regular troops for the action.[25] On 1 November, Indian civil administrators, accompanied by a small force, took over the administration of both Babariawad and Mangrol.

Meanwhile, Junagadh itself had become ungovernable, as Nehru had foreseen. Because of border tensions and the economic blockade, traders refused to enter into business transactions with Junagadh. This led to shortages of foodstuffs and other essential commodities. The state's revenues dried up and panic spread among officials of all ranks. 'Muslims of Kathiawar seem to have lost all enthusiasm for Pakistan,' Sir Shah Nawaz Bhutto wrote to Jinnah on 27 October, adding that the 'situation has ... so worsened that responsible Muslims and others have come to press me to seek a solution to the impasse.'[26] The Nawab had already fled to Karachi, taking with him the entire cash balances of the treasury.

On 5 November, the Junagadh State Council decided that it was 'necessary to have a complete reorientation of the State policy and a readjustment of relations with the two Dominions even if it involves a reversal of the earlier decision to accede to Pakistan.'[27] On 8 November, the Dewan, Sir Shah Nawaz, requested the Indian government to take over the administration of Junagadh. The request was promptly accepted and India took over the administration of the state on the following day. Mountbatten recorded, 'Either through a misunderstanding or purposely in order not to embarrass me (I am not sure which), I was not informed of what had happened until late in the evening of 8th November.'[28]

Whitehall and the 'Stand Down' Instructions

Pakistan had a strictly limited interest in Junagadh and, despite the warnings of Mountbatten and Lockhart, there was never any real danger of an India–Pakistan war in Kathiawar. Whitehall kept a generally low profile in the inter-dominion dispute, leaving it to the men on the spot—Mountbatten, Auchinleck and Lockhart—to restrain India from seeking recourse to arms over Babariawad and Mangrol. Mountbatten played his role by vividly portraying to his ministers the legal and diplomatic complications which might result from military action. The Commander-in-Chief on his part repeatedly stressed that the Indian army was in no position to undertake large-scale operations even though, in the context of Junagadh, the warning lacked credibility. The unpreparedness of the army for major military operations and their need to concentrate on the primary task of maintaining internal law and order became a refrain which the Commander-in-Chief was later to take up in Kashmir and Hyderabad.

The service chiefs, as we saw earlier, were guided by the 'Stand Down' instructions. Their joint letter to the government lacked political finesse and had to be withdrawn but the instructions themselves remained intact. Field Marshal Auchinleck's secret instructions of 30 September were later endorsed by the UK Chiefs of Staff and Alexander, the Defence Minister, sought Attlee's approval.

This question was discussed at a meeting of the British cabinet's Commonwealth Affairs Committee on 13 October, shortly before the outbreak of the Kashmir crisis. Alexander's proposal was that the decision to issue the code-word 'STAND DOWN' should be left to Auchinleck himself during the period of existence of the Supreme Headquarters for India and Pakistan. Ministers were in general agreement on the 'Stand Down' instructions but differing views were expressed on Alexander's proposal. Noel-Baker, the Secretary of State for Commonwealth Relations, raised the objection that the decision to issue the 'Stand Down' order would be of such great political and military importance that the final decision should be taken by ministers, not the Supreme Commander. This raised a fundamental question: what was the underlying logic of the 'Stand Down' instructions? Were they based on political principle or on expediency? Was it a matter of principle that British officers should take no part in an inter-dominion war and should 'Stand Down' if such a war became imminent? Or were the instructions designed to serve British political and strategic interests, requiring ministerial decision?

Auchinleck's approach was based on principle, Noel-Baker's on expediency. British ministers never directly addressed this basic question. The debate in the Commonwealth Affairs Committee on 13 October was confined to the practicability of Noel-Baker's proposal. Would there be sufficient time in an emergency to consult ministers? If not, should the Supreme Commander seek other advice? Noel-Baker was prepared to allow that in an emergency, if sufficient time was not available for a reference to London, the decision might be left to the Supreme Commander. The convoluted compromise which emerged was as follows:

> *The general view of the Committee was that, while the Supreme Commander should be given full discretion to act in the event of extreme urgency, it was most desirable that His Majesty's Government should, if possible, be consulted before the decision was taken to issue the code word 'STAND DOWN,' and that the Supreme Commander should be asked to make every effort to do so. In any event, before taking any action himself or making a submission to His Majesty's Government, the Supreme Commander should consult with the United Kingdom High Commissioners in India and Pakistan, or at least with former if he could not communicate with the latter.*[29]

The Committee 'invited the Minister of Defence, in consultation with the Secretary of State for Commonwealth Relations, to send instructions to the Supreme Commander.'

Following these deliberations, Prime Minister Attlee conveyed his approval of the 'Stand Down' instructions in a telegram to Auchinleck on 15 October.[30] The complex supplementary instructions to be sent by the Defence Minister did not follow till much later—in November. Thus, on the eve of the Kashmir conflict, the 'Stand Down' instructions were reinforced by the Prime Minister's endorsement and Auchinleck still retained full powers to order a 'Stand Down.' This was to have a major impact on the course of events in Kashmir at the end of the month.

III
Crisis in Kashmir

Mid-way through the Junagadh affair, a crisis of far greater dimensions erupted in Kashmir. The political events preceding the undeclared war between India and Pakistan have been the subject of several scholarly volumes.[1] The central concern of this study is the military and diplomatic history of the conflict and for our purposes an outline sketch of the immediate political background will suffice.

Kashmir was the largest of the princely states in territorial extent and the most diverse in cultural terms. In the central valley surrounding the city of Srinagar, the dominant language was Kashmiri, spoken alike by the Muslim majority and the Hindu minority. To the south lay the province of Jammu, where Dogri was the most widely-spoken language among inhabitants who were mainly Muslim in the western and Hindu in the eastern areas. The highlands of Ladakh in the north and east were populated by Buddhists with close religious and linguistic affinities to Tibet. Baltistan, west of Ladakh, was occupied by an ethnically related people who were, however, mainly Shia Muslims. Further north, the sparsely populated valleys of the Gilgit area harboured a fascinating range of local dialects and cultures. Finally, at the western extremity of the state of Jammu and Kashmir, running along the border with Pakistan, lay a strip of territory with close ethnic and linguistic connections across the border. This consisted of the principally Punjabi-speaking areas of Muzaffarabad and Mirpur districts and the intervening Poonch jagir, where a variant of Hindustani was in vogue. The populations of these areas were predominantly

Muslim, though there was a substantial Hindu and Sikh minority, particularly in Mirpur. The diversity of the state was aptly summed up by an Australian diplomat: 'The State of Jammu and Kashmir,' wrote Sir Owen Dixon in 1950, 'is not really a unit geographically, demographically or economically. It is an agglomeration of territories brought under the political power of one Maharaja. That is the unity it possesses.'[2]

Grievances against the Maharaja's autocratic regime led to the founding, in 1932, of a political party, the All-Jammu and Kashmir Muslim Conference. Its leader was the youthful and charismatic Sheikh Mohammed Abdullah. The party was essentially non-communal in its approach and it formally changed its name to the National Conference in June, 1939.

The secular ideals of the National Conference and its struggle for democratic rights led to the establishment of close links with the Indian National Congress. Since the late 1920s, the Congress had developed links with democratic movements in the princely states of India. The principal agency through which these ties were formed was the All-India State Peoples' Conference, established in 1927 with the aim of integrating the various movements in the princely states *inter se* as well as with the broad national movement. In 1941, the National Conference formally joined the All-India State Peoples' Conference and in 1946, on the eve of independence, Sheikh Abdullah became the President of the latter organisation.

In contrast with the Congress, Jinnah's Muslim League kept away from involvement in the internal affairs of the princely states. Jammu and Kashmir was a partial exception in the sense that the Muslim League was actively hostile to the secular approach of the National Conference. Jinnah appealed to all Muslims in the state to rally around the communal rump of the erstwhile Muslim Conference, now reconstituted as a separate party. Its leader, Ghulam Abbas, was not a Kashmiri-speaker and his following was largely confined to the Poonch and Mirpur areas.

In May 1946, the National Conference launched the 'Quit Kashmir' movement, demanding an end to autocratic government. 'We naturally visualise,' announced Sheikh Abdullah, 'that the Princes and Nawabs should quit all the States.... The rulers of the Indian States who possess one-fourth of India have always played traitors to the cause of Indian freedom. The demand that the Princely Order should quit is a logical extension of the policy of "Quit India".'[3]

The timing of Abdullah's initiative was awkward for the Congress. With independence around the corner, the Congress would have preferred to carry the princely states on a common front, instead of emphasising the intrinsic conflict of interests between a democratic movement and the princely order. But when the Maharaja's government arrested Abdullah and unleashed a policy of repression against the National Conference, Jawaharlal Nehru rushed to Kashmir to intervene on behalf of his friend. Nehru was detained at the border and pushed back into British India.

Thus, the salient features of the political scene in Kashmir on the eve of independence may be summed up as follows. A secular party, the National Conference, led the freedom struggle of the mainly Muslim citizens of Jammu and Kashmir against their Hindu Maharaja. The Congress was closely associated with the National Conference and its movement for democratic rights. The Muslim League, professed champions of Muslims of the subcontinent, denounced the secular democratic movement and its connections with the Congress.

The Question of Accession

This, in a nutshell, was the background against which Maharaja Hari Singh had to decide whether to accede to India or Pakistan. The Maharaja feared that if he acceded to India, he would be obliged to hand over authority immediately to Abdullah and the National Conference. Better terms could, perhaps, be negotiated with Jinnah but this was otherwise an unattractive prospect and accession to Pakistan would be bitterly opposed by the biggest political party in the state. The Maharaja appears initially to have toyed with the notion of an independent Kashmir but he soon realised the impracticability of this ambition. By mid-September, he had decided to offer accession to India, on condition that he would not be asked to institute immediate reforms or, in other words, to hand over power to Sheikh Abdullah. He appointed a new Dewan, Justice Mehr Chand Mahajan, and instructed him to secure an agreement with New Delhi on these lines.[4]

Nehru, however, insisted that Abdullah should be immediately released from prison and be associated with the governance of the state. The Prime Minister anticipated that Pakistan would attempt to seize Kashmir by force and was convinced that the Maharaja's forces would be unable to stop the invaders unless a popular resistance were organised. In a letter to Patel on 27 September, he offered the following perceptive assessment:

> It is obvious to me from the many reports I have received that the situation there [Kashmir] is a dangerous and deteriorating one. The Muslim League in the Punjab and the N.W.F.P. are making preparations to enter Kashmir in considerable numbers. The approach of winter is going to cut off Kashmir from the rest of India. The only normal route then is via the Jhelum valley. The Jammu route can hardly be used during winter and air traffic is also suspended....
>
> I understand that the Pakistan strategy is to infiltrate into Kashmir now and to take some big action as soon as Kashmir is more or less isolated because of the coming winter.
>
> Whether this strategy succeeds or not depends upon the forces opposed to it.... I rather doubt if the Maharaja and the State forces can meet the situation by themselves without some popular help.... Obviously the only major group that can side with them is the National Conference under Sheikh Abdullah's leadership....
>
> Indeed, it seems to me that there is no other course open to the Maharaja but this: to release Sheikh Abdullah and the National Conference leaders, to make a friendly approach to them, seek their cooperation and make them feel that this is really meant, and then to declare for adhesion to Indian Union. Once the State [accedes] to India, it will become very difficult for Pakistan to invade it officially or unofficially without coming into conflict with the Indian Union. If, however, there is delay in this accession, then Pakistan will go ahead without much fear of consequences, specially when the winter isolates Kashmir.[5]

In the run-up to independence and partition, Patel and Nehru had adopted rather different political approaches towards Kashmir. Under the Independence of India Act it was left to each princely ruler to decide which of the two successor states, India or Pakistan, he should accede to. Since it was the Maharaja who would decide on Kashmir's accession, Patel tried to calm the fears aroused in his mind by Nehru's support for the 'Quit Kashmir' movement. He wrote to the Maharaja on 3 July, urging him to accede to India 'without any delay' and reassuring him about the Congress' intentions. 'I am sorry to find that there is considerable misapprehension in your mind about Congress,' he wrote. 'Allow me to assure Your Highness that the Congress is not only not your enemy, as you happen to believe, but there are in the Congress many strong supporters of your State. As an organisation, the Congress is not opposed to any Prince in India.'[6]

But by September, sensing the approaching crisis, Patel and Nehru closed ranks. On 2 October, Patel advised the Maharaja to proclaim a general amnesty and release political prisoners. And on 21 October, after discussions with the recently freed Abdullah, he wrote to the Maharaja's Prime Minister, Mehr Chand Mahajan: 'it is my sincere and earnest advice to you to make a substantial gesture to win Sheikh Abdullah's support.'[7]

In response to pressing suggestions from Nehru and Patel, the Maharaja released Sheikh Abdullah from detention and there was an exchange of cordial messages between the two. The Maharaja continued, however, to drag his feet on the question of associating Abdullah with the governance of the state. The resultant impasse over accession remained unresolved till the last week of October. On 21 October, just hours before Pakistan launched its thrust towards Srinagar, Nehru wrote to Mahajan:

In view of all the circumstances I feel it will probably be undesirable to make any declaration of adhesion to the Indian Union at this stage. This should come later when a popular interim government is functioning. I need not tell you about the urgency of the situation and the dangers inherent in it.[8]

Raiders in Kashmir

Suspecting that the Maharajah was inclined to accede to India and knowing that Sheikh Abdullah opposed accession to Pakistan, Karachi decided to seize Jammu and Kashmir by force. British officers could not be taken into confidence and the armed forces could not be openly employed. The plan was to launch a clandestine invasion by a force composed of Pathan tribesmen, ex-servicemen and soldiers 'on leave.'

Colonel Akbar Khan, Director of Weapons and Equipment at the Pakistan Army Headquarters, was put in charge of the operation. He has left us a valuable historical account[9] which provides details of the role played by senior military officers under the supervision of Pakistani political leaders. His account confirms that among the military officers deeply involved in the operation were Brigádier Sher Khan, Director of Intelligence, Colonel Azam Khanzada of the Ordnance Corps, Lt Colonel Masud of the Cavalry, and Air Commodore Janjua of the Royal Pakistan Air Force. Ex-servicemen of the Indian National Army and members of the Muslim League National Guard were utilised for the actual operations.

Akbar Khan also confirms the central role of Pakistan's Prime Minister, Nawabzada Liaquat Ali Khan, to whose office he was attached as Military Adviser. Among other political leaders who were actively involved were the Premier of the North West Frontier Province, Abdul Qayyum Khan and a senior minister of the West Punjab government, Sardar Shaukat Hayat Khan.

Did Jinnah have a role in the plot? There has been a great deal of speculation on this question on the basis of circumstantial evidence. A definitive answer is now available. In a 1997 BBC television programme on Jinnah, Shaukat Hayat Khan confirmed that the raid into Kashmir had been approved by the Quaid-e-Azad himself.[10]

Pakistan initially sought to exploit a local agrarian uprising which had broken out in the jagir of Poonch. The agrarian system in the Poonch jagir differed from the rest of the state and the tax burden on landholders was more oppressive than elsewhere in Jammu and Kashmir. On the eve of independence, an agitation against revenue exactions and rising prices erupted in Poonch. After the end of World War II, thousands of demobilised soldiers returned to their villages in Poonch and joined the agitation. (Poonch, with its Satti and Sudhan 'martial communities,' was one of the favoured recruiting areas of the Raj.)

Pakistan sought to exploit these local circumstances. She first tried to channel existing economic grievances into a movement for accession to Pakistan. This met with no more than modest success. General Scott, the British Chief of Staff of the Kashmir Forces upto the end of September 1947, gave the following account to Grafftey-Smith, the UK High Commissioner in Karachi:

Kashmir has been quiet, except for trouble in Poonch late August and September.... Towards the end of August, a party of about 30 Muslims from the Punjab entered Poonch and incited the Sattis to march on the capital, to demand Kashmir's accession to Pakistan. A considerable number, swelling to 10,000 agreed to go to Poonch, primarily in order to represent their own local grievances, their principal complaint being the high prices of foodstuffs.[11]

The agitation resulted in the destruction of property and protestors were driven off by the state forces when they tried to enter the town of Bagh. There had been no further trouble in the State, General Scott reported, upto his departure on 29 September.

Pakistan, however, rapidly stepped up the level of infiltration, causing a material change in the ground situation. Large numbers of armed men—Pathan tribesmen, Punjabis and other Pakistani nationals—were sent in to carry out irregular warfare against the Maharaja's forces. Though Karachi disclaimed responsibility, the raiders received weapons, transport and overall direction from Pakistani authorities. Akbar Khan's account only confirms what was long evident to observers.

As a result of the stepped-up invasion, the Maharaja's forces suffered significant reverses and on 15 October, the Dewan sent a telegram to Attlee appealing to him to advise the Pakistani government to deal fairly with Kashmir. Whitehall, of course, ignored this inconvenient appeal.

Pakistan was thus able to mount clandestine military pressure against the Maharaja along a strip of border territory in Jammu province. This was an area where pockets of pro-Pakistan sentiment existed on account of cross-border ethnic affinities. Pakistan was able to exploit the fact that large numbers of Poonchi soldiers served in her army as a result of the decision to allot to her the Muslim units of the army of undivided India.

The tactics followed in the border areas of Jammu could not be replicated in other areas of the state where there was little local support for Pakistan. Thus it was envisaged that the conquest of the central vale of Kashmir would be effected through a massive tribal invasion along the main highway linking Rawalpindi to Srinagar via the towns of Domel and Muzzafarabad. In the absence of any significant political support in the Kashmir valley, the 'raid' could only take the form of an outright invasion by tribal irregulars, with all the attendant horrors of arson, loot and rape visited on the civilian population.

On 22 October, Pakistan launched the invasion of the valley. At 4:30 a.m., thousands of well-equipped tribesmen crossed over the bridges at Muzaffarabad and sacked the town. Provided with motor transport, they moved swiftly up the Jhelum valley road to the environs of Uri. Here they met spirited resistance from a small force of the Maharaja's army, led in person by the newly-appointed Chief of Staff, Brigadier Rajinder Singh. Numbering no more than 200, the state forces managed to delay the invaders' advance, gaining a critical advantage for the defence of the capital. The gallant Brigadier Rajinder Singh laid down his life in the action. From Uri, the raiders headed to Baramula. Here they encountered heroic resistance from local civilians led by the martyr Maqbool Sherwani. After an orgy of massacre, pillage and rape, in which even the sisters of the European convent were not spared, the invaders continued their march. By 27 March, they were poised to launch the final assault. Its objective was the Maharaja's summer capital, Srinagar.

IV
The Defence of Srinagar

With Pakistan's escalating involvement in Poonch, the Maharaja's government appealed to India for military equipment. An indent for supplies was sent on 1 October and this was soon followed by a request that Indian forces be stationed near the border so that they could come to the state's rescue if the need arose.[1] The Indian government, as stated in Chapter 3, anticipated that Pakistan would try to seize Kashmir by force of arms. It, therefore, took a prompt decision to assist the state with military supplies. Patel wrote to the Defence Minister, Baldev Singh, on 7 October:

> I hope arrangements are in train to send immediately supplies of arms and ammunition to Kashmir State. If necessary, we must arrange to send them by air.
>
> I think the question of military assistance in time of emergency must claim the attention of our Defence Council as soon as possible. There is no time to lose....[2]

The decision that arms should be supplied to Kashmir on top-priority basis was simply derailed by the Commander-in-Chief, General Lockhart, acting in collusion with Field Marshal Auchinleck. Lockhart took the position that no arms were available in Delhi. Army Headquarters asked Supreme Headquarters to let them know what arms were available and where in depots elsewhere in the country. The latter raised the question: could arms be supplied to states which had not yet acceded to either dominion. In this connection, reference was made to a decision taken by the Joint Defence Council that no arms should be made available to Hyderabad without the Council's approval. Though the decision was specific to Hyderabad, it furnished a pretext for stalling action on the government's decision.[3] Auchinleck and Lockhart knew that Pakistan would protest vigorously if military supplies were sent to the Maharaja and they were reluctant to get drawn into an inter-dominion controversy. Despite increasingly urgent appeals from the Kashmir state authorities, no arms were made available by the Indian army right till 22 October, when Pakistan launched the invasion of the Jhelum valley by tribal lashkars.

The Indian government first learnt of this grave development on the evening of Friday, 24 October, when a desperate appeal for assistance was received from the Kashmir state authorities. The Governor-General and Prime Minister were both present at a dinner party that evening at the Thai Embassy and Nehru took Mountbatten aside to inform him about the crisis. A meeting of the Defence Committee was held the next morning in order to consider India's response. Over the next two days—the weekend of 25 and 26 October—the Government of India would take decisions of great historical importance.

25 October 1947

The fact that the crisis was discussed in the Defence Committee rather than in a plenary meeting of the Cabinet was not simply a matter of administrative detail. It permitted Mountbatten, as Chairman of the Defence Committee, to play a critical role in policy-making, a role from which he would have been excluded if the initial deliberations had taken place in a meeting of the full Cabinet. Moreover, the meeting on 25 October established a precedent: till the end of 1947, all important questions relating to Kashmir were decided not in the Cabinet but in meetings of its Defence Committee. This allowed Mountbatten to play a role which far exceeded that of a constitutional figurehead and which culminated, at the end of the year, in the decision to refer the Kashmir issue to the United Nations.

The Defence Committee met at 10 a.m. on 25 October, under Mountbatten's chairmanship. General Lockhart informed the members that he had received a telegram on the previous day from the acting Commander-in-Chief of the Pakistan army, Lieutenant General

Sir Douglas Gracey. This conveyed that a force of 5,000 tribesmen had entered Kashmir and seized Muzaffarabad and Domel on 22 October. It warned that the force was about to attack Kohala. The Prime Minister added that he also had information about large-scale raids in the Jammu area, right up to Poonch. He pointed out that the trucks and arms which had been supplied to the raiders could have been provided only with the assistance of the Pakistan authorities. He had received information that the invasion had been planned a fortnight earlier at a conference in Rawalpindi.[4]

By the time Gracey's cable was received, it was already outdated. It suggested that the target of the raiders was Kohala, a border town located a few miles south of Muzaffarabad. In fact, by the time the cable was received on 24 October, the raiders were already in the neighbourhood of Uri, almost halfway to Srinagar, the summer capital of the state. Thus, when it met on the 25th morning, the Defence Committee was not fully aware of the gravity and immediacy of the threat to Srinagar.

Against this background, Nehru and Patel brought up the question of the weapons which the army had been instructed to send to Kashmir. When General Lockhart came up with the excuses noted previously, Patel at once pointed out that the Joint Defence Council decision was being misinterpreted. The minutes of the meeting made it clear that the Council's decision concerned Hyderabad alone. Mountbatten agreed that this was the case. The Commander-in-Chief having been overruled, the Cabinet Defence Committee decided that Army Headquarters should depute officers that very day to pick up arms from the various depots and supply them to Kashmir. Chartered aircraft were to be placed at their disposal for this purpose.

What else was required to save Kashmir from the invaders? The Prime Minister reiterated his view that the only way in which the Maharaja's government could save the situation was through full cooperation with the popular forces represented by Sheikh Abdullah. Abdullah should be invited to lay down the policy to meet the situation and the National Conference should agree to cooperate with the Maharaja. There was no advantage in taking up the question of accession before this condition was met. The Prime Minister's position, as we saw in Chapter 3, was based on his conviction that the invasion could be successfully opposed only if the Kashmir authorities were backed by popular support. Nehru insisted that the Maharaja's accession should have the support of the biggest mass organisation in the state.

Sensing that his ministers were determined to go to the assistance of the Kashmiris, the Governor-General argued that it would be a folly to send troops into a 'neutral' state. Pakistan, he felt, could do exactly the same thing, thus precipitating an inter-dominion war. Mountbatten urged that assistance should not be provided before the state had temporarily acceded to India. Pakistan would then have no right to intervene. Drawing a parallel with Junagadh, he proposed that the will of the people concerning accession should be ascertained as soon as law and order had been generally restored. This, he felt, would avoid provoking Pakistan.

Sardar Patel questioned Mountbatten's reasoning. In his view, Pakistan would object to India's coming to the assistance of the state whether or not it was preceded by accession. He saw no reason why India should not respond to a request for assistance from a friendly state which had been subjected to invasion. Nehru agreed with Patel that it would be perfectly legitimate for India to respond to the appeal received from the Jammu and Kashmir government. He added that he accepted the principle that a final settlement on accession should be made after consulting the people. The debate on prior accession ended on an inconclusive note.

It was left to Patel to pose the question whether India was in a position to render military assistance to Kashmir on an effective scale. Mountbatten offered the view that, as far as the Vale of Kashmir was concerned, most reinforcements would have to be flown in by air, though some could be sent by road over the next two or three weeks. General Lockhart said that he could not confirm this without further examination; it was highly probable, however, that troops could be sent to Jammu. V.P. Menon proposed that the Indian army should take over the Jammu front, permitting the Maharaja to concentrate his own troops on the Srinagar front. This view was generally accepted. Nehru suggested that the Indian airforce should be brought into the operations, particularly for reconnaissance purposes and as a show of strength.[6] Mountbatten threw his weight against any precipitate action, emphasising the need for further information.[7]

The Committee finally decided to direct the Chiefs of Staff to 'examine and prepare plans' for (a) Indian troops to take over the Jammu front; (b) use of RIAF planes in Kashmir, particularly for reconnaissance and show of strength; and (c) the possibility of flying Indian troops to Srinagar.

Such were the limited and tentative decisions taken by the Defence Committee on 25 October, in the absence of fuller information. The Committee was not yet aware of the immediacy of the threat to Srinagar. It was understood that the plans the service chiefs were required to 'examine and prepare' were contingency plans for inducting Indian troops 'in case this should be necessary to stop the tribal invasion.'[8] The focus was on sending Indian troops to Jammu rather than Srinagar. In order to remedy the lack of concrete information, it was decided that V.P. Menon should fly to Srinagar in order to assess the situation and suggest what further action was required. It was agreed that Menon should discuss the question of accession with the Maharaja as well as the possibility of cooperation between the state government and the National Conference. He was not authorised, however, to offer any assurance regarding acceptance of accession.

Menon flew to Srinagar the same day and found the city gripped by panic. He later wrote:

> When I landed at the airfield, I was oppressed by the stillness as of a graveyard all around.... The road leading from the aero-drome to Srinagar was deserted. At some of the street corners I noticed volunteers of the National Conference with lathis who challenged passers-by; but the State police were conspicuous by their absence. Mehr Chand Mahajan [the Prime Minister] apprised us of the perilous situation and pleaded for the Govern-ment of India to come to the rescue of the State.... The Maha-rajah was completely unnerved by the turn of events. There were practically no State Forces left and the raiders had almost reached the outskirts of Baramula. At this rate they would be in Srinagar in another day or two.[9]

On Menon's advice, the Maharaja and his family immediately left Srinagar for the safety to Jammu. Later in the evening, just as he was preparing for bed, Menon received a frantic call from Mahajan, who said that rumours were circulating to the effect that the raiders had infiltrated into Srinagar itself and that it was no longer safe for Menon to remain in the city. Menon, Mahajan and the air crew bundled into an old jeep—the only transport left behind by the fleeing Maharaja—and took off for the airport.

26 October 1947

Menon's report to the Defence Committee on 26 October left no doubt that help was urgently required if Srinagar was to be saved from the invaders. General Lockhart provided the further information that the Commander of the Kashmir State Forces had requested that an Indian infantry battalion be flown to Srinagar that very day. However, the service chiefs, supported by Mountbatten, sought to dissuade the ministers from an airlift on the grounds that it involved great risks and dangers.[10] As they listed these hazards, Prime Minister Nehru countered each point:

- The service chiefs stated that a single battalion would be an inadequate force if a general uprising were to break out in Kashmir. Nehru ruled out this possibility. He pointed out that a great majority of the inhabitants of the vale were supporters of the National Conference; the general populace would be friendly, although there would be an unfriendly minority.
- Next, the service chiefs pointed out the considerable difficulties involved in keeping the battalion supplied after its initial induction. Nehru responded that the road from Jammu to Srinagar was likely to be open till the end of November and possibly for another three weeks thereafter. The Pathankot–Jammu road was usable. The service chiefs observed, however, that this road ran very close the Pakistan border for a certain distance and there was, therefore, danger of its being cut by irregular armed bands.
- The chiefs then noted that the battalion to be airlifted would have to leave behind its motor transport. The Prime Minister said that he understood that some transportation was available locally in Srinagar; he also hoped that it would be possible to send up the unit's own transport by road.
- Air Marshal Elmhirst stated that adequate numbers of aircraft were not immediately available; the RIAF could provide only four transport aircraft. The ministers agreed that civil aircraft could be used to fly troops to Srinagar. It was hoped that nine such planes would be readily available. It was agreed that if these planes, in addition to the four RIAF transport aircraft, were to make two trips each to Srinagar on the 26th, it would be possible to fly in almost a complete battalion.

- Finally, Elmhirst said that the RIAF officer who had accompanied Menon to Srinagar had reported that, in his opinion, the Srinagar airfield was likely to fall into the hands of the raiders within thirty-six hours. Menon said that he disagreed with this opinion: the raiders were advancing at a rate of about 6 miles a day and they were still 35 miles away from Srinagar.[11]

Lockhart disclosed that in keeping with the decision of the Committee the previous day, the 1st/5th Gurkha Rifles had been alerted to be ready for a possible operation. This posed problems: apart from the fact that it would be preferable to use Indian troops for the operations, the 1st/5th Gurkha Rifles had a large component of British officers. Objections could arise to the employment of these officers in Kashmir. It was therefore decided that the 1st Battalion of the Sikh Regiment would be earmarked for the airlift.

Finally, General Lockhart asked if Kashmir was of vital importance to India. Nehru and Patel both declared without hesitation that the future of Kashmir was vital to India's very existence.

Thus the government refused to be deterred by the cautionary counsels of the Governor-General and service chiefs. The Committee concluded that though there were military risks involved in airlifting a battalion, these were worth taking in the prevailing circumstances.

As regards accession, the Committee was agreed on the desirability of setting up an interim government under Sheikh Abdullah simultaneously with the acceptance of Kashmir's accession. It was also agreed that after law and order had been restored in the state, the will of the people would be ascertained on the matter of accession.

Faced with a desperate situation, the Maharaja was at last prepared to shed his earlier reluctance to appointing Abdullah to office. An assurance to this effect was given to the Government of India and the Governor-General speedily accepted the instrument of accession, noting at the same time India's intention to consult the people once law and order had been restored. Lord Mountbatten reported to the King:

The Commanders pointed out the extreme hazards of flying in troops, and I added my voice to theirs. But as soon as I saw my Ministers had made up their minds that the military risks must be accepted and Indian troops sent, I was clear that it was essential to send sufficient and in time.[12]

The Airborne Operation

Arrangements for the airlift now proceeded at breakneck speed. Patel at once requisitioned all available civil aircraft by means of a radio broadcast. This yielded a good catch since a substantial number of civil airplanes were operating ferry services for refugees to and from Delhi. Following the state's accession to India, the service chiefs shed their initial reservations and spared no effort to make the airlift a success. Preparations proceeded non-stop throughout the night and as dawn broke over the Safdarjung Airport on the 27th morning, the first batch of the Sikh battalion began to emplane. As it was not known whether the Srinagar airfield was already in enemy hands, the commanding officer of the battalion, Lieutenant Colonel Dewan Ranjit Rai, was instructed to circle overhead and land only if the airfield was free of the raiders. In case of doubt, his instructions were to fly to Jammu. At 10:30 a.m. Delhi received a wireless message from the Srinagar airfield conveying the news that Lieutenant Colonel Rai and his troops had landed.

After securing the airfield, Lieutenant Colonel Rai led a contingent of his troops to Baramula, having received reports that the raiders had reached that town. The National Conference was able to furnish the required transport as Nehru had anticipated. At Baramula, Lieutenant Colonel Rai found that he was heavily outnumbered by the invasion force. He therefore decided to withdraw to Pattan. At this point, the gallant officer fell in action. By his daring, he had secured the Srinagar airfield, making a vital contribution without which the planned operations would have been impossible. By the evening of the 27th, the Sikh battalion not only controlled the airfield but had also established itself at Pattan, which offered the only hilly terrain between Srinagar and Baramula. Occupying the heights at Pattan, the Sikhs were positioned to control the road to Srinagar. Thus, by the end of the first day, Srinagar had been saved. The raiders were in retreat.

The Supreme Commander

Mountbatten himself was surprised by the unqualified success of the airlift. Even as the operation was in progress on the 27th, he reminded Patel in writing about his misgivings. 'I must remind you,' he wrote, 'that the risk is great and that the chances of keeping the raiders out of Srinagar are not too good.'[13] But when the success of the airlift was finally established, he paid a fulsome tribute. Mountbatten, who was the Supreme Allied Commander in Southeast Asia during World War II, said that in all his war experience he had never come across an airlift of this order being undertaken successfully at such short notice.

How would Jinnah react to the Indian initiative? Nehru considered this question—and come to the wrong conclusion. He wrote on 27 October:

> *Kashmir has now formally acceded to the Indian Union and we have accepted that accession. This makes a big difference in the constitutional position and if the Pakistan Army goes into Kashmir State anywhere it means war. I rather doubt if they will do this ... as this would mean their having to protect their whole West Punjab border. In any event we must be perfectly prepared for all consequences.*[14]

Nehru assumed that his adversary's response would be based on cool-headed, rational calculation—a common error in judging the opponent's response in crisis situations. Enraged over the collapse of his scheme, Jinnah threw caution to the winds and ordered General Gracey on the 27th to launch the Pakistan army into Jammu and Kashmir. His order was to march into Baramula and Srinagar, to seize the Banihal pass and to send troops into the Mirpur district of Jammu.

Jinnah had not reckoned with the 'Stand Down' instructions. Gracey flatly refused to carry out his orders in the absence of instructions from the Supreme Commander, Field Marshal Auchinleck. He rang up Auchinleck at 1 a.m. that night to inform him about the development. In response to Gracey's urgent appeal, Auchinleck flew to Lahore in the morning to meet the Pakistan Governor-General.

In their meeting with Jinnah, Gracey emphasised Pakistan's military weakness and Auchinleck pointed out the 'incalculable consequences of military violation of what now is territory of [the] Indian Union in consequence of Kashmir's ... accession.'[15] Spelling out the implications of the 'Stand Down' instructions, the Supreme Commander told Jinnah in plain terms that all British officers would be withdrawn at once if the Pakistan army were to be sent into Jammu and Kashmir. Pakistan in the early years of independence was critically dependent on the services of British officers. Most of the senior military commanders were British[16] and in the technical branches of the services, even lower-level British personnel were irreplaceable. Confronted with the prospect of a 'Stand Down,' Jinnah reluctantly withdrew his orders while ventilating his anger at what he alleged was India's 'sharp practice' in securing Kashmir's accession. By invoking the 'Stand Down' instructions and emphasising the implications of Kashmir's accession to India, Auchinleck averted an open war between Pakistan and India at the end of October.

Throughout the month of October, British generals in the subcontinent looked to the Supreme Commander for guidance. In the earlier part of the month, Lockhart took the cue from Auchinleck and ignored the instructions of his government to supply arms to the Kashmir authorities. At the end of the month, under Auchinleck's instructions, Gracey refused to implement Jinnah's orders to send his troops into Kashmir. For Auchinleck as for Mountbatten, accession was the touchstone by which to judge the legality of military presence in a princely state. In the case of Junagadh, they had staunchly opposed Indian military action in view of the Nawab's accession to Pakistan. They were to reluctantly acquiesce in an Indian take-over only after this was requested by the Junagadh government itself. Applying the same yardstick, Auchinleck pointed out to Jinnah that sending Pakistani troops into Kashmir would constitute a violation of India's borders.

The Supreme Commander's days in India were, however, numbered. He had incurred the wrath of Sardar Patel for what the latter perceived as partiality towards Pakistan in the matter of division of military stores. His role in the Junagadh affair added fuel to the fire. Patel justifiably concluded that in the final analysis the British officers at the helm of the armed forces took their orders from the Supreme Commander, not the Indian government. He charged the Field Marshal with 'throttling the initiative of Headquarters Indian Army and acting as the advanced outpost of Pakistan.'[17] Mountbatten tried his best to defend Auchinleck but to no avail. By late September India was ready to move a formal proposal in the Joint Defence Council to close down Supreme Headquarters.

With great reluctance, Mountbatten advised the Field Marshal on 26 September to forestall the Indian move by taking the initiative himself to propose an early closure of his headquarters. Auchinleck deeply resented the doubts cast on his impartiality by the Indian government but he accepted the Governor-General's advice and submitted a paper to the Joint Defence Council in mid-October—a fortnight before his encounter with Jinnah at Lahore—recommending the closure of Supreme Headquarters by 30 November. Though the proposal was strongly opposed in the Joint Defence Council by Liaquat Ali Khan, in view of India's position Whitehall reluctantly came to the conclusion that there was no alternative but to withdraw the Supreme Commander and all British personnel at his headquarters. Supreme Headquarters thus ceased to exist on 30 November— much earlier than the originally intended date of 15 August, 1948. Auchinleck's initiative of dissuading Jinnah from launching the Pakistan army into Jammu and Kashmir turned out to be his last major act as Supreme Commander.

British generals in India and Pakistan maintained informal channels of communication on Kashmir developments. Gracey's telegram of 24 October finds a place in every history of the Kashmir conflict; less well-known is the fact that he had informed Lockhart about preparations for the invasion even before 24 October. He had alerted Lockhart earlier in a telephone conversation that well-armed Pakistan tribesmen were massing in the Attock–Rawalpindi area and were provided with civilian transportation. Lockhart was well aware of his government's concern over Pakistan-sponsored raids into Kashmir but he did not consider it necessary to pass on the report to the Indian government since Kashmir was not a part of the Indian Union at that date. Lockhart perceived no threat to India from the tribal movement since Kashmir was not at that time a part of Indian Union! At the end of December, Nehru came to learn about this telephone conversation; it led to Lockhart's immediate resignation, less than five months after his appointment as Commander-in-Chief.[18]

There is also evidence that Cunningham, the Governor of NWFP, had alerted Lockhart about the intentions of the tribesmen in a 'private' letter but it remains unclear whether this amounted to more than a broad hint. The Commander-in-Chief shared the contents of the letter with the other two service chiefs, who were both British, but not with the Indian government.[19] Lockhart's failure to alert his government was consistent with his flouting instructions to send military supplies to Kashmir. The intention in both cases was to avoid entanglement in a princely state which had yet to accede to India.

V
Reactions in London

In the immediate post-independence period, Britain had an unrivalled influence in the subcontinent. She hoped to preserve her political and strategic position by negotiating alliances with both India and Pakistan, either in the form of Commonwealth defence arrangements or through bilateral treaties with the two countries. Britain was pessimistic about the prospects of persuading India to enter into an alliance but in 1947–48 she had not yet given up hopes of doing so. On account of her size and resources, India was viewed as an influential factor in the Asian political scene. Pakistan was a more promising prospect as a military ally. She had already conveyed her eagerness to enter into a defence arrangement and her geopolitical location was eminently attractive to Western strategists. Moreover, Pakistan was deemed to be potentially influential in the 'Muslim world' and London regarded it as axiomatic that if Pakistan were given cause for offence, this would provoke a reaction throughout the strategically vital Middle East region. Thus, if Britain had more extensive political and economic interests in India, in Pakistan her strategic stakes were much higher.

An inter-dominion war was anathema to the United Kingdom. Not only would it be unprecedented in Commonwealth history but it would also make it difficult to simultaneously pursue British interests in both Pakistan and India. Britain could not afford to alienate one or the other side, particularly Pakistan, her potential ally.

The men on the spot—Mountbatten, Auchinleck and the British officers commanding the forces of India and Pakistan—sought to avert war on the basis of judicial impartiality. In Kashmir as in Junagadh, they unswervingly followed the principle that neither India nor Pakistan should send troops into a princely state which had not acceded to it and they made it clear that British officers would be withdrawn at once from both armies if war seemed imminent. Attlee himself had approved the 'Stand Down' instructions. Yet, at the end of October, Britain began to shift the basis of her policy. Judicial impartiality required acceptance of the full implications of Kashmir's legal accession to India and was thus inconsistent with the policy requirement of avoiding Pakistan's alienation. The legal fact of accession was not questioned but to a large extent it was ignored. The precise balance between legality and expediency was not clearly defined and there were frequent inconsistencies in British policy as it evolved through *ad hoc* reactions to specific developments.

Attlee's Position

After the Cabinet meeting on 25 October, Nehru cabled Attlee to alert him about the impending crisis. 'A grave situation has developed in the State of Kashmir,' he wrote. Large numbers of Pathans equipped with motor transport and automatic weapons had crossed over from Pakistan and invaded Kashmir state territory. The invaders were proceeding up the Jhelum valley towards the vale of Kashmir. An urgent appeal for assistance had been received from the Kashmir government. India would be disposed to respond favourably to such an appeal from any friendly state, and more so in the case of Kashmir, whose 'borders run in common with Afghanistan, USSR[sic] and China.' '[The] security of Kashmir ... is vital to [the] security of India.' The Indian government was thus giving urgent consideration to Kashmir's appeal for assistance. 'I have thought it desirable to inform you of the situation,' Nehru concluded, 'because of its threat of international complications.'[1]

Anxious to prevent a possible war, Attlee sent urgent messages to both Nehru and Liaquat Ali Khan, counselling restraint and bilateral discussions. In doing so, he refrained from commenting on the relative merits of the Indian and Pakistani positions on Kashmir.

'The future relations of this State [Jammu and Kashmir] with Pakistan and India has obviously from the first presented a problem of difficulty the merits of which I do not think it incumbent of me to discuss,' he conveyed to Nehru. 'You must of course give serious consideration to an appeal from the Ruler of the State, but I beg of you not to let your answer to this appeal take the form of armed intervention by the forces of India.... This could only lead to open military conflict between the forces of the two Dominions resulting in incalculable tragedy.' He informed Nehru that he was also sending a message to Liaquat 'begging his government to do their utmost to prevent the incursion into Kashmir of armed persons from outside.' He suggested that Nehru, Liaquat and the Maharaja might meet to discuss Kashmir's future.[2]

Simultaneously, Attlee shot off a cable to Liaquat Ali Khan appealing to him to 'use your influence with any such who have already entered Kashmir to return home' and repeating his suggestion for a meeting between the two dominion Prime Ministers and the Jammu and Kashmir Maharaja.[3]

Meanwhile, the situation in Kashmir was developing at lightning speed. By the time Attlee's message was delivered to Nehru on the 27th, the Indian government had decided to accept Kashmir's accession and had begun to airlift troops into Srinagar. Nehru explained the rationale of the decision to the UK Prime Minister at some length. The tribal raiders, he pointed out, had reached Baramula, a mere 35 miles from Srinagar. 'There was immediate danger of these raids reaching Srinagar and destroying and sabotaging that capital city and massacring large numbers of people both Hindus and Muslims.' Urgent appeals for help had been received not only from the Maharaja but also the National Conference, the largest popular organisation in Kashmir. When the Maharaja first asked for accession, the Indian government had hesitated to accept it but '[u]ltimately when this demand was insistently made on us and was supported by responsible popular elements in Kashmir,' India decided to accept the accession, while making it clear that a 'final decision could only be taken in accordance with the wishes of the people, to be ascertained as soon as law and order were established.' It was inconceivable that the tribesmen could have been armed and provided with motor transport without the knowledge and assistance of the Pakistan authorities. While disowning their involvement, the Pakistan authorities wanted to force their will on the government and people of Kashmir. India would have welcomed Pakistan's cooperation in halting the raiders but she could not wait for such assistance before dealing with an urgent and critical threat.[4]

Nevertheless, in deference to Attlee's request, Nehru proposed to Liaquat that they meet to discuss the Kashmir situation. He invited Pakistan's cooperation in preventing the raiders from entering Kashmir and reiterated India's position that the accession was subject to a reference to the people of the state, which would be made once Kashmir had been cleared of the invaders.[5]

Once again, events were moving at greater speed than the cable traffic. Even before receiving Nehru's telegram, Attlee had learnt about the Indian airlift from press reports. He now sought to contain the situation by proposing that any *further* movement of Indian troops into Kashmir should be undertaken only by agreement with Pakistan. At the same time, he renewed his appeal to Pakistan to control the tribesmen and he urged both premiers to meet immediately to discuss the 'best means of restoration of order in Kashmir as a preliminary to talks about the future of Kashmir once order has been restored.'[6]

In replying to Nehru's second cable, Attlee deftly avoided endorsing the rationale of the Indian action. 'I do not think it would be helpful if I were to comment on the action your government has taken,' he wrote. 'The immediate and grave problem… [is] to prevent Kashmir becoming the cause of a break between the dominions themselves. This cannot but be a matter of concern to me and my Government.'[7]

Nehru had hoped that his account of the threat to Kashmir and Pakistan's obvious connivance in the tribal invasion would evoke some expression of support. Attlee had no intention of playing the role of an impartial judge. He was prepared to make an appeal to Pakistan but not to criticise her or to side with India on legal grounds. Though disappointed with Attlee's response, Nehru correctly identified its basis. 'I would suggest that developments be judged by [the] test of time and not only by expediency,' was Nehru's acid response to his British colleague.[8]

Though as a matter of policy British ministers refrained from supporting the Indian airlift in public, they privately recognised that it was justified. On one of Nehru's telegrams, Noel-Baker—no friend of India—minuted that the Indian Prime Minister 'makes a very strong case for his action in stopping the tribesmen.'[9]

Attlee's appeals fell on deaf ears in Karachi. Jinnah had no intention of withdrawing the invaders. Furious over the Indian rescue operation, he ordered the regular army to follow the tribal raiders into Kashmir but was thwarted, as we saw earlier, by Auchinleck and Gracey. Vastly relieved that open war had been averted, London hailed the initiative taken by the two officers. Alexander, the Defence Minister, congratulated Auchinleck on his 'timely and courageous action' and Gracey for his 'wisdom, restraint and resolution in a most difficult situation.'[10] In restraining Jinnah, Auchinleck had explicitly declared that Jammu and Kashmir was now part of Indian territory on account of the state's accession to the Indian Union. This position of legal rectitude went beyond the public statements deemed politic by British ministers. Ignoring this inconsistency, London judged the Supreme Commander's initiative by its result.

Conflicting Advice

London received conflicting advice from its men in Karachi and New Delhi. The British High Commissioner in Pakistan, Sir Lawrence Grafftey-Smith, sent an impassioned telegram arguing that the 'Indian Government's acceptance of [the] accession of Kashmir is the heaviest blow yet sustained by Pakistan in her struggle for existence.' 'Strategically,' he wrote, 'the frontier of Pakistan, which must be considered as requiring defence, is very greatly extended' since India would gain direct access to the North-West Frontier and tribal areas where 'infinite mischief can be made with "Pathanistan" or other slogans.' 'Afghanistan policy will almost certainly change for the worse; and disturbances and disorders in Gilgit and the North West Frontier zone generally may ... excite Russian interest and appetites.' Moreover, from an economic point of view, the 'threat to Pakistan's irrigation systems, hydroelectric projects, etc. arising from Kashmir's accession to India is held to be both serious and real.' In addition to these dangers looming ahead, Pakistan faced the immediate prospect of a new flood of refugees which Karachi feared would result from a 'repetition in Kashmir of East Punjab methods by Sikhs and Dogras ... designed to change [the] entire composition of the population.' His imagination inflamed by this fanciful prospect, Grafftey-Smith protested that the 'rumoured presence of a Sikh battalion in Kashmir is excessively provocative.'[11]

Grafftey-Smith's line of reasoning created a deep impression in London. Whitehall came to regard it as axiomatic that Indian control of the western areas of Jammu and Kashmir would imperil the very existence of Pakistan. In this view, an Indian presence in the western areas of the state would pose a strategic threat to Pakistan. Moreover, Indian control over the irrigation headworks in Mangla could lead to the ruin of Pakistan's agricultural economy. Nor could Pakistan's fragile economy be expected to cope with a massive influx of refugees which might result if India were to bring the Poonch and Mirpur areas under her control. Whitehall's views on this point were accepted by Mountbatten and the circle of British officers in New Delhi and were to have profound consequences (as we shall see later) for the course of military operations in Jammu and Kashmir. Whitehall officials, used to viewing subcontinental issues in simplistic communal terms, were ready even to accept Grafftey-Smith's strictures against the deployment of Sikh troops in Kashmir. They were proved wrong by the friendly reception accorded to the Sikhs by the population of Srinagar, a fact confirmed by no less an authority than Field Marshal Auchinleck.[12]

From New Delhi, Ismay and Shone offered a different perspective. Ismay, Mountbatten's Chief of Staff, was in London during the crucial days when India decided to send her army into Kashmir. On returning to his post on 28 October, he was 'shocked' to learn of the airlift. But, as he reported to Noel-Baker on 31 October, 'after hearing [the] full story I am convinced that there was no option despite [the] grave political and military risks involved.' Ismay emphasised that the 'supreme object is to stop the fighting at the earliest and the only man who can do this without difficulty is Jinnah who controls [the] lines of communication of the tribesmen.' 'It would be immensely helpful,' he urged the British government, 'if Prime Minister could at once make it clear to Jinnah that his action in conniving or at least permitting the tribesmen to pass through his territory is thoroughly blameworthy and that H.M.G. cannot but attach considerable responsibility to him for the present situation.' Pakistan, Ismay observed, was in this matter the 'guilty State.'[13] High Commissioner Shone cabled his own endorsement of this view. 'Pakistan,' he pointed out, 'has been guilty of conniving in actual use of force in [the] case of Kashmir.'[14]

Ismay's opinions normally carried considerable weight in London. A distinguished soldier-statesman, he had served as Churchill's Chief of Staff during World War II and was later to rise to the posts of Secretary of State for Commonwealth Relations (1951–52) and Secretary-General of NATO (1952–57). Whitehall had no doubt that Pakistan bore at least some responsibility for the tribal invasion. Nevertheless, as a matter of policy, Attlee was not prepared to alienate Pakistan. Noel-Baker, the Secretary of State for Commonwealth Relations, informed Ismay that Attlee felt it was difficult to pass judgement on culpability in view of conflicting reports and that the 'Prime Minister is therefore unwilling to send a message to Jinnah which in effect charges him with the major responsibility.'[15]

Role of Noel-Baker

Noel-Baker did not share Attlee's reluctance to apportion responsibility between India and Pakistan. The draft telegram he had proposed to send in reply to Ismay set out a list of omissions and commissions on the part of each of the two governments but it was not approved by Attlee, who had no desire to enter into this exercise. Noel-Baker contented himself by setting out his views in a memorandum to High Commissioners Shone and Grafftey-Smith. This document provides an insight into the thinking of the CRO during the initial stage of the Kashmir conflict. Pakistan was taken to task for being 'most unwise in not trying to take any physical steps to prevent the tribesmen from crossing their territory and the tribesmen have doubtless acted with some connivance of local Pakistan authorities, particularly in obtaining artillery and transport.' Jinnah was, however, absolved of the responsibility of actually organising the invasion. As regards India, she had a strong case for sending troops to Srinagar to prevent massacres by the tribal invaders, which would moreover have had a grave effect on the communal situation throughout the country. However, India had made 'provocative mistakes' in accepting Kashmir's accession since this was not really required for sending military help; in not consulting with or even informing Pakistan before the airlift; and in sending Sikh troops to Kashmir.[16]

According to this convoluted reasoning, India should have given due warning to Pakistan, then flown in troops to Srinagar for the sole purpose of saving the Kashmiris from the tribal invaders, and rejected the requests of the Maharaja and the most popular political party in Kashmir to accede to India, thus compelling the state to accede to Pakistan which, as even the CRO recognised, was at least partly responsible for the invasion!

Noel-Baker viewed Kashmir's accession to India as an awkward fact in the context of his Pakistan policy. He had served as the Secretary of State for Air before coming to the Commonwealth Relations

Office earlier in the year. He was thus fully aware of the importance which British defence planners attached to securing strategic bases in Pakistan, particularly in the context of air warfare. His essentially pro-Pakistan approach reflected also the tendency of many CRO offi-cials to view developments in the subcontinent in exclusively com-munal terms. Thus, Grafftey-Smith's views on the employment of Sikh soldiers in Kashmir found a receptive audience in the CRO though they were totally unfounded. The underlying premise in Noel-Baker's approach was spelt out in the CRO memorandum. 'It would have been natural for Kashmir to eventually have acceded to Pakistan on agreed terms,' the CRO asserted, because of her predominantly Mus-lim population, because her communications with the outside world ran mainly through Pakistan and because she derived considerable revenues from trade with Pakistan under a Customs Agreement signed in 1870. This approach totally ignored the fact that Jinnah's call for Pakistan had failed to evoke much support in Kashmir as well as the fact that the major political organisation in the state had joined the Maharaja in requesting accession to India. As regards communi-cations and revenues, events demonstrated soon enough that these could not be regarded as impediments to Kashmir's accession to India.

Noel-Baker now took two initiatives which were later to have major consequences for the evolution of British policy. He submitted for Attlee's approval—successfully on this occasion—a draft telegram to Liaquat on the eve of Mountbatten's visit to Lahore. The telegram, issued in Attlee's name on 31 October, read as follows:

> I earnestly hope that the result of the conference at Lahore on Saturday may result in the two Governments agreeing on plans which seem to afford the most hopeful chance of early cessation of the fighting in Kashmir and of agreeing together that the recent course of events is not to prejudice in any way the ulti-mate decision of the future of Kashmir. **If such satisfactory results are achieved** I trust that you and the Governor-General will be willing to use all your great influence to make it plain that it cannot be in the Muslim interests that the present situation should be allowed to continue and to make such appeal in the way you will know best to ensure that those not immediately under your control may fully weigh your counsel to them[17] (em-phasis added).

Noel-Baker described this message as following the same lines as Attlee's previous cables to Nehru and Liaquat.[18] Yet it differed from Attlee's earlier position on a crucial point. Attlee had previously appealed to the Pakistani Prime Minister to use his influence with the raiders to persuade them to return home. Embedded in the artful language of the latest cable was the hint that this step might be taken only *after* Pakistan and India reached agreement on 'plans which seem to afford the most hopeful chance of early cessation of the fighting.' Liaquat did not miss the hint. In a crucial turnaround, Britain had accepted Pakistan's contention that she could make an effective appeal to the tribal invaders only after a solution had been found which was acceptable to her. A copy of the message was urgently communicated to Ismay (to be passed on to Mountbatten before his meeting with Jinnah) but, under specific instructions from Noel-Baker, its contents were not shared with the Government of India.

The 'Stand Down' Instructions

The Commonwealth Secretary's second initiative concerned the 'Stand Down' instructions. As we saw earlier, Attlee had approved Auchinleck's 'Stand Down' instructions following the meeting of the Commonwealth Affairs Committee in October. Supplementary advice was to have been sent to the Supreme Commander, suggesting the desirability of prior consultations with London, if possible, but these instructions were not actually sent at the time.

In early November, Noel-Baker decided to follow up on the question. The resultant telegram to Auchinleck was issued in Alexander's name but Noel-Baker's finger-prints are visible all over the text. Upto this point, the rationale of the 'Stand Down' order had been that British personnel ought not to participate in hostilities against any dominion. The telegram which issued on 6 November shifted the basis of the instructions. 'We are of the opinion,' Auchinleck was informed, 'that this [Stand Down] should take place only if there is danger of British officers actually taking the field against each other. Planning in each of the two Headquarters against each other is obviously highly embarrassing and distasteful but we doubt if it is in itself a reason for final withdrawal of all officers from both sides.'[19]

The Commonwealth Affairs Committee had merely agreed that the Supreme Commander might be advised to consult London, if possible, before ordering a 'Stand Down.' This limited decision envisaged no change in the circumstances in which the 'Stand Down' was to be invoked. Only a few days previously, Auchinleck had taken decisive action in accordance with standing instructions—specifically approved by the Prime Minister—which required all British personnel to 'Stand Down' in an inter-dominion conflict even though their command or administrative functions did not involve the risk of their actually fighting fellow British officers. Auchinleck had been commended for adhering to this approach in his confrontation with Jinnah. Alexander's congratulatory telegram had actually been drafted in the CRO and had been personally approved by Noel-Baker.

What then, was, the motive behind the sudden shift reflected in the 6 November telegram—a shift which could claim no sanction in the preceding decisions of the Commonwealth Affairs Committee? A passage in the cable provides a clue:

*Both the Dominion Governments already know that we shall withdraw all British officers if the two armies actually begin to fight each other. This should have some restraining influence though it is true it is **likely to have less effect on India than on Pakistan** (emphasis added).*

The Indian government had taken in its stride the threat of resignation of British officers over Junagadh policy. In contrast, Jinnah's climb-down at Lahore confirmed his critical dependence on the services of British personnel. Noel-Baker drew the conclusion that the application of the 'Stand Down' instructions on the lines already approved by the Prime Minister and communicated to India and Pakistan, would place the latter at a disadvantage.

Attlee's message to Liaquat on the eve of the Mountbatten–Jinnah meeting was intended to offset the weakness of Pakistan's legal and political position; the revised 'Stand Down' instructions were designed to offset her military weakness. Thus, by early November, British policy took a sharp turn in favour of Pakistan. The Indian government was deliberately kept in the dark about the changes in policy.

Subsequent events would show that Alexander had not grasped the full import of the telegram to which he had put his signature. The restriction on 'taking the field against each other' was artfully vague; it was subsequently interpreted by Noel-Baker in more ways than one, with profound consequences for the Kashmir operations. But we are anticipating developments and must now return to the Kashmir story as it unfolded in the last two months of 1947.

VI
Jammu Province

While the Indian army was engaged in clearing the invaders from the Srinagar vale, the raiders continued their advance in the Poonch and Mirpur areas of Jammu province. By the beginning of November, they had occupied Bhimbar, Rajouri and Rawalkot and were threatening the State Force garrisons in Mirpur, Kotli, Poonch and Naoshera. Thousands of refugees, fleeing from the raiders, sought shelter in the Poonch garrison. On 2 November, the Prime Minister of Jammu and Kashmir, Mehr Chand Mahajan, made a desperate appeal to Nehru to rescue the beleaguered garrison.

At this juncture, India's topmost priority was to remove the threat to Srinagar. In the state's Jammu province, the major task assigned to the army was to keep open the lines of communication from Pathankot, the main supply depot, to Srinagar. This was no easy task as the route ran close to the Pakistan border for over 63 miles. The threatened State Force garrisons were sustained by supplies dropped by the Indian airforce.

The Defence Committee met in early November to consider what response was possible to the urgent appeals from the Jammu and Kashmir state authorities. Air Headquarters expressed their inability to increase their supply commitments. The general view of the service chiefs was that it would be difficult to provide adequate help to the stranded garrisons in Mirpur, Kotli and Naoshera. Lieutenant-General Bucher, the officiating Commander-in-Chief, pointed out the undesirability of allowing operations in the Poonch and Mirpur areas to affect the main operations in the Srinagar sector. He said that the Jammu–Srinagar road could not be kept open for the three winter months and it was, therefore, necessary to stockpile supplies in Srinagar before the onset of winter. Any diversion of effort from this task would be disastrous.[1] Mountbatten, Chairman of the Defence Committee, added a further warning. In the Mirpur and Poonch areas, there was a substantial local element among the hostile forces. The local population was likely to include both friends and hostile persons. It would prove impossible to distinguish friend from foe and unfortunate incidents were likely to occur in the course of operations.[2]

Thus, the Governor General and Commander-in-Chief were opposed to offensive action in Jammu province. Nehru, who did not subscribe to Mountbatten's appreciation, wanted to afford whatever assistance was possible to the State Forces. However, he accepted the need to accord first priority to the Srinagar operations. Hence, on 4 November, the Defence Committee 'agreed that it was not a matter of high priority at the present time to send Indian troops into the Poonch area with the object of reinforcing or evacuating the Kashmir State troops there.'[3]

Within the next ten days, however, the military situation was transformed. Baramula was freed on 8 November and on 14 November Indian forces entered Uri, 65 miles from Srinagar. The town of Uri is located at the point where the road along the narrow Jhelum valley enters the broad vale of Kashmir. Thus, control of Uri put the Indian army in a position to guarantee the security of Srinagar. The threat to the capital having been removed, the Indian government decided to take a fresh look at the question of launching operations in Jammu province.

This brought to the surface the wide differences at the higher political level between Nehru and Mountbatten and, at the military level, between Kalwant Singh and Bucher.

On 14 November, Major-General Kalwant Singh, who had recently assumed charge as General-Officer-Commanding, Jammu and Kashmir Division, briefed the Defence Committee on the military situation. He informed the committee that a column had been sent from Jammu town to Mirpur and had already covered half the distance. It was stated that the intentions of the army were now as follows:

(a) To reconnoitre from Uri to Domel and Kohala; to deny the road to the tribesmen, and to try to reinforce Jammu State forces,

(b) *To continue the movement of the column from Jammu to Mirpur and Punch [Poonch], in order to relieve the garrisons of State forces still holding out,*

(c) *To send, at the appropriate moment, another column from Uri to Poonch, with the idea of meeting the column coming from Jammu. Thereafter, the Uri column could be maintained from Jammu,*

(d) *To continue to send in sufficient supplies to maintain the troops in Kashmir and Jammu through the winter.*[4]

Lieutenant-General Bucher painted a more sombre picture. He was deeply concerned about possible developments in the Poonch area. The tribal Lashkars could motor right up to the Poonch border and then infiltrate into the state in large numbers through the hill tracks. In the Kashmir valley, the tribal raiders had made the mistake of fighting like regular troops, thus providing good targets for the Indian army in open ground. They had probably learnt their lesson and might be expected in Poonch to play their own guerilla game in the hills. Bucher accepted the importance of evacuating isolated Kashmir state troops but he warned against a permanent commitment in Poonch.

The final decision, as recorded, was as follows:

(i) *It was of vital importance to deny the whole stretch of the Jhelum valley road to tribal ingress into Kashmir.*

(ii) *After this had been properly effected, it was necessary to begin replacing Indian Army personnel by State troops and police in order to concentrate them progressively in and around Srinagar. This concentration was to be a prelude to a general and sustained withdrawal to India, as the demands for aid to the civil power in Kashmir lessened.*

(iii) *In view of this and the poor flying conditions for air transport during the winter it was desirable that the Jammu–Banihal–Srinagar road should be kept open, if possible.*

(iv) *It was necessary to establish such a force in Jammu as was required to give aid to the civil power, to suppress disorderly elements and to protect the minority communities.*

(v) *It was further necessary to despatch small mobile columns to relieve and evacuate beleaguered garrisons near to the Jammu–Poonch–Uri road. These columns were also to*

> *evacuate non-Muslims living in close proximity to the road,*
> *if their lives were endangered.*
> *(vi) Lastly no effort in aid of the civil power over and above that*
> *in serial number (v) was to be embarked upon in Poonch,*
> *because the advent of winter, and lack of means, rendered*
> *winter action impossible.*[5]

These 'instructions' departed significantly from the 'intentions' set out by Kalwant Singh. In the Uri sector, the main task was defined on more or less similar lines but in Jammu province, the objective was limited to the evacuation of beleaguered garrisons near the Jammu–Poonch–Uri road. The net result of this approach would be to leave the raiders in uncontested control of a large stretch of territory. Moreover, after they had completed their task in the Jhelum valley, regular Indian forces were to be withdrawn altogether from the state, instead of being redeployed against the invaders in other sectors.

The recorded 'decision' reflected Bucher's views, not the government's. Nehru's understanding was that the army had been instructed to 'rid Jammu of raiders'; not simply evacuate beleaguered garrisons. This is clear from a letter he wrote to the Chief Ministers on 14 November soon after the conclusion of the Defence Committee meeting. He explained the objective of the operations in the following terms:

> *The position now in Kashmir is that our troops have taken Uri*
> *from which one road takes off to Domel on the Abbotabad fron-*
> *tier and another to Poonch where a Kashmir detachment has been*
> *beleaguered for quite some time. The Kashmir valley is now*
> *practically cleared of raiders, but for stragglers, and the threat to*
> *Srinagar has been removed. But the position in Jammu is not*
> *very good. We have not till now been able to divert to this region*
> *the forces necessary for the operations there; but we are doing so*
> *now, and the next phase of the campaign will be to rid Jammu of*
> *raiders. This will not be an easy task for the communications are*
> *difficult and the area is very close to West Punjab from which*
> *supplies can reach raiders easily. Nevertheless, it is a task which,*
> *I am confident, will be carried out satisfactorily by our army.*

Nehru was under no illusion that the task would be completed quickly. Apart from military difficulties, there were also political problems. He explained:

The Hindu–Muslim problem in Jammu is as bad as in West Punjab of which in fact this part of Kashmir is an extension geographically. While in the Kashmir valley, under Sheikh Abdullah's influence, there is remarkable communal unity, and Muslims, Hindus and Sikhs alike have demonstrated cohesion of purpose and effort in the phase of a common danger, in Jammu there is fierce communal passion, and the RSS, the Akali Dal and the Muslim League, operating in various degrees, have created a situation full of explosive possibilities. For this reason, our commitments in Jammu and Kashmir will, I fear, be onerous for quite some time to come.[6]

Kalwant Singh, on his part, seems to have interpreted the instructions received from Army Headquarters with a generous measure of flexibility. He proceeded broadly on the lines of the 'intentions' he had previously outlined. On 16 November, he issued orders for the early relief of Naoshera, Jhangar, Kotli, Mirpur and Poonch. With this object in view, he directed a force under Brigadier Paranjape to move immediately on the access Akhnur–Beri Pattan–Naoshera, Jhangar. After establishing a firm base in Jhangar the following day (17 November), the column was to advance to Kotli, which was to be relieved on 18 November and Mirpur, to be relieved by 20 November at the latest. A second force, commanded by Brigadier L.P. Sen, was to strike from Uri on 18 November, arriving at Poonch the same day. A detachment of this force was to proceed south from Poonch to effect a junction from Paranjape's force. After reinforcing the Poonch garrison with one battalion, the rest of Sen's force was to return to Uri. Paranjape's was to receive support from Jammu.

Bucher severely criticised this plan. The tasks envisaged by Kalwant Singh, he maintained, far exceeded the instructions conveyed to him in accordance with the record of the Defence Committee's decisions of 14 November. Bucher stated that the uncoordinated advance of the two columns, from Jammu and Uri respectively, was dangerous. Moreover, the planned advance from Uri to Poonch was almost foolhardy. Bucher emphasised that India could not afford to take any risk that might result in even a minor setback as this would lead to the immediate loss of the prestige gained by operations in the vale.[7] It will be seen that this extreme aversion to risk carried the implication that the Poonch area should be abandoned to its fate lest the army suffer even a minor setback.

Kalwant Singh replied to these charges on 20 November, noting that he had already ordered that the advance from Uri to Poonch should be stopped.[8] Meanwhile, operations proceeded with some delays and modifications. The column from Jammu relieved State Force garrisons at Naoshera (18 November), Jhangar (19 November) and Kotli (26 November). On 20 November, Sen was ordered to send a column from Uri to Poonch. This column was unexpectedly halted by a destroyed bridge at Kahuta but a part of the force was able to cross over and reach Poonch, thus enabling the garrison to hold out till the arrival of further reinforcements. Mirpur, however, could not be relieved in time. The State Force garrison evacuated the town on 25 November. The relief operation was thus substantially, though not completely, successful. By the end of the month, the situation in Jammu province had markedly improved. This would not have been possible if Bucher's policy of avoiding all risks had been followed.

At this point, it is necessary to mention a fortuitous circumstance which had a significant bearing on the operations. The Governor-General, Lord Mountbatten, left India on 9 November, to attend the wedding of his nephew, Phillip, with Princess Elizabeth. The Jammu operations could thus proceed without interference on his part. On his return on 24 November, Mountbatten faced a *fait accompli*. He later complained bitterly to Nehru about the change of military objectives during his absence. He wrote:

> ... I have on several occasions repeated my views on the question of sending Indian troops into these Western areas. At the last Defence Committee meeting before I left for London, I did not raise my voice against the stated intentions of the army to send columns from Jammu towards Mirpur and Poonch, and from Uri to Poonch in order to relieve the garrisons of State forces still holding out. But on the day I left, it was for this object and this object only, that these operations were planned to take place.
>
> During my absence in London this object changed. It then evidently became the purpose of the Government of India to impose their military will on the Poonch and Mirpur areas.[9]

Nehru responded:

> You will remember that from the very first date that we discussed the Kashmir issue, I have laid stress on the fact that we must

drive out the raiders and establish peace and order in Kashmir State.

It was only then that the question of plebiscite arose. At no time did I think of accepting the presence of outside raiders in any part of Kashmir State.[10]

As we saw in Chapter 5, Whitehall believed that Indian control of the western borderlands of Jammu would pose a grave strategic and economic threat to Pakistan. It is against this background that we must view Mountbatten's opposition to plans for clearing the raiders from the Poonch and Mirpur areas. Not surprisingly, the operational directives issued by senior British commanders were heavily influenced by the views of Whitehall and the Governor-General rather than the views of the Indian Cabinet. The divergence in the two approaches were to appear starkly in the deliberations of the Defence Committee over the next fortnight, culminating in late December in a climactic exchange between the Governor-General and the Prime Minister.

VII
The Governor-General as Mediator

At the meeting on 28 October in which Auchinleck prevented Jinnah from sending the Pakistani army into Kashmir, he had also put forward a proposal for a round-table conference between Jinnah, Liaquat Ali Khan, Mountbatten, Nehru, the Maharaja and the Kashmir Premier.[1] Jinnah readily agreed to invite the others to a meeting in Lahore. He could not have failed to see the resemblance between Auchinleck's proposal and Attlee's plea for a tripartite meeting.

Indian leaders were given the impression that the invitation originated from Jinnah and Mountbatten threw his full weight behind its acceptance. The proposal, however, ran into strong opposition in the Cabinet.[2] The Governor-General argued that a session of the Joint Defence Council was due in any case and this could be combined with the proposed talks. Though this round of the Joint Defence Council was scheduled to be held in New Delhi, Mountbatten urged that the venue might be shifted to Lahore as Liaquat was ill and unable to travel.

Patel strongly objected to the proposal. He maintained that since Pakistan was the aggressor, there was no reason why India's leaders should go 'crawling to Jinnah.' He was supported by other ministers who saw a parallel between the proposed trip to Lahore and Chamberlain's inglorious journey to Munich. Only Nehru was prepared to accept the invitation, though he was ill himself. Unwilling to leave any stone unturned in the quest for peace, he agreed to accompany Mountbatten to Lahore. Nehru, however, objected to the Maharaja's participation in the meeting. 'Mr. Jinnah wanted the Maharaja Saheb and you to be invited also to this meeting,' he wrote to Mahajan, 'but I did not encourage this idea. I think all our talks should be on the Dominion level. Of course, if anything affecting Kashmir is to be decided, the Kashmir Government must be consulted. In that consultation it is necessary that Sheikh Abdullah should be present. At present I see no reason why any of you should be go to Lahore to confer with Mr. Jinnah or anybody else.'[3]

At this point, the Pakistani government chose to issue a statement rejecting Kashmir's accession to India, describing it as being 'based on fraud and violence.' The public airing of this wild charge made it impossible for Nehru to accompany Mountbatten and he sent word to the Governor-General that he was too ill to go to Pakistan.

This left Mountbatten in an awkward position. An outright rejection of Jinnah's invitation would be a rebuff to the Quaid-e-Azam and would damage Auchinleck's credibility in Pakistan. Even more worrying was the danger that it might derail Attlee's efforts to promote a tripartite meeting. The Governor-General decided to salvage what he could of the initiative by flying to Lahore unaccompanied by any of his ministers.

Before his departure, Mountbatten succeeded in obtaining a major concession from Nehru. As we noted earlier, the Indian government had accepted Kashmir's accession, subject to its declared policy that such matters should be finalised in accordance with the will of the . people. The intention was that India herself would conduct the exercise in a fair and open manner after the invaders had been driven off and peace was re-established. This was the procedure followed later in Junagadh. Mountbatten now persuaded Nehru to agree that the exercise might be conducted under the auspices of the United Nations in order to demonstrate that it was free and fair. On the eve of the Governor-General's departure for Lahore, Nehru informed Mahajan about the decision. 'A plebiscite has to be impartial,' he wrote on 31 October. 'After full consideration of this problem we are inclined to think that it should be held under United Nations' auspices.'[4] The first step had been taken towards involvement of the United Nations.

Mountbatten–Jinnah Meeting

Mountbatten arrived in Lahore on 1 November without a brief from the Indian government and with no authority to negotiate. He was not altogether without guidance from London, however. As we saw in Chapter 5, Attlee sent a cable to Liaquat on 31 October hinting that Pakistan might persuade the raiders to return home *after* an agreement had been reached with India on plans affording a chance for an early ceasefire. A copy of Attlee's message was rushed to Ismay.

The role Mountbatten took upon himself was that of a mediator, though it was not formally described—or, possibly, even recognised—as such. It was a curious role for the Governor-General of a country that viewed itself as the aggrieved party. Mountbatten met with Liaquat in his sick-bed and, at much greater length, with Jinnah. His conversation with the latter lasted over three hours and ranged over the issues of Kashmir, Junagadh and Hyderabad, darting from one topic to another. Mountbatten made it clear from the outset that he was speaking 'not as Governor-General of India but as the ex-Viceroy who had been responsible for partition and was anxious to see that it did not result in any harm coming to the two Dominions.'[5]

Mountbatten tried to set at rest Jinnah's suspicion that the airlift had been planned long in advance as a plot to secure Kashmir's accession. He recounted the events as they had occurred and handed over to Jinnah a copy of a chronological statement of developments signed by the three British officers commanding India's armed forces. Jinnah expressed surprise at the remarkable speed of the operation but did not question the chronological statement or Mountbatten's own account. He complained instead that the Indian government had failed to inform him on 24 October itself that a crisis was developing in Kashmir. If only India had 'suggested that Pakistan should co-operate in dealing with the situation, all the trouble would have been ended by now,' he said disingenuously.[6] Jinnah repeated his charge that the accession rested on 'fraud and violence' and would never be accepted by Pakistan. Mountbatten rejected the allegation, pointing out that the question of 'fraud' did not arise since the Maharaja was fully entitled to make the accession. As regards 'violence,' this had come from tribesmen for whom Pakistan was responsible.

Mountbatten handed over to Jinnah a composite formula he had drafted on the flight from New Delhi for settling differences over Kashmir, Junagadh and Hyderabad. He said that though he had not yet shown the formula to the Indian authorities, he felt that they might find it acceptable. Mountbatten's formula ran as follows:

The Governments of India and Pakistan agree that, where the ruler of a State does not belong to the community to which the majority of his subjects belong, and where the State has not accepted to that Dominion whose majority community is the same as the State's, the question of whether the State should finally accede to one or the other of the two Dominions should in all cases be decided by an impartial reference to the will of the people.[7]

Jinnah rejected the proposal. He insisted that a plebiscite was redundant and undesirable when it was quite clear that states should accede on the basis of their communal majority. He offered instead to exchange Junagadh for Kashmir. Mountbatten observed that the Government of India would agree to changing the accession of a state only if a plebiscite showed that its people were not in favour of the accession. Jinnah argued that he could not accept a formula which covered Hyderabad, in addition to Kashmir and Junagadh. He disclaimed any deeper interest in Hyderabad but stated that the Nizam wished to remain independent and Pakistan could not be party to coercing him to accession.

Lord Ismay, who had accompanied Mountbatten, asked Jinnah how the fighting in Kashmir could be stopped. Jinnah's response was that both sides should withdraw simultaneously and immediately. Mountbatten enquired how the tribal raiders were to be called off. Jinnah replied that all he had to do was to give them an order to come out and to warn them that if they did not comply, he would cut off their lines of communication. He said that if Mountbatten was prepared to fly out with him to Srinagar, he would guarantee that the matter would be settled in a day. Mountbatten, tongue in cheek, expressed mild astonishment at the degree of control Jinnah had over the raiders! He refrained, however, from pressing for the withdrawal of the raiders as a first step for a settlement. Mountbatten doubtless bore in mind the latest turn in British policy, signalled by Attlee's telegram to Liaquat.[*]

When Mountbatten reverted to his proposal for a plebiscite, Jinnah claimed that he opposed the proposal for with Indian troops in Kashmir and with Abdullah in power, a plebiscite would not be free and fair. Mountbatten sought to meet this objection by suggesting a

---

[*] Mountbatten's views on Pakistan's involvement in the tribal raid differed from those of the CRO. He was not in favour of ignoring the Pakistani role or pretending that Karachi had no control over the raiders, His report on his talks with Jinnah exposed the latter's role. Mountbatten was careful, however, to refrain from any action which ran contrary to British policy.

plebiscite under United Nations auspices. Jinnah, however, insisted that only he and Mountbatten could jointly organise a plebiscite. Mountbatten pointed out that he could not accept such a role as a Britisher and as a constitutional Governor-General. Even if the Government of India were to agree, said Mountbatten, Attlee would not consent. Jinnah remained unimpressed.

On his return to New Delhi, Mountbatten suggested to Nehru that he send a cable to Liaquat setting out India's proposals for bringing the fighting to an end. He also submitted a 'very rough note' containing his own suggestions for proposals to form the basis of discussions with Pakistan. These included the following elements:

- 'a plebiscite should be held in Kashmir.... UNO might be asked to provide observers for this plebiscite.'
- 'a joint India–Pakistan force should hold the ring while the plebiscite is being held.'
- 'both Governments should agree on the form of the public announcement to be made in regard to the procedure for accession of those States in which this matter is in dispute.' The proposal presented by Mountbatten to Jinnah could form the basis of discussion.
- 'the above proposals should be the subject of a round-table discussion at the earliest possible date.'[8]

It will be seen that in drawing up these proposals, Mountbatten was mindful of British policy which sought to accommodate Pakistan in a major way. He ignored the Indian position that withdrawal of the raiders should be the first step toward a settlement, thereby accommodating Pakistan's position (discreetly supported in Attlee's cable of 31 October to Liaquat) that an appeal to the tribesmen could be made only after the two governments had come to an understanding on Kashmir's future. It was impossible for Mountbatten to accept Jinnah's suggestion for a plebiscite held by the two Governor-Generals. He had rightly pointed out that the arrangement would be inconsistent with his constitutional role and also unacceptable to the British Government. The latter point was soon confirmed in a telegram from the CRO to Grafftey-Smith advising that, even if India were to agree to the proposal, it would 'surely be awkward from [the] British angle' since 'Lord Mountbatten would be placed in a very invidious position as Joint Arbiter with Mr. Jinnah.'[9] Nevertheless, Mountbatten accommodated the underlying Pakistani concern by suggesting that a joint

India–Pakistan force should 'hold the ring' during the plebiscite. In other words, withdrawal of the raiders from Jammu and Kashmir would be followed by the induction of Pakistani army regulars. Finally, Attlee's proposal for a tripartite meeting, with the Maharaja as one of the parties, was duly reflected in Mountbatten's suggestion regarding a 'round table' discussion.

These proposals were inevitably still-born. The idea that a joint India–Pakistan force should 'hold the ring' flew in the face of Kashmir's accession to India. It implied a derogation of sovereignty which India could never accept. India was prepared to accept a plebiscite under United Nations auspices but not the induction of the Pakistani army into the state. Thus nothing more was heard of the Mountbatten proposals.

Indian and Pakistani Proposals

On 2 November, the day after the Mountbatten–Jinnah meeting, Nehru made a public offer to hold a referendum under United Nations auspices. He announced in a radio broadcast:

> We on our part have no intention of using our troops in Kashmir when the danger of invasion has passed. We have declared that the fate of the people is ultimately to be decided by the people.... We are prepared when peace and law and order have been established to have a referendum held under international auspices like the United Nations.[10]

Attlee rushed to congratulate Nehru on the initiative. He cabled:

> [I]f I may say so it seems to me that you have made a notable step towards the restoration of mutual confidence [with Pakistan] by the announcement in your broadcast yesterday that your Government was willing when order has been re-established to have a referendum under international auspices. Your statement that you will withdraw your troops after restoration of order is of course also of the first importance.[11]

The Pakistani reaction took Attlee by surprise. Liaquat Ali Khan rejected the Indian offer in the most violent terms in a cable to Attlee.

> [It is] full of most dangerous potentialities.... What the Indian Government calls restoration of law and order is no more than

an attempt to oppress, kill, terrorise and drive out the Moslem population of Jammu & Kashmir until, like the East Punjab and the Indian States in East Punjab, the composition of the population is entirely changed.... Pandit Nehru has even avoided use of the word plebiscite and has spoken of referendum which might mean anything. After the Indian Government have established complete mastery over the territories of Jammu & Kashmir, the holding of a plebiscite or referendum will be purely a farce.[12]

Liaquat spelt out the Pakistani proposals on the lines that Jinnah had indicated to Mountbatten. These, he said, comprised the following:

(1) To put an immediate stop to fighting, the two Governors-General should be authorised ... to issue a proclamation forthwith giving 48 hours notice to the two opposing forces to cease fire. Governor-General of Pakistan [has no?] control over the forces of the provisional Government of Kashmir or tribesmen engaged in fighting, but he will warn them in the clearest terms that if they do not obey [call?] to cease-fire immediately, the forces of both Dominions will make war on them.

(2) Both forces of the Indian Dominion and the tribesmen to withdraw simultaneously and with utmost expedition from Jammu & Kashmir State territory;

(3) ... the two Governors-General to be given power to restore peace, undertaking the administration of Jammu & Kashmir State, and arrange for Plebiscite without delay and under their joint control and supervision.[13]

Attlee commended these proposals as a 'promising starting point for discussions' but rejected Liaquat's allegations against Nehru and sought to minimise the differences in the two approaches. 'I cannot believe that Mr. Nehru's pledges have the sinister implications which you suggest,' he informed Liaquat. 'It seems to me therefore that both you and the Prime Minister of India have put forward proposals which, although they differ in form, are broadly based on the same principles.'[14]

In reality, the divergence between the two positions was formidable. Pakistan's attempt to seize Kashmir by the clandestine employment of irregulars had misfired, precipitating the state's accession to India. Pakistan now sought to reverse the events by diplomatic means. Her proposals totally disregarded the fact of accession; they sought also to set aside the authority of both the Maharaja and the most popular political party in the state by transferring control jointly to Jinnah and Mountbatten. India's stand was based on the fact that the state had legally acceded to India, with the support of its largest and most popular political organisation. She was prepared to accept a referendum under United Nations auspices but only after the raiders had been expelled and order had been restored. The idea that Pakistani irregulars should be replaced by regular Pakistani army troops was legally and politically unacceptable to her.

This was the chasm that Mountbatten sought to bridge through negotiations on the margins of the Joint Defence Council sessions in November and December 1947.

A Moment of Hope

As we saw earlier, by mid-November the Indian army had succeeded in removing the immediate threat to the Srinagar vale and was poised for further operations against the raiders. While progress on the military front was satisfactory, Nehru was sensitive to the need for allaying Pakistani misapprehensions concerning India's intentions and preventing the outbreak of a war between the two new states. He shared his thinking in one of his periodic circular letters to provincial Chief Ministers.

> *Recent events in Kashmir and partly our action in Babariawad and Mangrol have been a severe blow to the Pakistani Government. They have a terrible sense of frustration. Already they were being overwhelmed by their problems. The vast number of Muslim refugees who have gone to Pakistan are a terrible burden on them and they cannot look after them. Because of all this they are suffering from the delusion that the Government of India are conspiring to destroy Pakistan. That, of course, is completely false. There is no conspiracy and there is no desire to destroy their State in any way. Any such attempt would lead to grave injury to us. War is a dangerous thing and must be avoided. Only those who do not understand it or its consequences talk lightly of war. From the military point of view there is little doubt that if there was war between India and Pakistan, Pakistan as a State would perish. But, undoubtedly, India would suffer very great*

injury and all our schemes of progress would have to be pushed aside for many years. Therefore, we must do our utmost to avoid war, and that is our definite policy.... Both statesmanship and expediency, as well as humanity, require this.[15]

This spirit of goodwill came under stress on the eve of the Joint Defence Council meeting when, in telegrams to Attlee and Nehru, Liaquat Ali Khan dismissed Sheikh Abdullah as a 'quisling' and once more accused the Indian government of attempting to eliminate the entire Muslim population of Jammu and Kashmir. Smarting from these vicious attacks, Nehru was inclined to call off the talks but was dissuaded from doing so by Mountbatten.

On 27 November, the two Prime Ministers met in New Delhi in a frosty atmosphere. Neither broached the question of Kashmir and it was left to Mountbatten to introduce the subject by recounting his efforts towards paving the way for a plebiscite following the state's accession to India. Nehru and Liaquat followed by giving an account of developments from their respective view-points. Mountbatten then proceeded to draw up a list of proposals based on the discussions. He noted that there was full agreement on the following points: (a) that a plebiscite should be held under an independent body like the United Nations; (b) that as soon as the situation had cleared up, Indian troops would be withdrawn, except for small garrisons at vital strategic points to prevent further raids; (c) that full freedom of speech would be permitted; and (d) that refugees would be allowed to return to the state before the plebiscite. In addition to these, the Pakistani government wished that: (a) Sheikh Abdullah should form a coalition with the opposition party; (b) United Nations representatives should be sent for as early as possible to speed up the plebiscite process and to act as preliminary observers; or (c) alternatively, an entirely new administration should be set up in Kashmir, which the people of Pakistan would accept as impartial.[16]

The discussions continued on the following day. Mountbatten argued that the real difficulty was that the Pakistani government could appeal to the 'raiders, local rebels and the people in Pakistan who were assisting them' only after they were in a position to 'give them an assurance that the object had been achieved.' However, steps for achieving this objective could not be initiated until the fighting had stopped. What was therefore required, according to Mountbatten, was a 'public declaration giving the necessary assurances on the

basis that the fighting would stop.'[17] On his suggestion, Lord Ismay was asked to draft a paper for discussion, with the assistance of Mohammed Ali and V.P. Menon.
Briefly, the proposal drawn up by Ismay was that:

(i) *Pakistan should use all her influence to persuade the so-called 'Azad Kashmir' forces to cease fighting and the tribesmen and other invaders to withdraw from Kashmir territory as quickly as possible;*

(ii) *India should withdraw the bulk of her forces, leaving only small detachments of minimum strength to deal with disturbances;*

(iii) *The UN should be asked to send a commission to hold a plebiscite and, before it was held, to recommend to the governments of India and Pakistan and Kashmir steps which should be taken to ensure a free and fair plebiscite; and*

(iv) *Certain steps which it was intended to take towards this objective—such as release of political prisoners and return of refugees—should be announced immediately.*[18]

In essence, Ismay's proposal sought to reconcile the legal implications of Kashmir's accession to India with the requirements of Pakistan's expressed concern for a fair and impartial plebiscite. It implicitly acknowledged India's sovereign rights by permitting her to maintain a military presence in Kashmir after the withdrawal of the invaders, and by recognising the authority of the Kashmir administration. At the same time, it offered Pakistan an assurance that the plebiscite would be free and fair by restricting the Indian military presence to a minimal level and by expanding the role of the United Nations by giving it an advisory function in the run-up to the plebiscite. It thus conceded Liaquat's demand for the induction of a United Nations presence before the plebiscite but not his demand for reconstituting the state government.

An inconclusive discussion followed on these proposals, centred mainly on the question of a residual Indian military force in the state. The Pakistani Prime Minister was joined in these discussions by Ghulam Mohammed and Nehru by Sardar Patel. Liaquat and his colleague reiterated their stand that *all* Indian troops should be withdrawn without exception. This was of course opposed by the Indian participants. At one stage, Patel offered a complete withdrawal from the Poonch area. This aroused much interest among the Pakistani representatives, who gave the impression that they might accept retention of Indian troops in other parts of the state if total withdrawal from the Poonch area was guaranteed. Nehru, however, drew attention to the problem of defining the 'Poonch area' and the question was not pursued further. Liaquat Ali Khan proposed that the British government should be asked to make available British troops for the plebiscite, presumably because this would obviate the need for an Indian military presence. Nehru replied curtly: 'British troops will never again enter Indian territory' and Mountbatten expressed doubt whether the United Kingdom would agree to provide troops.

When Nehru observed that he would have to consult the Maharaja regarding the Ismay proposal, Liaquat promptly countered by observing that he, likewise, would have to consult the 'Azad Kashmir Government,' though he hastened to add that Pakistan did not recognise this 'government'! Sardar Patel at one stage declared that he would reject any proposal concerning a plebiscite in Kashmir unless Pakistan accepted the principle of a plebiscite for Hyderabad also. However, he did not press the point and this linkage fell by the wayside.

An incidental feature of the discussion was the light it threw on Pakistan's assessment of Abdullah's popularity in Kashmir. Liaquat Ali Khan observed that Sheikh Abdullah probably did have very great influence in the valley of Srinagar; he added however that as far as he was aware, Abdullah had little influence in Jammu and none in Poonch and Gilgit.[19] Despite his denunciation of Abdullah as a quisling, Liaquat had no difficulty in recognising the strength of his following, at least in the Kashmir valley.

From a chilly start, the mood had become remarkably cordial and, towards the conclusion of the meeting, both Prime Ministers agreed that an early discussion on joint defence plans against external aggression would be a practical and constructive step towards restoring goodwill between India and Pakistan. Their belief in shared interests held firm even at this time of a crisis in Indo–Pakistan relations.

Mountbatten was encouraged by the course of the discussions. Both Liaquat and Nehru had reserved their respective positions, neither having rejected the Ismay formula outright. Mountbatten formed the impression that Liaquat was willing to compromise on total withdrawal of Indian troops and on a change of administration in Jammu and Kashmir. Nehru, on his part, had not rejected the implied linkage between the raiders' withdrawal and an accord on conditions for a fair plebiscite. Nor had he dismissed the idea of a substantially expanded UN role. The Governor-General was hopeful about the prospects for progress on the lines of the Ismay proposals. Nehru, too, hoped for an accord on Kashmir. The successful outcome of negotiations on complex India–Pakistan financial issues in late November gave him added cause for optimism. Moreover, Mountbatten and the service chiefs had advised him that, for reasons of terrain and climate, it would not be possible for the army to complete the work of expelling the raiders during the winter months. A spring offensive was expected to produce conclusive results but Nehru was anxious to avoid, if possible, the suffering inflicted on the local population by continued hostilities.

Encouraged by Mountbatten, Nehru was inclined to accept the Ismay proposal in a spirit of accommodation. He explained his views in a letter to the Maharaja of Kashmir.

During the past week there have been discussions between the Governments of India and Pakistan about all manner of vital and controversial issues between us, quite apart from Kashmir. Surprisingly enough, we have come to a settlement in regard to nearly all these, although previously we had failed to do so....

Because of this I feel that the time is propitious for a settlement on Kashmir also.... The alternative is no settlement and carrying on this little war indefinitely and at the same time tension and conflict all over India with consequent misery to numberless persons....

In spring, we could drive out the raiders from the Poonch area also. But that means another four months; and meanwhile, the raiders and the Poonchi rebels will remain in possession of that area and harass the people of the State....

You must have seen the draft proposals which were discussed by us with Mr. Liaquat Ali Khan.... We are bound down to that proposal, provided, of course, there is a settlement.[20]

Impasse

However, the mood changed sharply in the first week of December as Pakistan stepped up the raids across the Poonch border. Mirpur town was devastated by the raiders and preparations were afoot for an attack on Jammu. Reports poured in of massacres and abduction of womenfolk for sale in West Punjab. Nehru protested to Liaquat,

During the last few days while we were supposed to be discussing possible terms for a settlement, these concentrations [of raiders] have been encouraged and additional raiders have been sent into Kashmir who have massacred thousands of persons there.... The Government of India cannot tolerate the continuance of the use of Pakistan territory for organising murderous raids into a part of Indian Dominion territory and must consider it as an act of hostility. This you will appreciate might involve far-reaching consequences.... It is hardly possible to conduct any negotiations while this state of affairs lasts.[21]

In New Delhi, the Cabinet pressed for a vigorous military response. Reinforcements were sent to Jammu and rifles were despatched for the Home Guards. Most significantly, at a meeting of the Defence Committee on 3 December, Nehru, Patel and Baldev Singh insisted, in the face of opposition from Mountbatten and the service chiefs, on air interdiction to establish a 'cordon sanitaire' along the Jammu–Pakistan frontier. This escalation of the conflict was only prevented by the Governor-General who, in connivance with the British service chiefs, largely sabotaged the Cabinet decision (as we shall see in Chapter VIII).

After some initial hesitation, Nehru finally decided to go to Lahore for the Joint Defence Committee meeting on 8 December. He was in an uncompromising frame of mind, determined to have a 'straight talk' with his Pakistani colleague.[22] Liaquat, too, was not prepared to make any concession.

At Mountbatten's invitation, the two Prime Ministers gave an account of developments from their respective points of view.[23] Nehru observed that Pakistani soldiers and army equipment had been captured in Kashmir, proving the involvement in the raids of persons in authority in Pakistan. He offered to produce proof that the North West Frontier Province government had provided arms and other assistance to the raiders. Moreover, there were concentrations of regular and irregular forces in Pakistani territory, close to the Kashmir border. He proceeded to give an account of the atrocities committed by the raiders on the local population. All this amounted to nothing less than an act of war.

Liaquat Ali Khan responded that the atrocities were not one-sided. As regards weapons, the frontier tribesmen had arms factories of their own and, if some Pakistani army rifles had been seized, they might have been taken from soldiers on leave. Ghulam Mohammed added—even more implausibly—that the raiders had also obtained arms from Afghanistan and the Soviet Union! Liaquat Ali Khan made much of the point that Pakistan could not stop the raiders without going to war against the tribes.

Turning to a possible settlement, while both sides agreed that the ultimate aim was to hold a fair plebiscite, they were sharply divided on the first step towards this objective. Nehru emphasised that the first step should be a declaration by the Pakistani government that it would do its utmost to influence the raiders to withdraw from Jammu and Kashmir. Liaquat was equally insistent that this step would only follow after India had declared that all her troops would be withdrawn and an 'impartial' administration was set up in Kashmir. Nehru responded that if all Indian troops were to be withdrawn simultaneously with the tribal raiders, the state would be left at the mercy of the so-called 'Azad Kashmir' forces. It was also out of the question to remove the first fully responsible government which had ever been set up in Kashmir. The Pakistani Prime Minister ignored Mountbatten's suggestion that the presence of a United Nations delegation in Kashmir would obviate the need for a change of administration.

Failing to make a breakthrough, Mountbatten tried to obtain a new concession from Nehru. Familiar with his Prime Minister's thinking on the Ismay proposal, Mountbatten pressed Nehru to make a *unilateral* statement on the lines of the Ismay draft! He argued that this measure would make clear to the world India's policy and it might also help Pakistan to persuade the raiders to withdraw. Nehru of course rejected a unilateral statement which would impose commitments on India without binding Pakistan in any way.

Mountbatten came to the conclusion that the impasse was now absolute and his efforts at mediation would yield no further results. He decided that the best course would be to throw the problem on the lap of the United Nations. He, therefore, suggested that the United Nations should be requested to send out advisers or observers in some capacity to solve the impasse. Nehru immediately rejected the idea, saying that he was prepared to approach the United Nations only for the purpose of the plebiscite and this could be done only after peace had been restored. Liaquat said guardedly that he would agree to the United Nations advising on the impartiality of the administration before the plebiscite.

Mountbatten took advantage of a break in the meeting to have a private word with Liaquat. He asked whether he could count on Liaquat's support for the proposal that the United Nations should be brought into the picture, in whatever form. The Pakistani Prime Minister readily agreed to cooperate.

Having coordinated his approach with Liaquat, Mountbatten sprang the proposal on Nehru when the meeting resumed and pressed for its immediate acceptance. It was the only way to stop the fighting, he argued, emphasising that this must be the main objective. Liaquat gave Mountbatten his full support, stating that he would not mind in what manner the United Nations was approached, even if it should take the form of an accusation by India that Pakistan was assisting the raiders. Nehru remained adamantly opposed to the proposal, insisting that the first step was to drive out the raiders. At one point, he declared in an outburst that, in view of Pakistan's position, the only solution was to clear Kashmir with the sword and that he would throw up his Prime Ministership and lead the men of India against the invaders!

Divergent Conclusions

The meeting ended without any result and marked the end of Mountbatten's efforts at mediation. His technique of mediation was to propose a compromise solution and, when this was rejected by Pakistan, to seek a unilateral concession from the party over which he had real influence—India. Thus Nehru's offer to hold a plebiscite under United Nations auspices was made in the absence of any gesture from the Pakistani side. The proposition dear to Patel that a plebiscite should be held in *all* cases of contested accession—including Hyderabad—was promptly jettisoned when opposed by Jinnah. Nehru was brought around to accepting the Ismay proposal. When this fell through because Pakistan would make no concession, Mountbatten once again sought to persuade Nehru to accept its obligations unilaterally. This time he did not succeed.

By the end of the meeting on 9 December, the Indian Prime Minister had finally reached the end of his patience. He had offered significant concessions which were not reciprocated. Despite his utter

6rt=6

6rt=6

abhorrence of war, Nehru's thoughts turned increasingly towards a full-fledged military solution.

Mountbatten, on the other hand, became deeply convinced that the only escape from war lay in an early reference to the United Nations.[24] His efforts at mediation had yielded some concessions on the part of India but none from Pakistan. This led him to progressively widen the terms of the proposed reference to the United Nations in a series of concessions to Pakistan. Mountbatten's initial proposal was to bring in the United Nations for the limited purpose of supervising or conducting a plebiscite. In order to accommodate Pakistan's insistence on an 'impartial' administration, Ismay expanded these terms of reference to include also an advisory role in the run-up to the plebiscite. When this, too, was rejected by Pakistan, Mountbatten came to believe that the United Nations should be called in to find a way out of the impasse which he himself had failed to break.

VIII
Military Plans

Right from the outset of the Kashmir conflict, Nehru had realised that objective military advice could not always be expected from the British officers commanding the Indian defence forces. It was only natural that their advice would be tailored to suit the requirements of what they perceived as British interests. On the very first day of the Kashmir operations, the Prime Minister had instructed the Defence Minister, Sardar Baldev Singh, to ask certain senior Indian officers to secretly prepare plans and appreciations independently of the service chiefs. On 27 October, he confided to Brigadier Hiralal Atal, his liaison officer in Srinagar:

> I have asked the Heads of our Services to prepare a full appreciation of possible developments and what we can do about them. I have separately asked the Defence Minister to get plans and appreciations from some senior Indian officers of the three Services. This will be kept secret by us.[1]

We do not know who these Indian officers were or what advice they gave to ministers, but it is necessary to keep this background in mind while studying the military planning process in November–December, 1947.

Military Appreciations

With Mountbatten's return to India on 24 November, Lockhart and Bucher felt that the time had come to review the whole situation from the political and military points of view. On 24 November, Lockhart, who had resumed his duties as Commander-in-Chief of the army, informed the Defence Committee that he had ordered two appreciations—one on Kashmir specifically and the other on the overall defence of India. He asked that further consideration of the military problem in Kashmir be deferred in view of the pending preparation of these appreciations. The Prime Minister agreed but he emphasised that the security of Kashmir must be considered the first priority for the military. The Committee concluded that the security of Kashmir was vital for the well-being of India and directed the chiefs of staff to take this into account in preparing their appreciations.[2]

It may seem strange that the Prime Minister should have had to spell out for the benefit of the service chiefs that priority was to be accorded to Kashmir. In the past few weeks, foreign invaders had occupied a part of the national territory and were now attempting to expand the areas under their control. Was it not self-evident that the armed forces should regard it as their prime task to defend Kashmir against the invaders? Yet the conduct of operations at the top-most levels of the military showed that this specific directive was, indeed, not superfluous. The Governor-General and the British service chiefs were seeking to limit and contain the inter-dominion conflict. Notwithstanding the immediacy and urgency of the task in Kashmir, the service chiefs did not assign to it higher priority than to meeting possible contingencies in Hyderabad or Punjab. While dismissing the possibility of a declaration of war by Pakistan, they held up the spectre of a weak government in Karachi being unable to prevent lawless elements and army deserters from launching large-scale raids into Indian Punjab. Hyderabad, where the internal situation was rapidly deteriorating, was another potential flashpoint.[3] These contingencies were accorded priority in military planning, along with Kashmir. As the official Indian account of the military campaign states in its matter of fact style:

This decision of the Defence Committee was of great significance; henceforth the defence of Kashmir became the chief task of the Indian Army. So far the attention of the Indian Army had been distracted by other equally urgent problems—Hyderabad and the defence of the East Punjab frontier. Later events were to vindicate this decision, for the trouble in Hyderabad proved a mere flash in the pan while the danger to the East Punjab frontier remained merely a threat.[4]

As instructed by the service chiefs, the Joint Planning Staff submitted a paper on Kashmir on 26 November. The paper concluded that control of the state territory, involving the stationing of troops in such places as Domel, Poonch, Mirpur and Kotli, would require deployment of at least four infantry brigade groups, each consisting of four battalions, plus strong administrative backing. Two brigade groups would have to be deployed in the Jammu–Naoshera–Mirpur–Kotli area; one in the Uri–Poonch area; and one in the Srinagar area. While the required number of troops could be found, providing supplies and maintenance for such a large force would be virtually impossible in the winter months, owing to the state of communications. Nor was sufficient time available to stock in supplies before the onset of winter.

The paper concluded that in the winter months it would be possible to maintain only three brigade groups (and supporting troops) in the state; two in Jammu and one in the Srinagar–Uri area. This was the crux of the problem. On this basis, it would be possible for the army to hold strongly only the district (and not the entire province) of Jammu and the Kashmir vale upto Uri. Military action west and south of Uri, as also west and north of Naoshera would be confined to vigorous patrolling and action by commando groups.

The Defence Committee met on 28 November to consider a paper submitted by the Chiefs of Staff on these lines on operational commitments during the coming winter. Mountbatten, once again in the chair, echoed the views of the service chiefs. He drew attention to the prevailing winter conditions and the poor state of communications. He emphasised India's limited capacity to maintain a large force in Jammu and Kashmir. Taking these factors into consideration, the Chiefs of Staff had recommended that no further operational commitments should be undertaken during the winter.

Nehru, however, pressed for an advance to Domel or even Kohala. He said that he failed to understand why the army had stopped at Uri; an advance to Domel was most important since it controlled the roads leading from Pakistan into Kashmir. If the army did not advance beyond Uri, it would not be able to prevent invaders from entering Kashmir over the bridges at Domel.

The Commander-in-Chief, General Lockhart, maintained that it would be risky to hold Domel on account of problems of maintenance and lines of communication. Maintaining a garrison in Domel would mean extending an already over-stretched line of communication. Should the road from Uri to Domel be cut by the raiders, the garrison at Domel would be isolated, with serious repercussions on the army's position. Nehru contested this line of reasoning. He said that a balance had to be struck between the risks involved and the psychological effect on the invaders of retaining the initiative in India's hands. He deprecated a defensive attitude. He thought it was unlikely that Indian troops would be cut off in Domel, keeping in view its geographical position and the nature of the terrain.

At this stage, the Chairman, Mountbatten, threw his full weight behind the Commander-in-Chief. He conceded the strategic importance of Domel but he emphasised the serious risks involved in an advance to the area, particularly when air supply facilities were practically unavailable.

Nehru had no alternative but to accept the fact that, in the last resort, the Defence Committee must be guided in purely military matters by the opinion of the service chiefs. But he once again reiterated his own view that it was important to push ahead to Domel. If the supply situation made it difficult to hold the town, at least the bridges across the Kishanganga river could be destroyed, creating a major obstacle for the invaders. At this point, Lockhart stated that he had asked Russell to examine the possibility of an operation of this type.

The Prime Minister having expressed his views with such force, the Committee only partially accepted the recommendations of the service chiefs. It:

(1) *agreed generally with the Chiefs of Staff paper with the exception of operations from URI and up to DOMEL,*
(2) *directed the C-in-C to examine with Maj. Gen. Kalwant Singh the feasibility of occupying DOMEL or sending a strong detachment to blow up the bridges in that area....*[6]

Jammu Province

Russell's paper on Domel turned out to be a plea for evacuating Poonch! He argued that the immediate task was pulling out the 'hostage to fortune' at Poonch, concentrating a brigade group at Naoshera, clearing up the enemy threat south of Jammu and providing firm protection to the Pathankot–Jammu–Naoshera lines of communication. Having assured the security of these areas, troops could then be moved from Jammu to Srinagar in the following spring. The destruction of the Domel bridge, if still considered desirable, should be possible in the spring and perhaps even earlier. After the winter, it would be possible to maintain in the Srinagar area the force of four brigade groups required for the Domel operation. Till then, the task of the army would be to control the Kashmir valley upto Uri and the Jammu–Naoshera area. Active patrolling would be undertaken from these secure areas. Mobile patrols from the base at Uri would progressively bring pressure to bear on the enemy, but they should not stick their necks out and should always remember that Indian troops could return to Uri without loss of face.[7]

Since the additional brigade required in the Jhelum valley could have been diverted from other parts of India, Russell's linkage between the proposed withdrawal from Poonch and an advance beyond Uri was, at best, tenuous. In essence, the paper sought to make out a case for an immediate withdrawal from Poonch while postponing to the spring a build up of forces at Uri which would allow the army to launch a major thrust towards Domel. In fact, Russell had already on 24 November issued operational instructions for the withdrawal of the Poonch garrison. These instructions had been overtaken by events and had not been implemented. His paper was an attempt to reinstate his previous directive.

Russell finalised this appreciation on 2 December. By then, however, his paper had once again been overtaken by events. In the past few days the air had been filled with stories of ghastly outrages perpetrated by the invaders in Mirpur and other occupied areas. Patel and Baldev Singh visited Jammu on 2 December to study the situation. They held discussions with Sheikh Abdullah, the Maharaja and senior officers of the armed forces present in Jammu. These included Major-General Kalwant Singh and Air Vice-Marshal Mukherjee. They returned with the information that with the active assistance of the Pakistani authorities, another large concentration of Pathan and Punjabi hostiles had appeared on the border and were poised to infiltrate into Jammu province. It was learnt that the Commissioner of Rawalpindi was generally directing the operations.

It was in this charged atmosphere that the Defence Committee met on 3 December. The cabinet was firmly determined to hold Poonch at any cost. Nehru outlined the military situation as he viewed it. In the northern sector, which included Srinagar, Uri and the Jhelum valley, Indian forces were well protected from any immediate threat. In the Poonch or middle sector, too, there was no immediate danger of being overwhelmed. Food stocks were adequate for the near future. There was no need to evacuate the town as long as military stores and ammunition could be supplied to the garrison. It was the southern sector which required urgent attention. India had recently suffered some reverses in this sector and if these continued there would be serious consequences in the middle and northern sectors. The priority tasks in the southern sector must include arrangements for the protection of the lines of communication from Pathankot to Jammu and from Jammu to Naoshera; protection of the bridges at Ramban on the Jammu–Srinagar road; and defence of the Akhnur area. After stabilising its position in these areas, the army should take the offensive.

It will be recalled that the Prime Minister had called for a show of strength by the airforce as early as 25 October. He now urged air action against tribal concentrations which had crossed over from Pakistan. Defence Minister Baldev Singh, supported by Deputy Prime Minister Patel, proposed establishing a ten-mile deep belt on the Indian side of the border in which extensive bombing operations should be conducted against Pakistani infiltrators. The ministers urged that a *cordon sanitaire* should thus be created along the frontier from Naoshera to Muzaffarabad. Patel mentioned that Kalwant Singh also had impressed on him the importance of air action in this border area.

Mountbatten at once marshalled arguments against air interdiction. He said that air action might cause casualties not only among the infiltrators but also among local muslims who were now Indian nationals. The ministers rejected the implication that air action would unavoidably cause harm to peaceful civilians. Nehru said that the territory to be bombed should be strictly defined and the objective should be to seek out and destroy insurgent concentrations. Patel pointed out that the muslim leaders of Kashmir had themselves called for offensive air action against the raiders in this area. The Governor-General then took refuge in strictly military arguments. Air action could be taken only during daytime and this might only lead to

infiltration by night. Moreover, he said he doubted if India had sufficient aircraft to take on this vast commitment. The ministers remained
unconvinced. It was obvious to them that air operations could act as
a significant check on the infiltrators even if it did not altogether prevent their ingress.[8]

At the end of this debate, the Defence Committee generally agreed
that a *cordon sanitaire* be created by air action and the Chiefs of
Staff were directed to examine this as a matter of great urgency. It
was also decided to arrange for reinforcing the army's strength in the
Jammu area by a brigade group so as to provide it with the desired
offensive capability. The Chiefs of Staff asked the Joint Planning Staff
to prepare papers on these two decisions.[9]

Failing to dissuade his ministers from pressing for a *cordon sanitaire*, Mountbatten decided to sabotage the proposal through the
service chiefs. He asked General Lockhart to stay back after the Defence Committee meeting and confided to him the real reason for his
opposition to the proposed *cordon sanitaire*. If established, he said,
it would probably once and for all do away with any hope of an agreement with Pakistan. He explained that he could not flatly contradict
the views so strongly expressed by ministers in the Defence Committee and had thus been obliged to moderate his opposition. This was
why he had arranged for the project to be examined by the Joint
Planning Staff. Mountbatten then suggested to General Lockhart the
lines on which the Joint Planning Staff could challenge the practicability of the *cordon sanitaire*.[10]

The Joint Planning Staff paper on a 'proscribed zone' or *cordon
sanitaire* dutifully advised that air action would be effective only in the
plains and in the areas around Kotli–Mirpur–Chaumukh and Bhimbar.
In other areas, the hilly terrain provided good cover to the enemy.
Low flying was necessary for detailed observation of the ground and
this would be restricted by hilly terrain. Bad weather would be a further impediment. Moreover, the area would have to be cleared of all
loyal local inhabitants, muslim and non-muslim, resulting in a heavy
inflow of evacuees to Jammu. The Jammu administration, already
hard-pressed by the refugee influx, would come under great strain.
The Joint Planning Staff paper concluded that in view of these factors, it would be advisable not to enforce a 'proscribed zone' as such
but to step-up the air effort against the hostile forces.[11]

Thus the quasi-political argument concerning the civil population,
which had originally been advanced by Mountbatten, was developed

further by the Joint Planning Staff. Indeed it was developed to an absurd point in the contention that a wholescale transfer of the civilian population was a prerequisite for the proposed *cordon sanitaire*. The paper was on more solid ground in pointing out that infiltration could not be entirely prevented by air action alone, though it may be questioned whether it did full justifice to the potential of air action, in light of the actual experience of airforce operations in support of the army in this sector.

The Joint Planning Staff had also been asked to prepare a paper on reinforcing the Jammu and Kashmir Division by four battalions with a view to conducting offensive operations in the area Jammu, Akhnur, Bhimbar, Naoshera and Jhangar. After labouring at length over the difficulties involved, the paper conceded that it would be possible to induct the additional force. However, it warned that the lines of communication, which ran close to the Pakistani border, would be vulnerable and liable to interruption by enemy action.

The most significant argument in the paper, however, concerned a different issue. At the meeting of the Defence Committee on 3 December, Nehru had emphasised the view that there was no immediate danger of losing Poonch town. The Joint Planning Staff paper sought to reopen the question of holding the town. It argued that maintaining the garrison at Poonch by road would present almost insuperable problems. It would require launching a major operation each time a convoy moved from Uri to Poonch and back. This point, of course, was generally understood. The Cabinet assumed that the Poonch garrison could continue to depend upon air supplies till such time as the situation on the ground changed in India's favour. The paper questioned this assumption, observing that air supply could be satisfactorily maintained only if the airfield could be extended to allow Dakotas to land and provided also that the garrison could keep the airfield secure. It recommended that a decision on Poonch should, therefore, await an examination of these problems by General Russell.[12]

Finalisation of Plans

The two Joint Planning Staff papers were considered in the Defence Committee on 5 December. The recommendations concerning the *cordon sanitaire* were approved without much discussion but the Committee specifically 'directed that our object should be offensive air action to prevent infiltration of the tribesmen and to deny the use of local facilities to them.'[13] It remains unclear whether the ministers fully realised that the formulation would be interpreted by the Committee Chairman as jettisoning the 'dangerous' idea of a *cordon sanitaire*.

On the other hand, the question of evacuating Poonch led to a heated debate. The Governor-General vigorously supported the Chiefs of Staff in calling for evacuation. Operations in Jammu, he said, were the 'exact inverse' of the operations in the Jhelum valley. In the Srinagar area, victory was certain. In the Jammu sector, however, India suffered from a serious strategic weakness since her lines of communication ran parallel to the Pakistani border. He compared the situation with the Imphal operations during World War II.

The Prime Minister questioned this approach. He called for bold action, urging an offensive at selected points in the Poonch area. A fighting force like the raiders could not hold together for long unless they were winning. A series of successful offensives by the Indian army would break the morale of the invaders and cause them to withdraw. Nehru rejected the parallel with operations in the Burma theatre. In the Burma operations, the main bases were far removed from the lines of communication; in Jammu, on the other hand, the main bases in east Punjab were not very far from the lines of communication. Even if the lines of communication were to be cut temporarily, it would not entail the same disastrous consequences as might have been the case in Burma.

The Governor-General brought the debate to an end by observing that ministers could only give policy directives; details of operations should be left to the Chiefs of Staff. He expressed the opinion that the policy might take the form of directing the Chiefs of Staff to keep at the front the largest force which could be adequately maintained, in order to prosecute operations vigorously. The Prime Minister agreed but added significantly that it was most important to adopt an offensive—and not defensive—approach. The Governor-General conceded that this should be an essential element of the directive. In regard to Poonch, it was agreed that a decision would await receipt of General Russell's recommendation but, meanwhile, there should be no withdrawal.[14]

Nehru was unshakeably determined to hold on to Poonch. Russell met him the day after the Defence Committee meeting in a final attempt to get him to reconsider his decision. The General once again emphasised the military risks involved in maintaining an isolated garrison and the problems involved in its relief. The Prime Minister declared emphatically that evacuation of the town should not even be contemplated. A withdrawal would give encouragement to the raiders at a critical juncture. Moreover, the refugees who had sought shelter in the town would meet a terrible fate at the hands of the enemy. The Prime Minister's unyielding stand settled the question. Russell accepted the decision and assured Nehru that he would do his utmost to implement it successfully though this would require a bit of good luck.[15]

The military plans for Jammu and Kashmir were now finalised and, on 10 December, Lieutenant-General Russell issued his instructions to the Commander of the Jammu and Kashmir Division, Major-General Kalwant Singh. The general task of the army was to secure the maximum possible area of the Jammu and Kashmir State, with a view to relieving Poonch and driving the raiders from the territory still under their control. More specifically, Kalwant Singh was charged with the following tasks:

(i)   *To build up a sufficient force on the central thrust line (Nao-shera–Kotli–Poonch) to relieve Poonch town. It was estimated that a brigade group would be required as an adequate striking force advancing north of Kotli to effect the relief. Additional troops would be required to protect the lines of communication, bringing up the total requirement to approximately six or seven battalions with supporting arms. Pending the relief operation, the Poonch garrison would have to be supplied by air.*

(ii) *To advance on Bhimbar, the important enemy-held road, head in the southern (Akhnur–Munawwar–Bhimbar) sector. Success at Bhimbar would also provide a degree of protection to the lines of communication for the central thrust toward Poonch.*

(iii) *To gain control of the Jhelum valley as far west as possible. The 161 Brigade based in Uri was no longer required to open the route to Poonch and it could now concentrate its resources on actions in the Jhelum valley. The number of troops in the sector was to be strictly limited to 4,000, unless Kalwant Singh could make his own arrangements to induct and maintain a larger force.*[16]

Conclusion

Thus the army's plans for the winter months emerged after a protracted debate between the Prime Minister and his colleagues on one side, and the Governor-General and service chiefs, on the other. Reflecting the official view in London, Mountbatten and the British officers at the head of India's armed forces had deep reservations concerning the government's political objective of establishing control over the entire territory of the Jammu and Kashmir state. Sensing these reservations, the ministers could not be certain about the objectivity of the military advice they received from the service chiefs. Hence they tended to consult separately with Indian officers in their confidence. The Prime Minister was also prepared to accept greater risks than were envisaged in the strictly conservative approach favoured by the service chiefs and he consistently pressed for bold action. In the final analysis, however, the Cabinet had no other option but to accept the assessment of the service chiefs. The latter, likewise, had to pay formal obeisance to the government's objective of driving the raiders from every corner of the state.

The plan which emerged had the aim of establishing Indian control over the entire state but it also accepted the impossibility of achieving this objective during the winter. The additional brigade required to expel the invaders from the Jhelum valley could be inducted only after the winter, when it would become possible to send supplies by road. It was also accepted that additional troops would be required in Jammu province; however, a timeframe for inducting these troops had not been worked out. The Cabinet successfully resisted plans for evacuating troops and civilians from Poonch. The service chiefs, however, finessed ministerial proposals for a raid on Domel to destroy the bridges across the Kishanganga and for large-scale air action to prevent ingress by the raiders in Jammu province.

IX
Counter-Attack or UN Appeal?

The idea of carrying the war into Pakistan was first mooted by Sheikh Abdullah at the beginning of November 1947. His view was that India should deliver an ultimatum to Pakistan to withdraw the raiders from Kashmir and declare war on expiry of the ultimatum. Nehru explained to him that this would be 'very injurious to Kashmir and to a lesser extent to India.' War with Pakistan would involve concentrating military resources elsewhere and might lead to diversion of Indian forces from Kashmir. India would ultimately win the war but, meanwhile, Kashmir would be ruined. 'It is to our great advantage to concentrate on Kashmir at the present and then consider the situation,' wrote Nehru to Abdullah.[1]

However, in mid-December the Prime Minister's views underwent a radical change. Two rounds of negotiations with his Pakistani colleague had concluded on 9 December with no results. The diplomatic breakthrough he hoped for had failed to materialise. Invaders operating from sanctuaries in Pakistan had stepped up the scale of their operations and ample evidence was now available to prove that they were equipped and directed by the Pakistani authorities. Nehru was dissatisfied with the defensive tactics employed by the army. The service chiefs maintained that there was no possibility of expelling the raiders from the Jhelum valley till the spring. In the middle sector, they pressed for evacuation of all besieged garrisons and it was only with the greatest difficulty that the government was able to prevail on them to maintain the Poonch garrison. By mid-December, it was clear that existing diplomatic and military approaches held out no promise of an early victory.

Nehru came to the conclusion that the solution lay in striking at the invaders' concentrations and lines of communication in Pakistani territory. He spelt out his views in an incisive policy note.

What is happening in Kashmir State is not merely a frontier raid but a regular war, on a limited scale, with the latest weapons being used on the part of the invaders. It is clear that the Pakistan Government is encouraging this in every way. Army officers and men are helping the invaders in every way.

After setting out details of Pakistan's involvement, Nehru carried out a critical appraisal of India's military response:

It seems to me that our outlook has been defensive and apologetic, as if we were ashamed of what we were doing and we are not quite sure of how far we should go. I see nothing to apologise for and a defensive way of meeting raiders seems to me completely wrong.

The first thing to be understood is that Kashmir is of the most vital consequence to us and that we are in deadly earnest about it.... I realise fully the difficulties of the terrain and the situation. Nevertheless I cannot get over the feeling that our tactics have been unsuccessful. There is a certain heaviness of thought and action which is peculiarly unsuited to a conflict of the type we are waging.... We cannot go on carrying on this little war for months and months and may be a year or more.

The Prime Minister drew the following conclusion:

Are we to allow Pakistan to continue to train new armies for invasion and allow its territory to be used as a base for these attacks? The obvious course is to strike at these concentrations and lines of communications in Pakistan territory. From a military point of view this would be the most effective step. We have refrained from taking it because of political considerations. We shall have to reconsider this position because a continuation of the present situation is intolerable.... This involves a risk of war with Pakistan. We wish to avoid war, but it is merely deluding ourselves to imagine that we are avoiding war so long as the present operations are continuing on either side.[2]

The Governor-General came to learn about this new thinking on his return from a tour of Jaipur and Bombay on 18 December.[3] He was alarmed at the imminent prospect of open war between the two dominions, an event he had striven hard to avert. An inter-dominion war would be a great setback to British and Commonwealth interests and, on a personal level, it would raise questions about his continuing to hold the office of Governor-General of India.[4] Mountbatten rose to the challenge and the exceptional skill with which he handled the situation fully justified the claim he had made earlier in the context of Junagadh that his 'presence as Governor-General of India was the best insurance against an actual outbreak of war with Pakistan.'

Mountbatten had consistently viewed a reference to the United Nations as an effective method of preventing or stopping an India–Pakistan war. This was why he had proposed, at the end of September, that the Junagadh issue be referred to the United Nations. In November, in his meeting with Jinnah, he had suggested a UN-supervised plebiscite in Kashmir. More recently, during the Nehru–Liaquat meeting in Lahore on 8–9 December, Mountbatten had expanded the proposal and suggested that an appeal be made to the UN to send over a team urgently in order to break the impasse and stop the fighting. Faced with the prospect of an open war, the Governor-General now insisted on a reference to the United Nations.

A Fateful Decision

Matters came to a head in a meeting of the Defence Committee on 20 December. The Prime Minister began by describing the overall situation as unsatisfactory and unacceptable. He observed that a regular war was being waged in Indian territory from bases in Pakistan. This situation could not be allowed to continue indefinitely. As things were, a settlement did not seem likely. It was necessary, Nehru said, to be clear about possible developments which might result from a political decision to conduct a limited strike into Pakistan. The Prime Minister said that this might mean Indian forces having to enter the districts of Sialkot, Gujarat and Jhelum in order to deny the raiders the assistance they had been getting at their bases. From an operational angle, he asked the Chiefs of Staff to view Kashmir and West Punjab as a single area.

Mountbatten interjected that he did not consider this ought to be issued as a directive to the Chiefs of Staff. The Prime Minister did not contest the point but insisted that it was essential that the Defence Committee should commence a study of this contingency. Mountbatten argued that the proper course would be to refer the whole matter to the UN. India had a cast-iron case. He was convinced, he said disingenuously, that the UN would promptly direct Pakistan to withdraw the raiders.

Faced with the Governor-General's non-cooperation, Nehru reluctantly agreed to a compromise. A reference would be made to the United Nations; meanwhile the Chiefs of Staff were instructed to draw up contingency plans for a military operation to evict the raiders from their bases in Pakistan.[5]

Upto this point, the Prime Minister had steadfastly resisted Mountbatten's attempts to involve the UN *before* the invaders had been expelled from Kashmir. The Prime Minister finally gave in on 20 December not because he expected the UN to take effective action against the invaders but simply in order to exhaust all peaceful means before taking recourse to military action against Pakistan. Though he had no great expectations from the UN, Nehru did not anticipate the extent to which the Security Council could constrain India's military options. Thus he wrote to General Bucher:

> We shall naturally continue our efforts in the political field, by reference to UNO etc., to bring about some cessation of fighting if it is possible. But I am sure that this will not result in fighting stopping at present. Indeed there is every chance of its spreading more and endangering our security. We have thus to be prepared for every contingency and to be prepared soon.[6]

The Cabinet met on 20 December after the Defence Committee session. Nehru presented the proposal for requesting the United Nations to call on Pakistan to cease her aggression in Kashmir. In presenting the request India would also make it clear that she reserved her right to take appropriate measures in self-defence. Before approaching the United Nations, India would formally request the Pakistani government to stop giving aid or encouragement to the invaders. These proposals were approved by the Cabinet. In addition to making preparations for a counter-attack by the Indian army, the Cabinet also envisaged raising a substantial force of irregulars, both in Kashmir and in East Punjab, for 'guerrilla warfare and frontier patrol' purposes, thus taking a leaf out of the Pakistani book. The irregulars were to be raised by political leaders but they would function under the general guidance of the army commanders. In Kashmir, Bakshi Ghulam Mohammad was given the responsibility of raising the force.[7]

During the inter-dominion conference on 22 December, Nehru handed over a letter to Liaquat Ali Khan to 'formally ask the Government of Pakistan to deny the raiders: (i) access to use of Pakistan territory for operations against Kashmir; (ii) all military and other supplies; (iii) all other kinds of aid that might tend to prolong the present struggle.'[8]

The fall of Jhangar, news of which had reached the Indian capital on 24 December, created a heightened sense of urgency. Nehru and his closest colleagues decided that military preparations should be speeded up and completed by the middle of January. General Thimayya was asked to come over from Amritsar for consultations with ministers. The government decided to send additional forces to Kashmir to be in 'full trim' by the middle of January.[9]

Nehru was well aware that a full-fledged war with Pakistan would affect the position of British officers in the armed forces[10] and, possibly, the Governor-General himself. He wrote to Sardar Patel: 'Among the consequences to be considered [by the Cabinet] are the possible effect on the British officers in the army. Also the reactions of the Governor General.'[11] Nevertheless, he appears to have assumed that Mountbatten and senior British officers would abide by the Cabinet decision to make contingency preparations for a counter-attack even if they had to resign their posts in the event of actual war. The compromise he had accepted in the Defence Committee involved a twofold approach—an appeal to the UN as well as contingency planning for an all-out war. He had accepted in good faith Mountbatten's proposal for an appeal to the UN and he expected the Governor-General and service chiefs to likewise implement the decisions taken collectively in the Defence Committee. This proved to be a fatal error. The Governor-General was determined to thwart the Cabinet.

Governor-General's Moves

Deeply concerned about an Indian counter-attack, Mountbatten addressed a long missive to Nehru on Christmas Day. The letter, which ran to some 2,000 words, repeatedly emphasised that the Governor-

General's consistent policy had been to stop hostilities. He recalled how he had consistently opposed extension of the fighting to the western areas of the state in Poonch and Mirpur and complained about the operations carried out in these areas in November, during his absence in London. He once again emphasised his view that the 'prospects of clearing the Poonch area of hostile elements within a reasonable time with the forces we can send (and their number is limited by administrative considerations however much it may be desired to throw the whole weight of the Indian army with this effort) are indeed remote.'

Coming to the main point, Mountbatten expressed his concern over the proposal to send the army into Pakistani territory in order to strike at the bases or nerve centres from which the raiders were operating. He hinted at international pressures, warning the Prime Minister that the 'idea that a war between India and Pakistan could be confined to the sub-continent, or finished off quickly in favour of India without further complications, is to my mind a fatal illusion.' Finally, the Governor-General recalled the proposal he had made to 'telegraph U.N.O. to send over a team as soon as possible' with the object of stopping the hostilities. What had happened since then had only reinforced his views and increased the sense of urgency. He urged the Prime Minister to broaden the terms of the reference to be made to the United Nations. 'Surely the main object should rather be to bring U.N.O. here at the earliest possible moment to get a team nominated, to come out and deal with the business and help to stop the fighting, within a matter of days?' he suggested. Mountbatten's letter was an urgent appeal to 'stop the fighting and to stop it as soon as possible.'[12]

Nehru sent a vigorous reply the next day. 'The invasion of Kashmir is not an accidental affair resulting from the fanaticism or exuberance of the tribesmen,' he wrote, 'but a well organised business with the backing of the State... we have in effect to deal with a State carrying on an informal war, but nevertheless a war.' India had thus far followed a 'cautious defensive policy' which had presented Pakistan with an advantage. By carrying on operations in a 'weak defensive way' India could not produce an effective impression on the adversary. 'From a strictly legal and constitutional point of view, it is our right and duty to resist this invasion with all our forces. From the point of view of international law we can in self-defence take any military measures to resist it including the sending of our armies across Pakistan territory to attack their bases near the Kashmir border.... Peace will come only if we have the strength to resist invasion and make it clear that it will not pay.' Nehru went on to say that the Government of India had accepted Mountbatten's suggestion and would make a reference to the United Nations but it 'cannot ask U.N.O. to arbitrate between raiders and the Dominion of India' or to make a joint reference with Pakistan on mutually agreed lines. India, as the aggrieved party, would draw the attention of the United Nations to the invasion and to the fact that Pakistan was aiding and abetting it and she would ask the UN to call upon Pakistan to refrain from doing so. Meanwhile, India must prepare for every eventuality. 'We have taken enough risks already; we dare not take any more. We can't even permit much longer the continuation of the use of bases in Pakistan to attack our troops and our territory in Kashmir. There is no question of small operations going on in Kashmir through the winter months, but of quick developments.'

The Prime Minister concluded that the government should immediately proceed on two parallel lines of action:

(i) *Reference to the UNO....*
(ii) *Complete military preparations to meet any possible contingency that may arise. If grave danger threatens us in Kashmir or elsewhere on the West Punjab frontier, then we must not hesitate to march through Pakistan territory towards the bases.*[13]

The Governor-General's Christmas Day letter was intended as much for Attlee's eyes as Nehru's. The full text of the letter, together with extracts from Nehru's reply and the relevant minutes of the Defence Committee, were promptly passed on to London through top secret cables from the UK High Commissioner.[14] Mountbatten's intention was to put on record his own role in restraining the Indian Cabinet and to inform Attlee of India's plans.

Mountbatten's anxieties had been heightened by the latest developments on the military front. Immediately after their success in Jhangar, the invaders mounted a new threat to Uri, which lay at the entrance to the vale of Kashmir. The Governor-General asked High Commissioner Shone to pass on the following message to Attlee:

Mountbatten's considered opinion is that the situation between India and Pakistan has reached a pitch where war will supervene

within a very short while unless immediate action is taken....
Main factor producing this is imminent danger that Indian troops
will suffer major military defeat in Kashmir on Uri and Naoshera
fronts. If this occurs, nothing that Mountbatten can do will prevent
Indian forces from marching in to West Pakistan to take posses-
sion of what Nehru calls 'bases and nerve centres of raiders.'[15]

The British High Commissioner followed up immediately with yet
another cable. He reported:

I learn privately that V.P. Menon ... informed the Governor-General
that the Inner Cabinet on December 26th had decided that if Uri
falls Indian forces must enter Pakistan to obliterate the 'bases
and nerve centres' of the raiders.[16]

Mountbatten had caused the alarm bells to ring in London. He
next sought a way to provide an opening for Attlee to intervene with
Nehru. Obviously, the British Prime Minister could not address Nehru
on the basis of secret information leaked by India's Governor-General.
Mountbatten thus urged Nehru to send a 'very full telegram' to Attlee,
since 'HMG have a right to know if war is becoming imminent.' Like
the earlier correspondence with Nehru, a copy of this message was
also sent to London, via Shone.[17]

Prodded by the Governor-General, Nehru sent a telegram to Attlee
about India's twin approaches at the military and diplomatic levels.
After outlining the mounting threat in the Jhangar, Naoshera and Uri
areas, Nehru went on to state:

These developments have created a military situation which is
full of peril not only to Jammu and Kashmir State, but to us.
Unless Pakistan takes immediate steps to stop all forms of aid to
the attackers, who are operating from bases in Pakistan and
therefore strategically enjoy a great advantage over us, our only
hope of dealing with them effectively would lie in striking at
them at their bases. This would involve our entering Pakistan ter-
ritory. Such a step would be justified in international law as we
are entitled to take it in self-defence. What is happening now is
definitely an act of aggression against us by Pakistan. However,
as we are most anxious to act in conformity with the letter and
spirit of the Charter of the United Nations we are asking the

Security Council to repeat to the Pakistan Government the request I made in my letter of 22nd December [to Liaquat Ali Khan].... This request is without prejudice to the freedom of the Government of India to take, at any time, such military action as they may consider necessary in exercise of their right of self-defence.[18]

Finessed

Alerted in advance by Mountbatten about India's thinking, Attlee responded without loss of time. His reply was a skillful combination of pleading and warning. Pressing for immediate action in the Security Council, Attlee said, 'In the meantime I beg you as a friend that, whatever the provocation, and whatever the immediate difficulties, you should do nothing which might lead to war, with all its incalculable consequences, between the two Dominions.' He added firmly:

May I say in all frankness that I am gravely disturbed by your assumption that India would be within her rights in international law if she were to send forces into Pakistan in self-defence.... It would, in my opinion, place India definitely in the wrong in the eyes of the world; and I can assure you that it would gravely prejudice India's case before U.N.O., if after having appealed to the Security Council, she were to take unilateral action of this kind.

And he concluded by repeating Mountbatten's warning against the possibility of a quick military solution. 'I think you are very optimistic,' Attlee said, 'in concluding that your proposed military action would bring about a speedy solution.'[19]

Attlee's message created deep resentment in the Indian government but it served the intended purpose. It dispelled the notion that Britain could be persuaded by an appeal to law and morality to jettison her interests in Pakistan and acquiesce in an inter-dominion war. It also provided a preview of the role Britain would shortly play in the Security Council. Over the next few weeks it would become abundantly clear that exercise of the intended military option would prove extremely difficult while the Security Council was seized of the Kashmir issue.

Mountbatten wanted Attlee to fly out and meet the Prime Ministers of India and Pakistan in order to defuse the crisis. This suggestion failed to find favour with Attlee, who felt that the chances of success of an effort at conciliation were extremely doubtful in the prevailing mood of the two governments. Moreover, an unsuccessful visit might lower the chances for Britain to play a helpful role in the Security Council. Attlee pinned his hopes on British moves in the Security Council.

In preparation for the Security Council meetings, the Commonwealth Relations Office briefed the American chargé d'affaires in London about the crisis, suggesting that the problem had to be tackled in two phases. The immediate priority was to stop a war which might begin within the next few days with an Indian attack towards Lahore. In the second phase, a way would have to be found to decide the long-term fate of Kashmir through a plebiscite or some other means.[20]

Thus primed, the United States Embassy in New Delhi addressed a note verbale to the Indian government seeking clarification of India's position. Donovan, the chargé d'affaires, also called on Prime Minister Nehru with the same object in mind. He reported back:

Nehru assured me GoI had no intention taking any steps against GoP which would cause situation deteriorate further.... He said GoI troops would not take offensive action against GoP but that he feared Kashmiri irregulars might raid into West Punjab in retaliation of raiders into Jammu by tribesmen from West Punjab.[21]

A formal reply was sent to the United States Embassy's note verbale setting out the Indian position on the lines of the complaint to the UN, which included an assertion of India's right to self-defence. However, the point had been registered that the United States, like Britain, would be seriously concerned if the fighting were to be extended into Pakistan territory.

Meanwhile, the last few days of December 1947 saw an improvement in the military situation on the ground. This made it possible to postpone the option of attacking the bases on the Pakistan side of the border. General Bucher, who was shortly to assume charge as Commander-in-Chief, advised Shone at the end of December that there was no ground for 'undue pessimism' since Indian forces had been reinforced.[22] A cross-border operation was no longer required

were made for a counter-attack across th
to take the item off the Defence Committ
contingency plans for striking across the
from which it did not re-emerge till the en

Thus the Prime Minister's moves were
General. Nehru believed that two parallel
be followed—a reference to the UN and
attacking the invaders' bases in Pakistan. F
point in good faith. Mountbatten and the se
the second point. Once the Security Coun
the Kashmir issue, it became politically alm
launch a counter-attack against Pakistan.
Jinnah from sending the Pakistani army int
thwarted Nehru from ordering the Indian ar

The course and outcome of the first Indo
understood if we overlook the fact that the tw
establish full national control over their resp
New Delhi, strategic decisions at the highes
Defence Committee which was presided by
naval officer on temporary deputation as Go
He and the British officers commanding th
India loyally as long as this involved no confli
Quite rightly, their primary loyalty was to Brit
that Mountbatten and the service chiefs did t
Indian government when it contemplated step
scale war with Pakistan—a contingency that
anxious to avoid.

The international factor is particularly import
world. Major powers are often able to influenc
come of these conflicts because of the vulnerab
to a variety of pressures—military, political an
wars, secrecy and surprise are vital factors not
also political context. Decisive results must b
before major powers can intervene. The role of /
British service chiefs made it virtually impossib
this requirement in 1947–48. Not only were bra
to strike at the invaders at their bases across the
ish government was kept informed at every s
enabled to take diplomatic steps to close India's

for protecting India's position at Uri or Naoshera. A move into Pakistan was not ruled out but it had ceased to be an imminent prospect.

On 1 January, 1948, India lodged a complaint with the Security Council about the operations carried on by Pakistani nationals and tribesmen against the Indian state of Jammu and Kashmir. In view of this aggression, India asserted her right under international law to take military action against Pakistan in self-defence. In her message to the Security Council, India stated:

In order that the objective of expelling the invader from Indian territory and preventing him from launching fresh attacks should be quickly achieved, Indian troops would have to enter Pakistan territory; only thus could the invader be denied the use of bases and cut off from his sources of supply and reinforcement in Pakistan. Since the aid which the invaders are receiving from Pakistan is an act of aggression against India, the Government of India are entitled, under international law, to send their armed forces across Pakistan territory for dealing effectively with the invaders.

However, since such action might involve armed conflict with Pakistan, India, in conformity with the principles and the aims of the UN Charter, requested the Security Council to ask the Government of Pakistan to (a) prevent their military and civil officials from participating or assisting in the invasion of Jammu and Kashmir; (b) call upon its nationals to desist from taking part in fighting; and (c) deny the invaders access to and use of its territory, military and other supplies, and other kinds of aid. The Indian government emphasised the need for immediate action and reserved for itself the 'freedom to take, at any time when it may become necessary, such military action as they may consider the situation requires.'[23]

The debate which followed in the Security Council soon revealed that the overriding concern of its members was to prevent an escalation of the conflict. As we shall see in Chapter 10, the British delegation worked actively behind the scenes to ensure that the debate focused on this aspect of the problem, rather than the complaint of aggression. As the international constraints on India's military options became evident, Mountbatten was able to persuade Nehru that there was no present need for the Defence Committee to consider the question of crossing into Pakistani territory. Several considerations

must have weighed with the Prime M........
military position, the attitude of the ....
sionment with the Defence Comm...........
Singh protested against the decisio...........
that:

> this does not mean that we shoul...........
> defend our territory or even to co...........
> on certain bases, if necessary, in ....
> impression ... was that such a pla...........
> fact had been prepared. If that is so...........
> tion of putting a stop to this plannir...........
> tage in putting up the plan we had...........
> crowd that attend the Defence Con...........

Nehru had in mind Mountbatten and ....
referred to the 'motley crowd' attend...........
meetings. The meeting on 20 Decemb...........
onstration of the Chairman's capacity t...........
No further session of the Committee wa...........
batten pressed for a last meeting befo...........
Nehru's reference to military plans—a...........
unclear—is less easy to place. General B...........
in-Chief, confided the US chargé d'affaire...........
ary that no steps had been taken to prep...........
attack across the Pakistani border. He ad...........
be necessary for such steps. Bucher said t...........
that he would advise London to transfer al...........
operational duties to advisory duties if ....
imminent.[25] Against this background, it ....
Minister was referring to ideas proposed in...........
High Commissioner Shone had informed L...........

> I ... understand that for some days past ....
> inet have not been discussing their mil...........
> Mountbatten or Lockhart but have be...........
> Indian 'military experts.'[26]

In any case, nothing further came of the...........
from Mountbatten, General Bucher saw to...........

X
The Security Council

London applauded Mountbatten's manoeuvre to thwart an Indian counter-attack across the border. Noel-Baker agreed with High Commissioner Shone that in view of the 'most dangerous turn' in the thinking of the Indian Cabinet, the 'effective choice may be between the early entry of Indian forces into Pakistan, and an appeal to the Security Council.... [T]he second is infinitely to be preferred.... We fully realize that it has been very difficult to bring the Indian Government to this decision, and that congratulations are due to those who induced them to make it.'[1]

Noel-Baker pointed out the lack of realism in the Indian decision. 'I understand, of course,' he wrote, 'the reasons which compelled the Indian Government to send in troops to defend Srinagar against [the] tribesmen. I understand the anger and frustration which they must feel at the continued support which we do not doubt, their opponents in Kashmir are receiving from Pakistan.' Nevertheless it was a 'dangerous political miscalculation' on India's part to hope that the Security Council would condemn Pakistan as the aggressor and authorise India to send her troops into Pakistan. The Security Council, he predicted, would not confine its task to the single point of Pakistan's complicity; it would also focus on the question of the plebiscite, which both parties had accepted.[2]

In preparation for the Security Council, the Commonwealth Relations Office formulated its views in close consultation with the Foreign Office which, at the time, was deeply preoccupied with Palestine.

After the end of World War II, Palestine was a magnet for survivors of the Holocaust. The Zionists were determined to create a Jewish State of Israel while the Arab majority in Palestine were equally resolved to prevent this development. The Arabs were adamantly opposed to Jewish immigration on a scale which threatened to alter the communal balance of the population. The British, anxious to prevent an Arab backlash in the Middle East, tried without success to set a ceiling on the inflow. They were opposed by militant Jewish groups, which in turn suffered reprisals from the Arabs. A violent civil war broke out which the British were totally unable to control. They placed the Palestine question before the United Nations in April 1947 and, in December, announced their decision to abandon the Palestine mandate by next May. Immediately after the British announcement, the UN General Assembly, under American pressure, adopted a resolution for partitioning Palestine into separate Jewish and Arab states. This precipitated fierce fighting among Arabs and Jews, accompanied by bitter Arab recriminations against the British and Americans. Such was the situation in the Middle East when India brought her complaint on Kashmir to the Security Council.

In the context of Palestine, the Foreign Office apprehended that Arab opinion might be further aggravated if British policy on Kashmir were to be seen as being unfriendly to a Muslim state. This fear reflected a failure to understand the nature of Arab nationalism; nevertheless, it was a determining factor in shaping the British position in the Security Council. It was summarised in a Foreign Office minute to Prime Minister Attlee.

> The Foreign Secretary has expressed anxiety lest we should appear to be siding with India in the dispute between India and Pakistan over Kashmir which is now before the United Nations Security Council. With the situation as critical as it is in Palestine, Mr. Bevin feels that we must be very careful to guard against the danger of aligning the whole of Islam against us, which might be the case were Pakistan to obtain a false impression of our attitude in the Security Council.[3]

The Foreign Secretary went to the extent of proposing that, as a reassurance to Karachi, the British delegation to the Security Council should include a person known for his advocacy of the Pakistani case, High Commissioner Grafftey-Smith. When it was pointed out that the High Commissioner could not leave his post at a critical time, Bevin urged Noel-Baker to consult Zafrulla Khan as to whether 'in the interests of our relations with Pakistan it would be well to supplement our delegation by someone known for his familiarity with the Pakistan case.' The question was dropped only after Zafrulla himself said that the step was not necessary,[4] in view of the assurances given by the British delegation.

Noel-Baker readily fell in with the pro-Pakistan line advocated by Bevin, a man he greatly admired. He shared Bevin's views on Pakistan's importance in the context of British strategy in the Middle East. He himself had always regarded Kashmir's accession to India as unfortunate, reflecting a tendency in the Commonwealth Relations Office to view subcontinental affairs in narrow communal terms. As we saw earlier, it was partly for this reason that the department felt that it would have been 'natural' for Kashmir to have acceded to Pakistan, despite the authoritative assessment of the man on the spot, General Scott, that there was little support for Pakistan among the Muslims of Kashmir.

Thus the 'preliminary and tentative' line which emerged at the beginning of January from the consultations between the Foreign Office and the Commonwealth Relations Office encompassed the following elements:

- As a first step, the Security Council should call on both parties to avoid action which might further aggravate the problem. This 'might not debar India from invoking Article 51 of the [the] Charter for action against Pakistan, [but] it would surely have a major deterrent effect.'
- A simple ceasefire call would not do since Pakistan would be unable to persuade the tribesmen to withdraw in the absence of agreed arrangements for a fair plebiscite.
- Such arrangements would involve:
  (i) replacement of the tribesmen by at least a token Pakistani regular force;
  (ii) withdrawal of Indian troops except for a force equal to the Pakistani force inducted into the state;
  (iii) appointment by the Security Council of a 'neutral' General to command both the Indian and Pakistani forces in Jammu and Kashmir;
  (iv) a 'neutral' administration to replace both the Abdullah and 'Azad' administrations. The 'neutral' administration could

consist of a small body of UN representatives, or a joint India–Pakistan administration.

- After agreement on a ceasefire subject to these conditions, the Security Council should be 'induced' to nominate a commission which would proceed to India and Pakistan to negotiate arrangements for a fair plebiscite.
- Thereafter, the Security Council should decide how best to give military support to the 'neutral' administration in Kashmir. A multi-national UN force would result in administrative and command problems. The force should, therefore, be provided by a single 'neutral' country, such as Belgium. Alternatively, Indian troops might be withdrawn to the Hindu majority eastern districts of Jammu and Pakistan troops to Muzaffarabad, Poonch and the western part of Jammu, with a small 'neutral' force in the Srinagar valley.[5]

Unlike the Ismay formula, this approach made no attempt to seek a mid-way solution between the Indian and Pakistan positions. The intention was to be supportive of Pakistan because of the perceived compulsions of the Middle Eastern situation. On every major point, the new approach endorsed the Pakistan position. The accession of Jammu and Kashmir to India was disregarded. Though Whitehall was well aware of the aid and assistance provided by Pakistan to the tribal invaders and despite Jinnah's own confirmation of his ability to 'call off' the raiders, the Commonwealth Relations Office accepted Pakistan's plea that she would be unable to restrain the tribesmen in the absence of plebiscite arrangements acceptable to her. On conditions for a 'fair' plebiscite, the Commonwealth Relations Office accepted Pakistani demands without any reservations—equal status for Pakistani and Indian military forces in the state and removal of the Abdullah administration. Since Britain herself was unwilling to provide the 'neutral' military force requested by Liaquat, she now contemplated a Belgian or some other proxy to meet Pakistan's requirement.

This approach arose more from the perceived compulsions of Britain's Middle Eastern policy than from her interest in securing military facilities in Pakistan per se. In fact the Chiefs of Staff raised practical and legal objections to the proposed military arrangements. They pointed out that it would take several months to induct a force from a 'neutral' country and that such a force would face serious administrative problems. The idea of a 'neutral' force, they felt was unsound. Likewise, experience had shown that a combined Indian and Pakistani force would be unworkable in practice. The UK Chiefs of Staff concluded that the 'only satisfactory military solution is for India to provide the support of the United Nations administration of Kashmir. It is constitutionally her responsibility and militarily we consider that any other solution would involve processes too lengthy and too complex to be effective.[6]

The Foreign Office rejected this recommendation on the grounds that it would be unacceptable to Pakistan. The idea of a force provided by a 'neutral' country was shelved but the Foreign Office and the Commonwealth Relations Office continued to insist that Pakistani troops should be deployed in Kashmir on an equal footing with the Indian army.[7] The only yardstick used by Bevin and Noel-Baker was acceptability to Pakistan. Indian reactions, not to mention legal or constitutional factors, were hardly taken into account. Had these questions come up in the Cabinet, other ministers with greater experience in subcontinental affairs—Cripps, for example—would certainly have insisted on a more even-handed approach. As it happened, however, the line to be taken in the UN Security Council was not considered in the Cabinet before Noel-Baker's departure for New York.

Nor did the Bevin–Noel-Baker scheme have the Prime Minister's approval. Attlee was inclined to lean towards Pakistan on account of the Middle Eastern factor but he was not prepared to push India beyond a point. His instructions to Noel-Baker were couched in general terms. He pointed out four important considerations which should govern the British line at the Security Council. First, it would be advantageous, through public debate in the Security Council, to bring it home to India as soon as possible that an Indian attack on Pakistan would shock and alienate world opinion. Second, in the prevailing circumstances, the Council should seek to devise a practical solution to the problem, rather than urging India and Pakistan to settle the problem by themselves. Third, '[w]e must be particularly careful to avoid giving Pakistan [the] impression that we are siding with India against her. In view of [the] Palestine situation this would carry the risk of aligning the whole of Islam against us.' Finally, the Indians also should be handled with care, since their emotions were running high on the Kashmir issue. 'Possibly however by playing on their respect for legal processes we might get them to accept whatever [the] Security Council can be brought to recommend.'[8]

First Steps in the Security Council

In 1948 the Security Council consisted of eleven members. In addition to the five permanent members–the United States, Soviet Union, United Kingdom, France and China (represented by the KMT)–it included Argentina, Belgium, Canada, Colombia, Syria and Ukraine. The Presidency of the Security Council rotates among its members in alphabetical order, each President holding the office for a month at a time. Belgium happened to preside over the Council in January 1948. Working closely with their Belgian ally, the British delegation faced no difficulty in obtaining a Presidential statement, on 6 January, making an 'urgent appeal' to the two countries 'to refrain from any step incompatible with the Charter and liable to result in an aggravation of the situation.' This was followed on 17 January by a Security Council resolution on similar lines, which additionally incorporated a ryder requesting each of the two parties to immediately inform the Council of any material change in the situation. This added stipulation proved to be significant in the latter part of 1948.

Meanwhile, undeterred by the absence of Cabinet approval, Noel-Baker pursued with single-minded zeal his objective of obtaining a resolution on the broad lines of his 'preliminary and tentative' proposals. His tactics were to operate from behind the scenes and to encourage the United States to seemingly take the lead. Through this ploy, he hoped to manoeuvre the Security Council into adopting a heavily pro-Pakistan approach, while deflecting Indian resentment to other parties.

Noel-Baker met with State Department officials in Washington on 10 January to press his proposals. These included the early despatch to the subcontinent of a UN Commission to implement a plan to be worked out in the Security Council. He emphasised that it was necessary for the details to be worked out in New York itself. It was necessary, he argued, to give Pakistan sufficient assurances to enable her to induce the tribesmen to go home and proposals which met this condition stood a better chance of being accepted by India if there were 'a loud trumpet call' from the UN. Noel-Baker's plan was to place Kashmir under effective UN control pending the plebiscite. The Security Council was to appoint a 'neutral' military commander to be stationed in Srinagar. He would be assisted by a UN Commission which would take over the administration of the state with the help of a Council consisting of both Indians and Pakistanis. Pakistani troops would occupy the north, Indian forces would be confined to the south and a mixed India–Pakistan force would be stationed in the Srinagar valley, together with one thousand 'international' troops. All troops in the state would function under the UN commander. The end result, in Noel-Baker's view, might be a partition of the state on communal lines.[9]

Noel-Baker emphasised that while the British wished to exercise leadership in this question, they did not wish to do so openly since that might look like a reimposition of the Raj! The United States, he said, enjoyed great prestige in both India and Pakistan and could thus play a decisive role.

The State Department reacted with a mixture of sympathy and caution. The United States was prepared to cooperate with the UK to the maximum possible extent but she did not wish to take the overt lead in the Security Council. The United States was also sceptical about the prospect of securing the agreement of India as well as Pakistan to the British proposals. She therefore favoured a less problematical three-point formula consisting of (a) a truce declaration; (b) the establishment of a UN commission to assist the parties in implementing the truce and finding a peaceful settlement of the question; and (c) calling for an early plebiscite and offering to assist the parties to that end through the Commission. The United States did not intend to advance this formula in the Security Council in rivalry to the Noel-Baker plan but she hoped that the UK would consider it as 'perhaps more palatable to [the] parties and other SC members and more in harmony with realities of SC capabilities.' The State Department specifically acknowledged that its suggestion 'differs from the UK plan in one essential point about which Noel-Baker expressed himself strongly: namely, that the process of conciliation should take place in NY and be supported by SC decision rather than left to SC Commission in the area.'[10] In other words, the United States was initially reluctant to issue Noel-Baker's 'loud trumpet call.'

However, in the end Noel-Baker's persistence carried the day. Building on the principle of allied solidarity, he was able to persuade the Americans to participate actively in the debate and advance the proposition that the key issue before the Security Council was not the invasion of Kashmir by Pakistani tribesmen but conditions for a 'fair' plebiscite. As we shall see, the United States was not prepared to follow Noel-Baker in totally brushing aside the implications of Kashmir's legal accession to India but she was persuaded step by step to move in that direction.

When the Security Council met on 15 January, Gopalaswami Ayyangar and Zafrulla Khan presented the case for India and Pakistan respectively. Ayyangar outlined the genesis of the problem and furnished evidence of official Pakistani complicity in the tribal invasion. He asked the Security Council to persuade Pakistan to cease participating or assisting in the invasion; to call upon her nationals to desist from fighting in Jammu and Kashmir; and to deny the invaders the use of her territory for operations against Kashmir, as well as military and other supplies and all other kinds of aid. In a marathon five and a half hour reply, the Pakistani Foreign Minister elaborated not only his stand on Kashmir but on the entire range of India–Pakistan issues. He accused India of attempting to undo the partition of the subcontinent; of carrying out a campaign of 'genocide' against Muslims in East Punjab, Delhi and other areas; of forcibly and unlawfully occupying Junagadh; of obtaining the accession of Jammu and Kashmir by 'fraud and violence'; and of threatening Pakistan with direct military attack. The objective of these 'various acts of aggression,' he alleged, was the 'destruction of the State of Pakistan.' Zafrulla concluded by demanding that Jammu and Kashmir be cleared of both the raiders and the Indians,

> whether by joint administration under the two Governors-General, by joint occupation of predominantly Muslim areas by Muslim troops from Pakistan and predominantly non-Muslim areas in Kashmir by Indian troops, by inviting Commonwealth forces; non-Indian forces altogether; or whether through the United Nations.[11]

The Belgian representative, in his capacity as President of the Security Council, produced a draft resolution providing for the establishment of a three-member commission invested with the dual function of investigating the facts and of carrying out directions given to it by the Security Council. As a compromise between the Indian and Pakistani positions, the facts to be investigated related, first, to Jammu and Kashmir and, second, 'when the Security Council so directs,' to the other issues raised by Pakistan.

The 'Belgian' draft was, in fact, inspired by the British delegation and was crafted to serve Noel-Baker's intention that the commission should play only a subordinate and symbolic role, while the real work of formulating a 'settlement' should proceed in New York.[12] Hence, while all parties were agreed on the urgency of the problem, no move was actually made to constitute the commission and hasten its departure for the subcontinent.

Noel-Baker turned his efforts to orchestrating moves with his Western allies in order to obtain a resolution setting out conditions for a plebiscite on the lines demanded by Pakistan. He had previously sought to assure the sceptical Americans that such a plan would be accepted by India. Since this assurance would shortly be put to the test, he now took the line that the New Delhi's position had hardened considerably 'perhaps as a bargaining device,' and that more pressure was required to 'soften up' the Indians.[13] Austin weakly questioned the desirability of introducing a substantive resolution at this stage but he soon gave in to the British minister. Indeed, in his efforts to oblige Noel-Baker, he even threatened Ayyangar that, in the absence of a settlement between India and Pakistan, conditions would not be sufficiently stable to permit establishment of Indo–US political and economic relations of a permanent character. This move was counter-productive. Prime Minister Nehru instructed Ayyangar to inform Austin that India sought no favour from any country in the area of bilateral relations and that conditions in India were quite stable.[14]

In the Security Council, the Western powers—the UK, the US, Canada and France—supported the Pakistani stand that the raiders could not be induced to withdraw without a change of government in Jammu and Kashmir. The question raised by India—namely, Pakistan's involvement in the invasion—was pushed aside. The Council, said the British delegate, was 'confronted with the question of how to stop the fighting. What will stop it and in what way should it be stopped?' The American delegate provided an answer: 'One cannot have cessation of hostilities and violence unless one also has an understanding.' A few days later he elaborated the implications. The Council, he declared,

> must consider it [the Kashmir problem] as a whole, because unless it does, there cannot be a cessation of hostilities. How is it possible to induce the tribesmen to retire from Jammu and Kashmir without warfare and without driving them out? That is the only way it can be done, unless the tribesmen are satisfied there

is to be a fair plebiscite assured through an interim government that is in fact, and that has the appearance of being, non-partisan.

Noel-Baker now emerged from behind the scenes with eloquent support for this argument.[15] The American delegation had lost sight of Marshall's caution that it should not overtly take the lead.

The Belgian delegate, Ambassador Van Langenhove, presented draft resolutions (a) providing for a plebiscite under the authority of the Security Council; and (b) specifying the duties of the commission (to be set up in terms of the earlier resolution) in bringing about cessation of hostilities. The Indian delegate protested in vain that the Council had failed to address its duty of calling upon Pakistan to deny assistance to the invaders. In vain did he cite the recent case in which the Council had called upon Albania to desist from assisting the Greek rebels.

As the debate proceeded, the extent of Noel-Baker's success in orchestrating Western positions became increasingly apparent. The Western group supported Pakistan on three crucial issues: that Pakistan could take no effective action to stop the invaders until a formula was found for a solution of the Kashmir problem acceptable to her; that the Abdullah government would have to be replaced by an 'impartial' interim administration; and that the United Nations should not merely observe the plebiscite but actually hold it under its authority. It was left to China to point out the need for a more specific direction to Pakistan to stop the hostilities and to question the need for establishing an entirely new regime in Kashmir. Colombia extended some support to China on the former point.

Shortly after his arrival in New York, Noel-Baker had translated his ideas into a draft resolution which was sent to London for approval, with the explanation that it had been cast in this form simply as a convenience 'to crystallize ideas.' This became the subject of correspondence between Whitehall and the UK delegation in New York with the aim of drawing up an agreed draft for submission to the UK Chiefs of Staff and the Cabinet.

Without waiting for London's approval, however, Noel-Baker had proceeded in New York along the lines of his plan. At the beginning of February, when Canada took over the Presidency of the Security Council from Belgium, Noel-Baker 'privately' showed his draft resolution—still unapproved in London—to General McNaughton, the

Canadian delegate.[16] It was arranged that under the auspices of the President (Canada) and with Belgium as the Rapporteur, talks would be held with the representatives of India and Pakistan to make progress towards a solution. Not surprisingly, the proposals framed by Canada drew their inspiration from Noel-Baker and were totally unacceptable to India. On 3 February, Nehru instructed Ayyangar to ask for an adjournment. A majority in the Cabinet, he informed Ayyangar, felt that 'we should get out of this [UN] entanglement as gracefully as we can unless [the] Council shows greater consideration for our point of view'.[17] On 12 February, the Security Council reluctantly accepted India's request for an adjournment.

Ignoring the Indian reaction, Noel-Baker decided to utilise the recess to obtain fuller American support for his plan. He showed his draft resolution also to Senator Austin and the Belgian delegate, Van Langenhove.

The initial American reaction was not encouraging. Secretary of State Marshall had 'grave doubts' about fundamental features of the plan. He pointed out that it envisaged a 'virtual UN trusteeship of Kashmir' for an indefinite period and he thought it 'highly doubtful' that India would acquiesce in such a plan. 'By providing no acceptable alternative to acceptance by India of Pakistan troops in Kashmir and by setting up [a] UN interim government which would completely supersede [the] present regime [in] Kashmir, [the] British exclude any possibility [of a] compromise solution' acceptable not only to Pakistan but also India. Moreover, greater emphasis was required on measures for stopping the fighting: it was 'essential to include under this heading provision for GOP [Government of Pakistan] to withdraw material assistance [to] tribal elements and Kashmir insurgents.' Finally, the 'accent given therein [the British plan] to communal aspects should be eliminated.'[18]

Marshall regarded it as essential that a UN plan should have the agreement, or at least acquiescence, of both India and Pakistan. Such a plan should call for a truce under UN observation, in which Pakistan would be required to take all possible peaceful steps to bring about withdrawal of the tribal invaders and cessation of fighting by the insurgents. Pakistan should withhold material assistance to any of these elements who did not cooperate in the truce. Concurrently with the withdrawal of the raiders, India should progressively withdraw its forces from combat zones but would have the right to retain them in Kashmir. To ensure a fair plebiscite, the Kashmir administration should be reorganised to include representatives of other major political groups and one or more ministers chosen on the basis of their technical qualifications to supervise the electoral machinery and the administration of law and order. If this interim government wished to use Indian or Pakistani troops, or both, it might do so in agreement with the two dominions. (Thus, Pakistani troops could not be introduced into Kashmir without India's consent; and while India's right to retain troops in Kashmir was recognised, these could be employed by the Kashmir government only with Pakistan's concurrence.)[19] The interim government would be left in charge of normal administration and the UN commission would have the right to interfere only in matters directly concerned with the plebiscite. These proposals would give greater prominence to Pakistan's obligation to stop assisting the raiders, recognise India's legal rights in Kashmir, and accept the continuance in authority of the Kashmir state government, albeit with certain changes and limitations.[20]

The fundamental difference between the American and British positions lay in the fact that the United States was prepared in 1947–48 to recognise India's sovereign rights in Kashmir. The difference between the American and British approach emerged clearly in an exchange of views between their officials at the end of February. To quote from the State Department record:

> The US representatives pointed out that they were disturbed by the possibly far-reaching implications of a Security Council resolution recommending the use of foreign troops from one party to a dispute in the territory of another party to the dispute.... The British representatives at first attempted to minimize such an analogy by asserting that Kashmir was 'territory in dispute.' The US representatives agreed that Kashmir was a state about which a dispute had arisen between India and Pakistan but stated that they found it difficult to deny the legal validity of Kashmir's accession to India. In the end, the British representatives agreed with the US point of view that we had to proceed on the assumption for the time being at any rate India had legal jurisdiction over Kashmir.
>
> When it was pointed out that a second objection to a SC recommendation that Pakistan troops be used in Kashmir was that it was extremely doubtful that India would permit the implementation of such a recommendation, the British hastened to state that, of course, they had assumed that India would in the last analysis agree to the use of Pakistan troops but only if 'morally compelled' to do so by virtue of a UN recommendation.[21]

The weak point in Marshall's position lay in his insistence that the United States should adopt a common position with Britain. He was 'particularly anxious [to] avoid presentation [of] competitive formal proposals by [the] British and ourselves and hope[d] that recommendations may be devised which both we and [the] British can support. We must take care not to be responsible for adoption of recommendations which [the] British from [the] wealth of their experience might consider unworkable.'[22] These instructions meant that the American views could be aired in public only to the extent that they were consistent with the British position.

Noel-Baker took full advantage of this fact. His ceaseless efforts to push the Pakistani viewpoint earned him Karachi's gratitude. Passing through London in early March, Zafrulla met Bevin and 'expressed great gratification over the help given to him by Mr. Noel-Baker behind the scenes.'[23]

A Policy Review

As early as 1 February, Patrick Gordon-Walker, the junior minister in the Commonwealth Relations Office, had warned that the 'Indians will be mortally offended if we put forward the idea [of admitting Pakistani troops into Kashmir] publicly' and had urged a more balanced approach in which the first step would be to call on the Pathan raiders to withdraw from Kashmir.[24]

India's strong reaction to Noel-Baker's one-sided approach at the UN gave grounds for concern about its consequences for Indo–British relations. Nehru originally suspected that the Western bias was the result of America's search for military and economic concessions in Pakistan; but after Ayyangar's briefing about the moves in New York, he realised that Noel-Baker was the 'villain of the piece in spite of his pious professions.'[25] Nehru complained angrily to Attlee that Noel-Baker had, in a conversation with Sheikh Abdullah, dismissed as untrue the charge that Pakistan had assisted the raiders. 'You will forgive me if I say frankly,' he cabled, 'that [the] attitude revealed by this conversation cannot but prejudice continuance of friendly relations between India and the U.K.'[26] Though Noel-Baker denied the charge, Attlee was left in no doubt that his minister's initiatives in New York were casting a long shadow on Indo–British relations.

This impression was reinforced by a strong message from Mountbatten, calling for a more even-handed approach which would not permanently alienate either dominion. 'Everybody here is now convinced that power politics and not impartiality are governing the attitude of the Security Council,' he reported. Despite his own efforts to dispel the belief, 'Indian leaders counter this by saying that the Anglo–United States block apparently attaches so high a value on the maintenance of Muslim solidarity in the Middle East that they are even prepared to pay the price of driving India out of the Commonwealth into the arms of Russia.' Mountbatten warned that if the Soviet Union were to come to India's rescue by exercising a veto in the Security Council, she 'would appear throughout the country as the saviour of India against the machinations of the United States and the United Kingdom.'[27]

Bajpai, the Secretary-General in the External Affairs Ministry, played on the Soviet factor with characteristic skill. He told Gordon-Walker that he did not want to appear to be using a threat—and indeed India was in no position to do so—but the fact was that Indian policy was at a watershed between the East and the West: there would be a powerful popular pro-Russian sentiment if the Soviets at a critical moment were to cast a veto in India's favour. Gordon-Walker warned his minister that though India was 'fundamentally anti-Russian,' the 'danger of a reaction against us in favour of Russia should not be lightly dismissed.'[28]

Ministers who had a long-standing interest in the subcontinent were deeply concerned about the line taken by Noel-Baker in New York. Among these were Sir Stafford Cripps, the Chancellor of the Exchequer, and Viscount Addison, the Lord Privy Seal. Prime Minister Attlee shared many of their misgivings and in mid-February he instructed his Secretary for Commonwealth Relations to return to London for discussions.

On 27 February, the Commonwealth Affairs Committee of the British Cabinet discussed the Kashmir question for the first time. There was a wide divergence of views and during the next six days the Committee held three more meetings on the same subject. Defending his initiatives, Noel-Baker maintained that the Security Council offered the best means for obtaining a settlement. As usual, he made light of India's objections to his proposals, claiming that there were new signs of a more accommodating temper on India's part as a result of the Security Council debate.[29] This contention was vigorously challenged. Gordon-Walker, the Parliamentary Under-Secretary in his own ministry, who had recently returned from an extended tour of the subcontinent, reported the disappointment and bitterness which the Security Council discussions had produced in India. He said that Grady, the American Ambassador in New Delhi, had spread the report that the American delegation would have adopted a more sympathetic attitude to India, had it not been for the pressure exerted by the British delegates. Gordon-Walker favoured a 'completely neutral' attitude on the part of the UK; any deviation from this, he said, might drive out either India and Pakistan from the Commonwealth.[30]

There was general support for a solution acceptable to both India and Pakistan. Under the Committee's direction, officials drew up a formula on the following lines:

- Pakistan was to take all possible steps to secure the withdrawal of the raiders from the state and to prevent new infiltration from her territory. She should also ensure that no help was given to those fighting in Kashmir.
- After the cessation of all fighting, India was to withdraw her forces from Poonch, Mirpur and Muzaffarabad,[31] including the garrison in Poonch Town. Indian forces in Jammu and Kashmir were to be reduced in number and concentrated in garrisons.
- The Abdullah government was to continue in office but would invite representatives of other parties to join them in the normal administration of the state. For maintenance of law and order and for carrying out the plebiscite, they would rely on local personnel in each district.
- The UN Commission was to be invited to appoint liaison officers to report on the implementation of the truce. The state government was to delegate to the Commission all powers required for holding the plebiscite.
- An Advisory Council (composed of equal members of Indian and Pakistani nominees) was to be set-up to advise the Commission.[32]

Noel-Baker attempted to shift the discussion to a different track. He observed that the difficulty in the Committee's proposals lay in the fact that it envisaged exclusive reliance on impartial local forces for the maintenance of law and order. These forces were not capable of carrying out the task. For this reason, he would have preferred to employ regular forces from both India and Pakistan. Noel-Baker said that the US proposals sought to overcome this difficulty, while in

other respects they bore a close substantive resemblance to the
Committee's proposals. He admitted that the Americans doubted
whether India would agree to induction of Pakistani troops in Kashmir, adding that their proposals specifically required agreement of
the two countries for employment of Indian or Pakistani forces.

Noel-Baker's attempt to secure Cabinet support for the 'American'
proposals—which, in fact, reflected the concessions he had been
able to extract from the State Department—proved unsuccessful.
The general view of the ministers was that India would react strongly
to the suggestion that Pakistani troops should be brought into Kashmir and would reject any proposal incorporating the idea. At least
one minister expressed his views with great force. In the impersonal
language of the Cabinet minutes:

> The view was expressed that the United States proposals....
> Would be wholly unacceptable to the Government of India and
> that the relations between His Majesty's Government and the
> Government of India would be seriously prejudiced if the former
> were to support them. The United States document made no
> mention of the undoubted fact that the tribesmen had passed
> through Pakistan territory before entering Kashmir, or of the fail-
> ure of the Pakistan Government to prevent this; it provided for a
> United Nations administration to be superimposed on the admin-
> istration in Kashmir; it mentioned the possibility that Pakistan
> troops may be permitted to enter Kashmir; and it was suggested
> that the Indian troops should be placed under the command of
> the Plebiscite Marshall [sic]. These were the sort of terms which
> might be imposed on a defeated country.[33]

Yet there were reservations in the Committee about its own proposals. Tentative soundings in London with Mohammed Ali and
H.M. Patel raised doubts about the acceptability of the proposed
package to the two governments. After much discussion, it was
finally agreed that the British delegation at the United Nations should
'undertake informal and exploratory discussions' on the basis of the
Committee's proposals to ascertain whether they offered a basis for
an agreed settlement. The delegation was instructed to support any
proposal for an interim resolution calling for the withdrawal of the
raiders and requiring Pakistan to prevent infiltration across her border and to stop assistance to the raiders. It was also decided to

inform the American delegation of the reasons why the UK was unable to support its proposals.[34]

These decisions required a major reversal of Noel-Baker's policy in New York. The Cabinet recognised the primary importance of requiring Pakistan to deny all assistance to the raiders, without necessarily linking it to a simultaneous agreement on the plebiscite terms. The Cabinet rejected Noel-Baker's proposition that Pakistani troops should be brought into Kashmir. Finally, London saw no reason for replacing the Abdullah government; the Cabinet felt it would be quite sufficient if the state government were to include representatives of rival groups and to delegate to the UN Commission such powers as they required to ensure a fair plebiscite.

The extent of the shift was reflected in the Cabinet's instructions concerning the US draft. The UK delegation was asked to inform the Americans that the draft was not acceptable since (a) it contained no language to show that the Indian complaint against Pakistan had been taken into account; (b) it would take administration out of the hands of the state government and reconstitute it under instructions from the Security Council; (c) it envisaged the presence of Pakistani troops in Kashmir; and (d) it would place Indian troops under the virtual control of the UN Plebiscite Marshal.[35]

The US position on all these points had largely evolved under Noel-Baker's influence. Indeed, the Americans themselves had questioned the propriety of bringing in Pakistani forces into territory that was legally Indian. They had reluctantly agreed to include a formulation which would allow the introduction of Pakistani troops provided India agreed and had made it clear that this was the furthest they would go to accommodate the British. If the UK delegation was to faithfully carry out the Cabinet's decision it would have to admit to the Americans that Noel-Baker's earlier initiatives had not been authorised by London!

The Chinese Proposals

The Security Council resumed discussion of the Kashmir issue on 10 March in circumstances which favoured pursuit of the new British plan. The presidency of the Council had passed from Canada to China, which had showed itself to be more favourably inclined to the Indian case than any other delegation. On 18 March, the Council President, Ambassador Tsiang Ting-fu, presented a new three-part draft resolution. The first part dealt with restoration of peace and order: it called on Pakistan to try to secure the withdrawal of the raiders and to prevent any further intrusion. The second part dealt with conditions for a fair plebiscite. It called on India to set up a Plebiscite Administration. The Director and Regional Directors of this body would be nominated by the UN Secretary-General but would act as officers of the Jammu and Kashmir government. The final section envisaged an interim government in the state constituted on the basis of adequate representation of all major political groups and the appointment of a high Indian official to ensure fulfilment of the state government's obligations under the plan.

The Chinese proposal went a long way towards meeting India's concerns. It accorded priority to the restoration of peace and order, a priority that was missing in earlier proposals. It was also consistent with India's sovereignty in Jammu and Kashmir: it did not question her exclusive right to maintain forces in the state, nor did it impose the authority of a UN administration over the state government. It did, indeed, envisage effective UN control over the plebiscite administration and the expansion of the state government to give adequate representation to all parties, but these arrangements were to be instituted under a legal formula which was consistent with Indian sovereignty. For these reasons, the proposal was welcomed by India as 'worthy of serious consideration' and, for the same reasons, it was rejected by Pakistan.

The State Department felt that the Chinese proposal offered a framework for a fair settlement though it was not prepared to vote for it in its original form. The department favoured amendments to provide more specific indication of the role of the UN Commission, confer on the Plebiscite Director powers to maintain law and order to the extent he considered this necessary for the purpose of the plebiscite, and to include provisions for the maintenance of law and order in areas from which the tribesmen and Indian forces were to withdraw. The State Department did not insist on a possible reference to induction of Pakistani forces—thus withdrawing the concession they had made earlier to Noel-Baker.[36]

The State Department's position was thus quite close to that of the British Cabinet. It would have been relatively simple for Noel-Baker to lend his support to the Chinese draft with a set of limited amendments to accommodate both the British and American viewpoints. But the Secretary for Commonwealth Relations made no serious effort to implement the Cabinet directive. He continued to press for far-reaching amendments to meet Pakistani demands. He pressed, for example, for removing Abdullah from office—a proposition which had no place in the Cabinet directive.[37]

The procedure adopted by the Security Council was to hold semi-formal meetings of limited groups of members to consider amendments. The active delegations were the UK, the US, Belgium and Canada, apart from the President himself. India and Pakistan were kept informed about amendments, and their reactions—or at least the latter's reactions—were reflected in subsequent amendments. Within twelve days, the Chinese draft went through no less than three revisions, each offering new concessions to Pakistan.

Nehru, who had received an assurance earlier in the month that new instructions had been issued to the British delegation, was greatly disturbed by the trend in New York. He concluded that there was 'unfortunately no reason to suppose that countries such as the U.S.A., Canada and Belgium will follow an independent policy. They will doubtless continue to play second fiddle to the U.K. and we must reckon with Mr. Noel-Baker pursuing his unfriendly part whatever may be his instructions from London.'[38] Krishna Menon conveyed to Attlee and Cripps his Prime Minister's strong feelings over the divergence between the instructions said to have been issued from London and the policy actually followed by Noel-Baker in New York.[39]

Attlee himself came to a similar conclusion about Noel-Baker's activities in the Security Council. In an extraordinary exchange of 'Top Secret and Personal' telegrams, he took the Commonwealth Secretary to task. On 1 April, he cabled:

... I am disturbed as to the extent to which the President's draft of 18th March has been amended. It appears to me that while India has made a very considerable advance, Pakistan has remained obdurate. Yet the last amended draft makes even more extensive demands on India. We have never authorised the new Article 5 involving the possible introduction of Pakistan troops into Kashmir. The proposal to set up parallel courts in Kashmir is also certain to be strongly resisted by India. Nor have we authorised the subordination of Indian troops to the plebiscite authority for any purposes other than those directly concerned with the carrying out of the plebiscite....

I am not therefore prepared for you to support the amended proposals of the President, to which I hope you have not committed yourself in any way.

Failing agreement between India and Pakistan you should... press for a shorter Resolution omitting these contentious details but containing the preamble calling upon Pakistan to secure the withdrawal of tribesmen from Kashmir and recommending the acceptance of a fair plebiscite and urging both sides to work for accommodation.[40]

Noel-Baker replied that the new Article 5 was proposed by Tsiang on his own initiative and supported by the Americans. Moreover, he claimed, Ayyangar had left him with the impression that India might well accept it! As regards parallel courts and subordination of the Indian army to the plebiscite authority, these proposals were, in his view, consistent with his instructions.[41]

This caused Attlee to administer an unambiguous rebuke.

I find it very hard to reconcile the view which you express as to the attitude of the Indian Delegation to the amendment inserted in Tsiang's draft with the representations I have received through the High Commissioner from India here.

From statements made to me it would appear that the Indian Delegation have expressed to their Government concern at the extent to which you seem to be supporting these increased demands on India.... It appears to me that you give a very wide interpretation to the heads of agreement when it is a question of pressing increased demands on India, but you do not appear to take a line against proposals put forward by your U.N. colleagues although they were not such as in our opinion India should be asked to accept.

It appears to me, and I know that Addison and Cripps share my view, that all the concessions are being asked from India, while Pakistan concedes little or nothing. The attitude still seems to be that it is India which is at fault whereas the complaint was rightly lodged against Pakistan.[42]

Noel-Baker now took refuge in the argument that it was not possible for him to change course at this stage. 'Since the other members of the Council know ... our plan for a fair plebiscite in February when

[the] Indian Delegation withdrew, how can I convince them now that Pakistan would be making no concessions by accepting Tsiang's draft of March 30?' he asked. Likewise, 'after what has passed,' he would be unable to push through the alternative of a short resolution limited to reproving Pakistan and exhorting the parties to arrange a fair plebiscite.[43]

Attlee resignedly accepted the *fait accompli*. 'We accept your view as things have gone revised Chinese draft may be accepted as basis for Council's action,' he cabled. This was however conditional to the draft being modified in some significant respects. The language of the resolution should make it clear that Pakistani troops could not be brought into Kashmir without India's consent. Furthermore, Jammu and Kashmir state troops and police would function under the plebiscite authority only to the extent required for purposes of the plebiscite.[44]

The April Resolution

These changes were duly incorporated but by now the document bore little resemblance to the original Chinese draft of 18 March. Colombia, in the person of Ambassador Adolfo Lopez, had assumed the Presidency of the Security Council. An informal group, consisting of the UK and US together with the present and past Presidents—Belgium, Canada, China and Colombia—had taken over the drafting process. Their labours, inspired mainly by Noel-Baker and Austin, resulted in a jointly sponsored resolution which was presented to the Security Council on 17 April.

This resolution, which was adopted on 21 April, consisted of two parts. The first part provided for an increase in the membership of the UN Commission from three to five and instructed the Commission to 'proceed at once' to the subcontinent in order to 'place its good offices and mediation' at the disposal of India and Pakistan with a view to facilitating the restoration of peace and order and the holding of a plebiscite.

The second part set out the Council's *recommendations* to India and Pakistan for achieving these objectives. To bring about the restoration of peace and order, Pakistan should 'use its best endeavours' to secure the withdrawal of the raiders—tribesmen and other Pakistani nationals—from Jammu and Kashmir state. After fighting had ceased, India should withdraw its forces and reduce them to the minimum level required for the support of the civil power in the maintenance of law and order. As far as possible, personnel recruited locally in each district should be utilised for maintaining law and order but, if these were to prove inadequate for 'pacification,' the Commission might employ for this purpose troops of either dominion, 'subject to the agreement of both the Government of India and the Government of Pakistan.' (Thus, Pakistani troops could not be introduced into the state without India's consent, while India's right to maintain a minimum military presence for law and order purposes would be recognised.)

For the purpose of the plebiscite, India was asked to ensure that the state government invited the major political groups to 'share equitably and fully' in the work of administration and that they delegate to the Plebiscite Administration necessary powers for holding a fair and impartial plebiscite including, 'for that purpose only,' supervision of the state forces and police. India should also make available to the Plebiscite Administration such assistance as it required from the Indian forces. The Plebiscite Administration would act as an officer of the Jammu and Kashmir state government but would be nominated by the UN Secretary-General and would, in turn, nominate his assistants. He would have the right to communicate directly not only with the state government and the UN Commission but also with the Governments of India and Pakistan.

Pakistan sought an amendment to the provision calling on India to make available from her forces assistance required by the Plebiscite Administrator; she wanted the UN Commission—not India—to provide the troops. Pakistan, however, failed to find any support for her view. A proposal for an amendment which would have enabled the Administrator to deploy Indian or Pakistani troops at his discretion, without obtaining the consent of *both* these governments, was defeated by seven votes to nil with four abstentions (Argentina, Syria, Ukraine and the Soviet Union).

The 21 April resolution was not accepted by either India or Pakistan. India objected that it did scant justice to her complaint and tended to make her look like a 'co-accused' with Pakistan. It was 'niggardly in its recognition of the merits of the matter, vague and indefinite in the wording of the action to be taken by Pakistan.' It sounded 'apologetic to Pakistan for reminding it of its duty.' It did not take into full account the fact that the Jammu and Kashmir state had acceded to India and that the accession would subsist unless the plebiscite were to go against India. 'Pakistan has no constitutional position in Jammu and Kashmir' and there was no justification for allowing her to intervene in the plebiscite. India was 'willing to give all guarantees and safeguards which would satisfy an international body like the Security Council but those safeguards cannot import into the State a position for Pakistan for interference as a matter of right.'

Pakistan complained that the 'one-sided' resolution amounted to a retreat from positions earlier taken in the Council. Ceasefire should be made a matter of cooperation between India and Pakistan. Pakistan should be entitled to employ her armed forces in the state in Muslim-majority areas, while Indian troops should be stationed only in non-Muslim areas. The provisions relating to the state's interim administration were vague: these should provide for equal representation of the National Conference, the Muslim Conference and 'Azad Kashmir.'

Neither government, however, declined to receive the Commission set up by the Security Council. India stated that she was unable to accept the recommendations of the Council but 'if the Council should still decide to send out the Commission ... the Government of India would be glad to confer with it.'

XI
A Private Initiative

At the end of 1947, Nehru discovered that his Commander-in-Chief, General Lockhart, had received an early indication about the tribal invasion of the Kashmir valley but had withheld the information from the Indian government. Lockhart handed in his resignation and was succeeded by the fellow British officer who, he believed, had 'betrayed' him to the Prime Minister.[1]

The new Commander-in-Chief, General Sir Roy Bucher, was endowed with the skills of a courtier. In a report to the War Office, the Military Adviser to the UK High Commissioner described him as follows: 'Though he has told me on several occasions he is "just a simple soldier" politics are the breath of life to him'.[2] The General succeeded in gaining the confidence of both Nehru and the British High Commissioner. After Bucher's appointment as Commander-in-Chief, Nehru wrote appreciatively: 'Bucher has done good work here and I rather like him. On the Kashmir issue he feels strongly that Pakistan has misbehaved and is generally responsible for much of what has happened.'[3] When the Commander-in-Chief handed over charge after a year, High Commissioner Nye recorded in a telegram to Whitehall: 'Bucher has not only been ready to accept advice [from Nye] but has consistently sought it.... He has consistently opposed all proposals likely to widen the existing breach between the two Dominions and has done so with some success.'[4]

On 13 February, the British High Commissioner, Sir Terence Shone, had an 'entirely off-the-record talk' with the new Commander-in-

Chief, General Bucher. The High Commissioner wished to ascertain India's military intentions in the Poonch sector. As we saw earlier, the British were particularly solicitous about Pakistan's interest in the Poonch and Mirpur areas of Jammu province. An Indian presence along the boundary in this sector would deprive Pakistan of defensive depth in the Rawalpindi area, her principal military centre. The British also shared Pakistani apprehensions that control of the Mangla headworks would enable India to divert the waters of the Jhelum river from the irrigation system of West Punjab, thereby wreaking havoc in Pakistan's economy. Finally, the British were inclined to accept Karachi's view that Indian military operations in the Poonch and Mirpur areas would result in an exodus of refugees, placing a heavy burden on the fragile Pakistani economy. Shone must have had these factors in mind when he asked Bucher about his plans for operations in this area.

Shone reported to London that his conversation with the Commander-in-Chief left him with the impression that 'India' (he presumably meant Bucher) had never seriously considered the proposition of extending her control over the entire length of the Poonch border. Bucher expressed the view that it would be almost impossible for India to hold the entire Western Poonch frontier with Pakistan in view of its length and the number of troops required. Shone, however, cautioned London that, with Cariappa's assumption of the East Punjab and Delhi Command, 'General Bucher may as time goes on be less and less informed of India's actual military plans in this area.' A couple of days later there was a further 'confidential talk' during which Bucher informed Shone that he had sounded Defence Secretary H.M. Patel about the Indian government's intentions. The Commander-in-Chief's assessment was that India would take no further military action in the Poonch area if she succeeded in extricating the large mass of Hindu and Sikh refugees from the town.[5] Bucher's assessment proved inaccurate but it shaped his moves in March 1948.

Shortly after these conversations with Shone, Bucher flew to London as a member of an Indian defence delegation. In early 1948, the UK suddenly reduced India's oil supplies. Apart from an impact on the economy, the reduction had obvious implications for India's capacity to carry out military operations. Nehru believed that the move was intended as a means of exercising pressure on India in the context of the Kashmir operations.[6] It was decided to send H.M. Patel and the Defence Financial Adviser, A.K. Chanda, to London on an arms purchase mission and also to seek a larger oil quota. Nehru accepted Mountbatten's suggestion that Bucher be included in the delegation as he might be helpful in explaining the Kashmir situation to the authorities in Whitehall, especially to General Scoones, the Principal Staff Officer at the CRO. The delegation returned in March after obtaining restoration of the original oil quota. Bucher doubtless explained the Indian position to the authorities in Whitehall and it would be surprising if the latter, in turn, did not appraise him of the British point of view on Kashmir.

On his return from London, Bucher took an extraordinary step. Without the knowledge of the Indian government, the Commander-in-Chief held secret negotiations with his Pakistani counterpart, General Gracey, in order to explore some sort of a private and informal truce arrangement. Gracey's presence in New Delhi for a Joint Defence Council meeting on 19 and 20 March 1948 provided a convenient opportunity for these discussions.

Before dealing with the issues discussed by the two Commanders-in-Chief, it would be useful to situate these in the context of military operations in Jammu province in the early months of 1948. A brief digression is therefore necessary to take into account developments on the battlefield.

Winter Operations in Jammu Province

The fall of Jhangar on 24 December 1947 was a serious blow to India. Jhangar lay at the junction of the roads connecting Mirpur to Poonch and Naoshera respectively. Its seizure thus placed the raiders in a position to mount threats to both Poonch and Naoshera.

This major setback prompted Army Headquarters to review their military plans. Major-General Kalwant Singh prepared an appreciation proposing the following steps:

- Immediate reinforcement of the Poonch garrison by a battalion;
- Organising a brigade group for freeing Jhangar at the earliest opportunity;
- Building up forces at Chhamb with a view to taking Bhimbar;
- After securing Jhangar and Bhimbar, to take Mirpur;
- After securing Mirpur, to relieve Poonch.

The Commander-in-Chief, General Lockhart, rejected the proposal for pressing an advance to the Pakistani border at Mirpur. He agreed, however, that Poonch town must be held at all costs (as required by the Cabinet); that early steps should be taken to free Jhangar in order to open the lines of communication to Poonch; and also to developing a threat from Chhamb to Bhimbar.[7]

At this point, a change occurred at the top-most level of the Delhi and East Punjab Command, which was responsible for the Kashmir operations. Both the cause and consequences of the change had important political implications. In November 1947, Lieutenant General Sir Dudley Russell, GOC-in-C of the Delhi and East Punjab Command, decided to go on a tour of Kashmir in order to acquaint himself at first hand with the situation at the front. His professional zeal cost Russell his job. Mountbatten, who evidently saw himself as the guardian of the 'Stand Down' instructions after Aunchinleck's departure from India, took objection to Russell's initiative. He pointed out to General Lockhart that Russell's tour amounted to a contravention of London's policy forbidding British officers to take part in the hostilities in Kashmir.[8] Russell resigned as GOC-in-C but was retained in an advisory capacity.

This application of British policy produced an unintended result. It brought an Indian officer to a crucially important post and thereby diminished Britain's ability to control the course of military operations. As noted previously, by the last week of February, High Commissioner Shone had started to express misgivings about the intentions of General Cariappa, who succeeded Russell as GOC-in-C.

Cariappa lost no time in implementing plans to strengthen Indian positions around Naoshera, where an enemy attack was expected. Towards the end of January, intelligence reports were received indicating a build-up of the Pakistan-sponsored 'Azad Kashmir' forces at Kot, a village near Naoshera from where they launched attacks on the Indian lines of communication. In order to remove the threat, Indian forces attacked and occupied Kot in an action designated 'Operation Kipper.' ('Kipper' was the nickname by which Cariappa was known to his colleagues.) This was the first major reverse inflicted on the so-called 'Azad Kashmir' forces in prepared positions. On 6 February, the 'Azad' raiders launched the expected all-out attack on Naoshera. After fierce fighting they were beaten back with heavy losses. The Indian Commander, Brigadier Usman, gained well-deserved fame as the 'Hero of Naoshera.'*

Having consolidated his position at Naoshera, Cariappa launched 'Operation Vijay,' with the aim of regaining Jhangar. On 18 March, after two weeks of heavy fighting, Indian forces succeeded in freeing Jhangar. The raiders thus lost control over the main approach from Mirpur to Poonch and Naoshera.

The stage was now set for an advance from Naoshera to Rajouri. On 13 April, Indian forces entered Rajouri town. There followed a series of raids and counter-raids in the Rajouri and Naoshera areas but, by early May, the Indian army succeeded in removing the Pakistani threat to the Jammu–Naoshera lines of communication.

Cariappa took an unusual, if necessary, precaution to ensure the success of operations 'Kipper' and 'Vijay.' He kept Army Headquarters in the dark about his operational plans. In the words of his biographer, Brigadier Khanduri, 'Cariappa appeared to be fighting two enemies—Army Headquarters headed by Roy Bucher and the Pakistan Army headed by Messervy.'[9]

Meanwhile, in accordance with the Cabinet's decision, the Poonch garrison remained in place. Reinforcements were flown into Poonch from Jammu in January. Food and ammunition supplies were airlifted by Indian airforce Dakotas. Realising that the beleaguered garrison was almost totally dependent on its airstrip, the so-called 'Azad Kashmir' forces brought up 3.7 inch howitzers and 4.2 inch mortars to the neighbouring hills and, on 17 March, they commenced shelling the town and airstrip. In order to counter this threat, the Indian airforce flew in two 25 pounders under the cover of darkness. These outranged the enemy guns and enabled the garrison to defend itself. The airforce also provided valuable support by strafing and bombing enemy positions. The 'Azad Kashmir' attackers were thus repelled by coordinated action on the part of the Indian army and airforce. The bold decision of the Indian government to hold on to Poonch against the advice of the Commander-in-Chief was amply vindicated.

---

* This gallant officer laid down his life in July 1948, while repulsing a Pakistani assault on Jhangar. Prime Minister Nehru paid him a memorable tribute in a letter to his brother. 'It was a soldier's death and a brave man's death.... So, while we naturally grieve we rejoice also at that courage which triumphs over death and which, in the ultimate analysis, makes a nation.' *Selected Works*, Vol. 7, p. 319.

Bucher–Gracey Talks

Thus, on 19 March, when Bucher began his secret discussions with Gracey, the military background may be summed up as follows. The Indian army had consolidated its position at Naoshera and had just re-taken Jhangar. It was set to advance to Rajouri, securing firm control over the lines of communication between Jammu and Naoshera. The beleaguered Poonch garrison was engaged in repelling a major attack, directed particularly at its vitally important airstrip; in carrying out this task the garrison received invaluable help from the airforce. Meanwhile, preparations were in progress for the planned spring offensive of the Indian army.

This was the context in which Bucher proposed to Gracey that they come to a secret understanding to maintain what would amount to a truce. The content of the discussions between the two Commanders-in-Chief was conveyed to London in top secret telegrams from the British High Commissioners in Pakistan and India. On 26 March, Grafftey-Smith reported to London that General Gracey had informed him that he was carrying on negotiations with his counterpart in India, General Bucher. The High Commissioner cabled:

> *These discussions at C-in-C level seem to have proceeded from General Bucher's indication to his opposite number in Pakistan that he had no wish to pursue an offensive into what is effectively Azad Kashmir controlled territory, i.e. the Mirpur and Poonch sector. General Gracey therefore proposed an agreement, with which Sardar Mohammed Ibrahim, the Azad Kashmir leader, has willingly associated himself, under which the Azad Kashmir forces will give safe conduct to the Indian armed forces now beleaguered in Poonch, and to the considerable non-Muslim elements in the town, to withdraw to territory now controlled by the Indian Army. In return, General Bucher appears to have undertaken*
>
> (a) *that the forces withdrawing from Poonch should not damage the town before leaving it and*
> (b) *that present irresponsible bombing by Indian air force, which is causing intense resentment among the civilian population, should cease forthwith. Shelling of Poonch by Azad forces is also to cease. Similar arrangements are under discussion for the evacuation by Indian elements of Rajouri.*

In addition to these arrangements, General Gracey claims to have discouraged the Azad forces from their present tactics of raiding behind the Indian front on the Uri sector.

The object of these arrangements is to reach a situation in which each side would remain in undisputed military occupation of what are roughly their present positions and, more importantly, will remain there strictly on the defensive. An atmosphere of truce might then replace the present somewhat futile and certainly wasteful military offensive on both sides.

I understand from General Gracey that some effect is already being given to these plans....

An essential part of the process agreed by the two Commanders-in-Chief is that three battalions of the Pakistan Army should be employed in Kashmir, opposite the Indian forces at Jhanjar, in or around Poonch and at Uri. Their role would be wholly defensive and primarily directed to preventing the tribesmen from further offensive action.... General Gracey is emphatic that, whatever arrangements for a plebiscite might be made, it will be essential for some Pakistan Army troops to be employed in the Uri sector....

The Pakistan Prime Minister is aware of the exchanges I have reported above, but I understand, he feels unable at present to endorse them officially....[10]

High Commissioner Shone in New Delhi was aware of the discussions between the two Commanders-in-Chief even before he received the Karachi telegram; but he had refrained from referring to them in his voluminous cable traffic, presumably because he thought that this was a highly sensitive matter which should not lightly be put on paper. His version of the exchanges was rather different and is best told in his own words. In response to the Karachi telegram, Shone reported on 28 March:

I knew something of the correspondence which has taken place between the two Commanders-in-Chief because General Bucher asked me to see him privately at his house on Sunday, 21st March, to say that he had received two confidential messages from General Gracey.... These messages which followed private talks between the two Commanders-in-Chief which took place at the time of the meeting of the Joint Defence Council held a few days previously had caused some perplexity to Bucher who

had first shown them to Brockman, Private Secretary to the Governor-General. Brockman had suggested that Bucher should
consult me privately in order to ascertain whether I agreed that
Bucher should immediately inform Pandit Nehru of receipt of the
messages. I had no hesitation in endorsing this suggestion.
...[Bucher] has given me the following information confiden-
tially. In the first place Bucher made it quite clear to Gracey
when he was in Delhi that India had no intention at present of
pursuing an offensive into interior of Mirpur and Poonch....
Bucher also has given no undertaking to Gracey to withdraw
Indian troops from Poonch Town. The position will be that once
civilians have gone the commitment of the Indian Army will be
less. Bucher cannot admit an irresponsible bombing by Indian
Air Force but says that bombing has been restricted recently because of weather and other difficulties. Moreover, it is the Indian
policy to maintain purely defensive military action while the
Kashmir dispute is under discussion at Lake Success.
    Bucher states categorically that India cannot agree to Paki-
stan troops entering Kashmir territory. Finally, Bucher does not
adhere to Gracey's appreciation that whatever arrangements for
a plebiscite might be made it will be essential for some Pakistan
troops to be employed in the Uri sector.[11]

The accounts of the two High Commissioners differed in some
respects but both cables suggest that Bucher conveyed that he would
not launch an offensive into territory controlled by the so-called 'Azad
Kashmir' forces in the Mirpur and Poonch areas. He also indicated
that he would contrive to withdraw Indian troops from Poonch town
and from the environs of Rajouri if he were allowed to evacuate the
besieged soldiers and civilians without interference. He had also offered
to halt Indian bombing operations (presumably by finding technical
justifications). Gracey, on his part, was to stop further shelling of
Poonch by 'Azad' forces, to provide 'safe conduct' to troops and civilian being evacuated to areas under Indian control, and to restrain
'Azad' forces from raiding behind the Indian front in the Uri sector.
    Gracey had insisted that three battalions of the regular Pakistani
army would have to be sent into Kashmir for deployment opposite
the Indian forces in Jhanjar, in or around Poonch, and at Uri. Gracey
seems to have formed the impression that Bucher accepted the proposed deployment but the latter's version differed on this point.
Shone, who drafted his messages with great skill and precision,

reported that Bucher had explained that 'India cannot agree to Pakistan troops entering Kashmir territory' and that 'he [Bucher] does not adhere to Gracey's appreciation that … it will be essential for some Pakistan troops to be employed in the Uri sector' (emphasis added). Did Bucher imply that while the Government of India would not accept entry of the Pakistani army into Kashmir, he, Bucher, might be able to turn a blind eye in the Poonch sector (after cessation of Indian military activity in the area) but that he would not be able to do so in the Uri sector?

Gracey, a straightforward soldier, failed to understand the delicacy of Bucher's position. The Commander-in-Chief of the Indian army was negotiating behind the back of his government and the offer he made clashed with government policy. The Indian government was determined to hold on to Poonch town at any cost. Bucher, as we have seen, had formed the incorrect impression that his government's principal concern related to the safety of the refugees who had taken shelter in the town. This led him to believe that he could persuade the authorities to accept a withdrawal once the refugees had been safely evacuated. Withdrawing Indian troops from the Rajouri area would not only be in conflict with government policy but would imply abandoning Cariappa's plans to occupy the town. More generally, putting the army in a strictly defensive posture was inconsistent with the Indian government's intention of expelling the raiders from the entire territory of Jammu and Kashmir. Bucher appears to have achieved some success in curbing Indian air activity in the Poonch sector 'because of weather and other difficulties' and this sheds light on his *modus operandi*. The Commander-in-Chief hoped to reshape government policy by doctoring his technical advice on military questions.

Gracey failed to understand that Bucher's proposals were in the nature of a private and informal understanding between the two Commanders-in-Chief. He dutifully submitted the proposals to the Pakistani authorities, thus raising them to a formal and official level. Sardar Mohammad Ibrahim Khan must have been delighted at the recognition of his 'Azad Kashmir government' implied in an agreement between his Commander and India's Commander-in-Chief permitting the presence of so-called 'Azad Kashmir' forces in Jammu and Kashmir state. Liaquat also gave his blessings to the initiative but shrewdly refrained from openly endorsing it, no doubt because he suspected it would be unacceptable to the Indian government and also, perhaps, in keeping with Jinnah's tactics of holding out till the last moment to see if further concessions could be secured.

Gracey's formal proposals put Bucher in a serious quandary because of the difficulty of explaining their origins to the Indian authorities. Advised by Brockman and Shone, he finally decided to reveal to the Indian authorities the contents of Gracey's cables, though in what form or with what gloss remains unclear. The government, of course, rejected the proposals and instructed the Commander-in-Chief not to engage in such discussions in the future. Bucher had no option but to inform his counterpart in Pakistan that India would 'revert to normal action' after 31 March.[12] To Shone, he explained away the collapse of his scheme in the following terms:

> *negotiations had led to a position in which there was an implied understanding that offensive action would be held up by both sides pending discussion of ways and means of securing evacuation of non-Muslim refugees from certain areas, e.g. Poonch and Skardu. The shelling of Poonch had ceased but in other areas the leader of the Azad forces had been unable owing to faulty communications and because of the scattering of his forces to fulfill the agreement.*[13]

Sardar Mohammed Ibrahim Khan put out a different account. He issued a press statement on 31 March to the effect that his 'government' was approached by India for a ceasefire order on 19–20 March and that an agreement was finalised on 24 March, only to be cancelled the following day on orders of the Indian Prime Minister.[14]

The most intriguing feature of the Bucher–Gracey talks concerned the induction of regular Pakistani troops into Jammu and Kashmir. It seems incredible that Bucher should have entertained such a proposal unless this is seen against the background of Noel-Baker's efforts at the United Nations to secure a Pakistani military presence in Kashmir. Towards the end of March, when Zafrulla Khan reverted in the Security Council to the question of employing Pakistani troops in connection with a plebiscite, the Commonwealth Relations Office in London speculated that his move might have been based on knowledge of the Bucher–Gracey exchanges.[15]

XII
The Spring Offensive

We have seen that at the end of 1947, the Indian government reluctantly come to the conclusion that a decisive offensive to expel the invaders from Kashmir would have to be postponed to the spring. They were advised by their service chiefs that an advance from Uri to Domel would be possible but only after the winter months. Preparations were made accordingly to launch a major offensive when spring arrived.

On the eve of the spring offensive, the Commander-in-Chief of the Pakistan Army, General Sir Douglas Gracey, visited New Delhi for one of the periodic Indo–Pakistan meetings on the division of defence stores. Gracey called on Mountbatten on 2 May and held a discussion with him on the general military situation. Mountbatten's record of the meeting includes the following exchanges:

> ... I asked him how the Pakistan armed forces stood in relation to war. How ready were they if war came between the two Dominions? General Gracey shrugged his shoulders and said, 'Pakistan has not got a hope. The air force can hardly take the air, and it will be years before the Royal Pakistan Air Force is efficient. The army, such as it is, is quite efficient, but it is half the size of the army of India and has no proper backing. The Pakistan army would run out of ammunition very quickly indeed in the event of any large scale engagements, and there were no ammunition factories of any type in Pakistan to replenish stocks. In fact, in

*any war between the two Dominions, Pakistan would be com-
pletely defeated militarily in a fairly short space of time, although
the Muslim soldiers would fight with great gallantry and to the
death.'*

*I urged him to make it abundantly clear [to the Pakistan gov-
ernment] that in the event of war, Pakistan would be finished,
however gallantly they fought, in a very few weeks unless they
had adequate stocks of ammunition and some war factories,
which could not occur for several years.*

*I told him that I proposed to bring to the notice of the Govern-
ment of India the military situation of India which, although far
stronger than Pakistan's, was still not such as to permit of any
other war than the one in Kashmir[1].... In fact I pointed out that if
we could get the two governments to feel themselves thoroughly
militarily impotent, then this appeared to be the best chance of
reducing the risk of war after my departure.[2]*

British interests required prevention of an all-out inter-dominion
war and to ensure this Mountbatten projected a deliberately exaggerated picture of India's military limitations vis-à-vis Pakistan. The military advice offered by the service chiefs to the Indian Cabinet must be
seen against this background.

On 5 May—within three days of the Mountbatten–Gracey conversation—General Bucher offered the following military appraisal to
the Defence Minister, Sardar Baldev Singh:

*As regards KASHMIR ... in my opinion, with the forces now
available, INDIA could not achieve more than the limited objectives which were being pursued. These were an advance to
DOMEL and thereafter the removal of the non-Muslim population from POONCH City.*

*I further said that in so long as the Poonchis, Mirpuris and
Muzaffarabadis offered resistance, it would NOT be possible for
INDIA to over-run these areas.*

*Reference the EAST PUNJAB, I said that the Indian forces there
were now barely sufficient for their overall defensive role.[3]*

In other words, the Commander-in-Chief offered the assessment
that the Indian army was in no position to drive out the raiders from
the entire territory of Jammu and Kashmir. An advance to Domel was

all that could be attained and even in this sector, Muzaffarabad was beyond the range of possibilities. As regards the Poonch area, the Commander-in-Chief urged that the objective should be limited to evacuating non-Muslim refugees from Poonch town—a view he had long espoused. Needless to say, the possibility of an Indian thrust into Pakistani territory to attack the rear bases of the invaders—the option proposed by Nehru in December 1947—was not even considered by the Commander-in-Chief. The posture in East Punjab was to be purely defensive.

We have seen in an earlier chapter that Prime Minister Nehru had lost faith in the institution of the Defence Committee, as then constituted, by the end of 1947. As a result, the Defence Committee did not meet for almost five months after December 1947. Anxious to limit the impending Indian offensive in Kashmir, to forestall military plans for Hyderabad and to avert the possibility of all-out war after his departure from India, Mountbatten now caused the Defence Committee to be convened.[4]

When the Defence Committee met on 13 May, however, its proceedings did not follow the script planned by Mountbatten. Right at the outset, Prime Minister Nehru drew attention to a directive that Army Headquarters had issued to Cariappa to evacuate refugees from the Poonch area. He criticised the directive for not reflecting the correct objectives: evacuation of refugees might be desirable to free the hands of the army for military operations but the main objective was to drive out and exterminate the raiders. What was required, the Prime Minister said, was quick occupation of strategic points such as Domel and Kohala in order to bottle up the raiders that remained behind. Nehru observed that about 15,000 refugees had already been evacuated from the Poonch area without any special effort on the part of the army. (This may have been unfair to Bucher in view of his secret initiatives with Pakistan in March!)

Bucher argued that in the prevailing law and order situation, troop deployments were barely adequate to meet the internal defence requirement. Nehru rejected this view, pointing out that law and order must be maintained essentially on the basis of a government's popularity and prestige; the physical presence of the army was only a supportive factor.[5]

Nehru's comments on Poonch effectively demolished Bucher's ploy for securing a withdrawal. The Commander-in-Chief hoped, however, that the focus on Domel could serve to restrict operations in the

Poonch and Mirpur areas. High Commissioner Shone informed the CRO the next day:

> *I understand privately that Ministers here have been expressing the desire that the raiders should be cleared out of the State as soon as possible and that military operations should be intensified to this end. It has been pointed out to them that the best means of driving out raiders and preventing further ingress would be an advance down the main road from Uri to Domel rather than offensive operations in Mirpur and Poonch areas. Ministers have agreed to this. Accordingly developments on the Uri front may perhaps be expected before long.*[6]

Pakistan Army Moves into Kashmir

While Bucher strove to convince the Indian government that his army was incapable of overcoming local resistance in the Poonch, Mirpur and Muzaffarbad areas, the Pakistani authorities entertained no such illusion. They were well aware that the so-called 'Azad Kashmir' forces would collapse before an Indian onslaught if they were not bolstered by the regular Pakistani army. In anticipation of India's spring offensive, Pakistan decided to send her army into Jammu and Kashmir while hoping that this would not provoke escalation into a full fledged war.

In April, General Gracey presented the case in an impassioned memorandum to the Pakistani government. The impending Indian offensive, he counselled, was likely to be directed at Bhimbar–Mirpur and Poonch in the south and Muzaffarabad–Kohala in the north. Gracey believed that this would almost certainly create a 'big refugee problem' for Pakistan. 'Occupation of Bhimber and Mirpur will give India the strategic advantage of ... sitting on our doorsteps, threatening the Jhelum bridge which is so vital for us. It would also give them the control of the Mangla headworks, thus placing the irrigation in Jhelum and other districts at their mercy.' Furthermore, the 'loss of Muzaffarabad or Kohala will ... have the most far-reaching effect on the security of Pakistan. It would enable the Indian Army to secure the rear gateway to Pakistan through which it can march in at any time it wishes to.... It will encourage subversive elements such as Khan Abdul Ghaffar Khan and his party, Ipi, and Afghanistan....'

Gracey concluded: 'If Pakistan is not to face another serious refugee problem …; if India is not to be allowed to sit on the doorsteps of Pakistan to the rear and on the flank at liberty to enter at its will and pleasure; if civilian and military morale is not to be affected to a dangerous extent; and if subversive political forces are not to be encouraged and let loose in Pakistan itself, it is imperative that the Indian Army is not allowed to advance beyond the general line Uri-Poonch-Naoshera.'[7]

Even before Gracey's memorandum, Pakistan had begun to infiltrate army battalions into Kashmir behind a frontal screen of irregulars. 'Rumours' of these movements were first reported to London on 15 March by Duke, an official of the UK High Commission in Pakistan.[8] The presence of Pakistani troops in Kashmir was confirmed by High Commissioner Grafftey-Smith on 4 May.[9] (The fact that it took him almost seven weeks to check and confirm Duke's report reflects the rather lacklustre quality of Grafftey-Smith's coverage of important developments, especially when contrasted with the steady flow of detailed and up-to-date cables originating from his colleague in New Delhi.) On 10 May, Grafftey-Smith finally supplied some details. He reported that General Gracey had informed him and his Military Adviser that the Pakistani army had three battalions in Kashmir, one in the Mirpur area, one west of Poonch and one south-west of Uri. Gracey explained that these battalions were acting in a 'long stop' defensive role against an Indian advance.[10] The reader will note that the deployment pattern was on the lines discussed in March between Gracey and Bucher.

Almost simultaneously, the American Embassy in Karachi informed Washington about the movement of regular Pakistani troops into Kashmir. On 8 May, the US Military Attaché, Lieutenant Colonel Hoskot, cabled the Director of Intelligence in the War Department, Lieutenant General Chamberlin:

Information received this morning indicates possibility armed conflict India Pakistan imminent unless present conditions change drastically, quickly. Pakistan has three regular Pakistan Army battalions Kashmir now, one vicinity Uri, one vicinity Poonch, one vicinity Mirpur, all lying well back present fighting but on war scale prepared immediate action event India advances any above three places should cause serious withdrawal Azad forces.… Pakistan army on practical war footing along entire Indo-

Pakistan border Bahawalpur State to Domel. 10th Division Lahore with brigade[s] Lahore, Sialkot, Rawali has complete war plan ready to be put into action. By bringing 7th Division which is mobilized on war footing in Pindi into action sending 3rd Armored Brigade from Rimalpur into positions along border north of Jhelum and robbing 9th Division Peshawar, Pakistan can throw at most corps into action. Lack supplies and reserves would mean short but bloody engagement with India certain and quick victor....[11]

The Indian Offensive

In preparation for the spring offensive, India inducted additional troops into the Uri front. Army Headquarters had estimated that three brigades would be required in the valley for the advance to Domel. By early May, with the induction of the 77 Para Brigade, the planned force level was in place. Headquarters, Jak Force, was disbanded on 1 May and replaced by two new Division Headquarters—one responsible for operations in Jammu and Poonch and the other for operations in the rest of Kashmir. The latter, designated Sri Div, under the command of an outstanding soldier, Major-General K.S. Thimayya, was given the task of driving the invaders from the Jhelum valley.

On 18 May, India launched its long-awaited spring offensive. The plan envisaged that the 161 Infantry Brigade, commanded by Brigadier L.P. Sen, would advance along the Uri–Domel road upto the Pakistani border. The 163 Infantry Brigade, under Brigadier Harbaksh Singh, was to execute an outflanking movement along the hills to the north of the Jhelum river towards Tithwal, from where the force was to move southwards to Muzaffarabad and Domel. Meanwhile, the 77 Para Brigade, under Brigadier P.S. Nair, was to guard the Uri bowl and the lines of communication.

The main thrust along the Uri–Domel road immediately ran into heavy opposition not only from Pathan raiders and Poonchis but also from regular Pakistani troops. After fierce fighting it was able to advance a few miles along the road but by 25 May it was brought to a virtual halt. The northward thrust met with greater success. Tithwal was taken on 23 May. Thimayya then sought to capture the higher ground west of Muzaffarabad and Domel, with a view to denying the enemy the use of the bridges on the Kishanganga and Jhelum rivers and the Domel–Uri road. A thrust was launched from Uri (Operation Surya) toward Muzaffarabad and another (Operation Gagan) toward the Chinari–Chakothi segment of the Jhelum valley road. The forces available however proved to be insufficient and neither operation could be completed according to plan. By 5 June, the Indian offensive had been halted. The advance to Tithwal was a significant gain but the offensive had failed to attain the objective of gaining control of Domel and Muzaffarabad and to seal the main access route from Pakistan to the Kashmir valley.

Meanwhile, the raiders had launched an attack against Indian positions in the northern sector. Moving in from the west, they attacked Kargil and Dras in mid-May. The attack on Kargil met with immediate success. Dras held out against the invaders for several weeks but it had to be evacuated finally on 6 June.

Apart from the loss of territory, the fall of Kargil and Dras exposed Srinagar to possible Pakistani raids. Army Headquarters offered the following appreciation on 9 June:

> *Enemy activity in the NORTHERN sector has increased and a threat to SRINAGAR by the occupation of KARGIL and DRAS is still a possibility, until these places are re-taken. To achieve this more troops will be required which can only be obtained by curtailing the advance to MUZAFFARABAD.*[12]

Thus by early June, the Indian offensive had been effectively halted. It had advanced less than ten miles west of Uri. The northward advance had met with greater success and Indian forces were established in Tithwal but progress beyond this point toward Muzaffarabad or Domel proved unattainable. Moreover, developments in Kargil and Dras required diversion of troops to this sector. On the basis of Army Headquarters' appreciation the Defence Committee decided on 10 June that:

> *... the present position in Uri–Chakothi–Tithwal area should be stabilised with a view to making an advance on Muzaffarabad provided it could be done without weakening other sectors and without taking undue risks.*[13]

In short, the government reluctantly suspended the long-planned advance to Domel.

There remained the possibility that Indian commanders in the field might even now take initiatives leading to the escalation of the conflict. To guard against this possibility, Bucher issued a detailed directive to Cariappa on 6 July instructing that no major operation should be undertaken without the approval of Army Headquarters. Cariappa was told to concentrate on stabilising existing positions.[14]

In a telegram to London, High Commissioner Shone reported:

> General Bucher told me yesterday that he had been impressing on the Indian political authorities the difficulty and dangers of the military situation in Kashmir now that large numbers of Pakistan forces including artillery were involved. He was particularly anxious to avoid a head on clash with Pakistan forces which might well result from some precipitate action on the part of an Indian Commander (e.g. Cariappa). He had therefore been advocating a defensive rather than an offensive policy in which I gathered he had considerable success.[15]

The arrival of the UN Commission in the Indian sub-continent in July enhanced the propitious environment for Bucher's advocacy of restraint. Though India did not accept the terms of the resolution providing for the despatch of the Commission, the fact could not be ignored that the Commission's report would significantly affect prospects for a resolution of the Kashmir issue. The Indian government had already accepted the assessment of Army Headquarters that a decisive push was not militarily feasible for the time being. Thus there appeared to be no justification for prejudicing the prospects of a generally favourably report by undertaking inconclusive offensives. Toward the end of July, Bucher was able to inform the British authorities that Nehru had issued instructions to the army to refrain from initiating offensive action while the UN Commission was in India.[16]

Bucher did not rest content with his successful advocacy of a defensive posture. In pursuit of his objective of limiting the scale of hostilities, Bucher also seems to have explored secret understandings with Gracey. A glimpse of these arrangements—which were not always successful in practice—is afforded by an exchange of telegrams between the UK missions in New Delhi and Karachi at the end of July. Acting High Commissioner Symon reported from Delhi on 26 July that Bucher had told him that he was worried about reports which had been coming in from the front during the past twelve hours about a fresh Pakistani offensive in Kashmir. If these reports were confirmed, he said, India would be forced to take strong retaliatory action. This possibility was causing Bucher anxiety.[17]

Symon's colleague in Karachi promptly sent a reassuring reply. He said that Bucher's reports apparently stemmed from the fighting near Chakothi, west of Uri, and Tithwal. He had no information that Pakistan intended to launch a general offensive and he regarded such a possibility as very improbable.[18] On 30 July he followed up with another message conveying the information that the US Military Adviser, who had just returned from a visit to the Chakothi area, had reported that Pakistan's intention in the recent fighting was to recapture the high feature north of Chakothi, overlooking their lines of communication. India's earlier seizure of this feature had made daylight movement impossible. The cable reported that in the view of the US Military Adviser 'recent operations are [the] result of [an] advance by [the] Indian Army *beyond line understood to have been given to General Bucher by General Gracey* as [the] limit beyond which any Indian advance would compel [a] Pakistan count-option [sic]' (emphasis added).[19]

Did Bucher Know about the Pakistani Move?

India's operational plans for the spring offensive, including force level decisions, were based on the assumption that the opposing force consisted of Pathan tribesmen, Poonchis and other irregulars. These calculations were upset by the presence in strength of regular Pakistani forces. The question must be asked if the Commander-in-Chief of the Indian army was aware, before launching the offensive, that it would run into opposition from regular Pakistani army units.

It is obvious that, at the very minimum, Bucher's secret conversations with Gracey in March gave him ample grounds to suspect that regular Pakistani troops would be sent into Jammu and Kashmir before the spring. Did Bucher possess more definite information? Bucher denied foreknowledge but Whitehall believed that Gracey had informed him about the Pakistani moves. Noel-Baker specifically instructed his officials to desist from seeking confirmation of their surmise. Notings on file on this question arose from the inordinate delay on Bucher's part in acknowledging a Pakistani army presence in Kashmir.

When Major-General Thimayya assumed charge of Sri Div at the beginning of May, he was told by Brigadier L.P. Sen, the officer commanding the infantry brigade deployed in the area, about the presence of three regular Pakistani army battalions in the Chakothi–Chinari area. Sen informed Thimayya that he had been regularly reporting the presence of this force for the past two months but his reports had not been accepted as factual. Thimayya himself had no difficulty in accepting Sen's assessment.[20]

Brigadier Sen's estimate of the size of the Pakistani presence may have been exaggerated but the fact that there was such a presence was confirmed as soon as the spring offensive commenced. Sen had expected that with the advance of the Indian infantry brigade towards Tithwal, Pakistani regular troops would be moved back. This was belied by an artillery attack on Indian positions in the early hours of 19 May, featuring 4.2 mortar bombs. Since neither the 'Azad Kashmir' forces nor the tribesmen were known to possess these mortar bombs, the shelling confirmed the presence of regular Pakistani forces. This observation was duly reported to Army Headquarters but was rejected as unfounded.[21]

Shortly thereafter, the Indian army took into custody Prisoners-of-War belonging to a regular Pakistan army unit. By 20 May, Prime Minister Nehru had no difficulty in concluding that the 'Pakistan Army is definitely taking part in the Kashmir operations, or at any rate, some battalions of that army are taking part plus also supplying guns.'[22] But Army Headquarters at the highest level continued to maintain silence. With additional evidence pouring in, Prime Minister Nehru publicly declared on 6 June that India had clear proof that Pakistan had placed units of her armed forces in Kashmir. Incredibly, even at this stage, Army Headquarters professed doubts about a Pakistani presence. This was reflected in a conversation between Loring, the Military Adviser to the UK High Commissioner, and Kalwant Singh, who presumably reflected the views of his Commander-in-Chief. The UK mission reported to Whitehall:

Kalwant Singh said that while reports given by prisoners suggest that regular units of the Pakistan Army are in Kashmir, he himself is not yet satisfied that the Indian Army authorities have sufficient proof of this.... He said he wished that the Prime Minister had not made any reference to this in his Delhi speech.[23]

It was only on the following day—8 June—that Kalwant Singh informed the UK Mission that he and General Bucher had personally interrogated a 'reliable prisoner' and were now satisfied that there was definite proof of the presence of Pakistani regulars.[24] By the time the Commander-in-Chief accepted the fact of the Pakistani army's presence, India's spring offensive had already been stalled.

It was extraordinary that India's Commander-in-Chief should have delayed the acceptance of a steady stream of reports about the presence of regular Pakistani forces till he had personally interrogated a 'reliable' POW. What makes this action doubly suspect is the fact that he had been informed by two British journalists as early as 18 May—that is, at the outset of the offensive, almost three weeks previously—about the presence of three Pakistani army battalions in Kashmir. The journalists, Laing and Hennesy of the Kemsley Press, had told Bucher that the presence of these troops in Kashmir was common knowledge in Pakistan.[25]

This prolonged silence on India's part caused mystification in London. High Commissioner Shone threw some light on the subject in a cable to Carter on 11 June:

So far ... as I can understand they [the Government of India] have had their suspicions of this for some time but Service Chiefs, particularly Bucher, had been counselling them to keep quiet until they were absolutely sure of their facts. This is borne out by the way Kalwant Singh spoke to Loring on Monday 7th (c.f. my telegram No. 1771) and the different line he took a day later (c.f. my telegram No. 1804 Milsit) after the A.H.Q. had eventually got what they thought was entirely reliable evidence.[26]

In London, General Scoones at the CRO had set out his own 'deductions' even earlier in a note dated 1 June. He wrote:

So far as General Bucher is concerned, it seems possible that during the talks between General Bucher and General Gracey regarding methods of withdrawing refugees from Kashmir, certain military moves were contemplated. This may have been put into operation by General Gracey and General Bucher might not have told his subordinate Commanders nor the Prime Minister about these plans. It may, therefore, be difficult for him now to make them known...

*So far as General Gracey is concerned, it appears that he is get-
ting more outspoken about this matter and has even gone so far
as to increase the number of battalions from 3 to 4 in conversation with press representatives. It is strange that he should do
this, specially with a press representative, if he feels that India
are unaware of the fact and might remonstrate.*

On this, Noel-Baker minuted: 'It may be better not to probe, at any
rate at this stage.'[27]

Stand Down?

In October 1947, General Gracey had refused to obey Jinnah's order
to send the Pakistani army into Kashmir. Yet, a few months later, the
same Gracey urged the Pakistani government to deploy their troops
in Kashmir. On this occasion the British refrained from raising the
question of a 'Stand Down.' What explains this volte-face? Did the
British authorities have prior knowledge of Karachi's intention of des-
patching its regular troops to Kashmir? The answers to these questions are complex and partly unclear.

Gracey's own version was that the British government knew in
advance of Pakistan's decision to send its regular army into Kashmir.
He revealed this in a conversation with General Bucher on 27 July.
Greatly agitated, Bucher rushed to the British mission to inform Deputy High Commissioner Symon about the conversation. The Commander-in-Chief was not outraged over British perfidy; his agitation
arose from concern that Gracey might have shared the information
with others as well! He reported that 'General Gracey told him a short
while ago—and may have told others too—that H.M.G. in the United
Kingdom knew in advance about the decision to send regular Pakistan troops into the State. Bucher expressed much concern as to the
reactions on the Indian side if public opinion in India gets hold of the
idea that H.M.G. were consulted about the Pakistan units moving
into the State or that the movement took place with their approval.
He feels that if this idea gets abroad it is likely to lead to strong anti-
British feeling in India.'[28] Symon tried to calm Bucher by reassuring
him that there had been no prior consultations with the British
government.

Symon's assertion was consistent with the initial reaction of CRO
officials when Grafftey-Smith informed them of the Pakistani move in

early May. The CRO had described the development as 'very serious' and 'threatening' and had chided Grafftey-Smith for not reporting it earlier.[29] The archives show that, at least at the level of departmental officials, Whitehall had no foreknowledge of the Pakistani move. Yet Gracey's statement is backed by much circumstantial evidence suggesting that Karachi had consulted Noel-Baker in advance.

In the first place, there was a curious failure on the part of the CRO to respond to the telegram from New Delhi about the Gracey-Bucher conversation and Gracey's categorical statement concerning London's foreknowledge. A note on the CRO file reads: 'Shown to Sir A. Carter, who is awaiting political [illegible—indication?]. He agrees that matter is serious.'[30] There is no further entry recording the 'indication,' if any, received from the political level—in other words from Noel-Baker.

Noel-Baker's role in the UN is also consistent with complicity in the Pakistani plan. Without Cabinet approval, he had pressed in the Security Council for a resolution which would allow Pakistani troops to be inducted into Kashmir. In this endeavour, he worked hand in glove with Zafrulla Khan. The latter appears to have consulted him informally when Pakistani troops were ordered into Kashmir. In early May, Liaquat told General Gracey that Zafrulla had reported to him that the Pakistani presence in Kashmir was well known at Lake Success.[31]

Finally, we must take into account Noel-Baker's position on the 'Stand Down' order and, more specifically, his moves to reinterpret it to Pakistan's advantage. He made sure that the instructions were not interpreted in the same way as in October 1947 since a 'Stand Down' would have made it impossible for Pakistan to deploy her forces in Kashmir.

We saw in Chapter 5 that in November 1947 Noel-Baker was responsible for a significant modification of the 'Stand Down' instructions. The new instructions, issued over the signature of Alexander, the Defence Minister, envisaged a 'Stand Down' only if there was danger of British officers 'actually taking the field against each other.' Participation in military planning in each of the two Headquarters might be 'distasteful' but might not in itself be sufficient reason for ordering a 'Stand Down.'

The revised instructions specifically recognised the fact that Pakistan, unlike India, was critically dependent upon the services of British officers in her armed forces. Auchinleck's earlier instructions, which had been approved by Prime Minister Attlee, called for a 'Stand Down' in the event of inter-dominion hostilities. The vaguely worded revised instructions issued in November could be interpreted to permit British officers to continue in service and participate in military planning so long as they did not actually 'take the field against each other'—whatever that might mean.

Alexander himself did not grasp the full implications of the 6 November telegram. Thus in early June, on receiving reports of Pakistani deployments in Kashmir, he expressed concern and raised the question of the 'Stand Down' order. He was dissuaded from pursuing the question by Noel-Baker, who advised that any formal enquiries 'might tend to disturb a delicate situation.' Noel-Baker wrote:

> You will remember that in the talks between the Staffs of India and Pakistan in Karachi [i.e. the private discussions between Bucher and Gracey in March], which was stopped by Pandit Nehru, it was proposed that three Pakistan battalions should go into Kashmir; I think this is the origin of the whole thing, and explains why India have never raised it.[32]
>
> For this reason and also because our information [about the Pakistani military presence in Kashmir] comes from a delicate source (viz. General Gracey), we took the view... that it was better for the present not to probe the matter further with Pakistan.
>
> As regards British officers, there are no British officers serving with the Pakistan Army in Kashmir. We are also assured that there are no British officers, serving with the Indian Army in Kashmir....
>
> Accordingly, I hope you will agree that we had better not press any enquiries about these Pakistani troops, though of course both High Commissioners will report to us any further information they may succeed in picking up.[33]

Noel-Baker thus argued that Britain should turn a blind eye to the Pakistani presence in Kashmir and that the 'Stand Down' instructions should be interpreted only as barring the physical presence in Kashmir of British military personnel in the opposing armies. The Defence Minister fell in with this plea. The assumption here was that no British officer had been sent into Kashmir with the Pakistani forces. It turned out that the assumption was not entirely correct. Grafftey-Smith reported in July that a few British technical officers were serving in Kashmir owing to the serious shortage of trained Pakistani personnel.[34] A few days later, he reported that one of these officers, one Major Sloan of the Royal Engineers, had been killed while clearing mines in Kashmir.[35] Even under the restricted interpretation of the 'Stand Down' policy, this called for a British response. Grafftey-Smith was therefore instructed to approach Zafrulla Khan at once and demand the immediate withdrawal of all British officers from Kashmir. He was to make it clear that London would not tolerate use of British officers 'in conditions in which they may be involved in hostilities with forces of another Dominion.'[36] Pakistan promptly complied with the demand.[37]

When the CRO instructed Shone to seek a similar assurance from the Indian government, the High Commissioner counselled restraint. He sent his deputy, Symon, to consult Bucher unofficially. The Commander-in-Chief confirmed that no British personnel were serving in Kashmir and there was no intention of employing them in the state. But he urged that the matter should not be taken up formally with New Delhi. Bucher knew that the Indian government viewed this as an act of self-restraint rather than compliance with a British demand. Doubtless with the case of Junagadh in mind, he told Symon that a formal demarche would almost certainly lead the Indian government to re-examine the need for further retention of British officers, including the question of his own replacement by an Indian officer. He claimed that 'there had been an agitation for some time by a group of senior Indian officers led by General Cariappa against further retention of British officers even in an advisory capacity on the ground that they cannot be employed when they are most needed e.g. Kashmir.' The High Commission pointed out that 'if Bucher is replaced ... we shall lose one of the most stabilising and restraining influences in India.' London reluctantly agreed to defer the question.[38]

Thus, one element of the 'Stand Down' policy as it came to be interpreted in 1948 was that the British officers would stay out of Kashmir state territory. The requirement was never communicated to New Delhi—though Mountbatten had applied it earlier in General Russell's case—lest it precipitate a decision to terminate the services of all personnel who did not owe full allegiance to India. A second element of the policy was that a 'Stand Down,' if ordered, would apply to both dominions simultaneously. This element came to be clarified in correspondence between Attlee and Liaquat but once again, India was not kept informed.

The Attlee–Liaquat correspondence arose from an Indian charge that Pakistan was planning to use her air force to attack the RIAF in Kashmir. Information available in London did not bear out this charge.[39] Indeed, it would have been foolhardy for Pakistan to employ her fledgling airforce in this manner since it would inevitably have led to Indian retaliation against the bases in Pakistan from which the attacks were launched. The possibility of the war spilling across the borders of Jammu and Kashmir was a matter of deep concern to Britain. Attlee therefore sought an assurance from Liaquat that the RPAF would not be launched against the RIAF in Kashmir. Liaquat provided the anticipated assurance, which Attlee conveyed to Nehru.

In thanking Liaquat for this response, Attlee spelt out his reasons for taking up the question. 'My object in recalling to you that, in the event of war, we should have to withdraw all British officers serving with the forces of India and Pakistan, was simply to remind you of this factor in the situation,' he cabled. 'Such a step (which we should only take with the greatest reluctance) would be dictated not by any consideration of the rights and wrongs of the dispute, or of the resulting advantages or disadvantages to one side or the other, but simply to prevent a situation in which British officers would be fighting one another. This we could never contemplate.'[40]

The same message was transmitted to Nehru and this drew a protest from Liaquat. The logical implication of Attlee's position was that British officers would be withdrawn from both armies in the event of an Indian counter-attack across the Pakistani border. 'I am surprised at your view that the withdrawal of British officers would not be dictated by any consideration of the rights or wrongs of the dispute,' he wrote. 'Surely if you withdraw British officers from the aggressor State, the question of British officers fighting one another cannot arise…. The disadvantages to India resulting from the loss of British officers are small compared with corresponding disadvantages to Pakistan. By the decision to withdraw British officers from both sides, and by informing India of your intentions to do so, you are encouraging India in her career of aggression.'[41]

Attlee replied that 'the position is that the withdrawal of British officers from India alone or Pakistan alone on the ground that one or the other was the aggressor State is a step which we could not contemplate unless it were in pursuance of some decision of the Security

Council.'[42] This message—which was deliberately not communicated to Nehru—added a further twist to the 'Stand Down' policy. At first sight it seemed to be a reiteration of position taken in Attlee's previous telegram but the question of a Security Council decision opened up a new possibility. Later in the year, it encouraged expectations in Pakistan which produced a major change of military posture.

Pakistan did not publicly acknowledge its military presence in Kashmir until 1 August. However, by the end of July India had definite information about Zafrulla's admission to the UN Commission for India and Pakistan concerning this presence. Thus on 28 July, High Commissioner Krishna Menon called on Attlee to draw his attention to the Pakistani admission and to express India's concern over the role of British officers in the Kashmir operations. He argued that the British government could not possibly approve of the participation, direct or indirect, of British officers in this illegal act of intervention.[43] On 5 August, after Pakistan had publicly acknowledged her military involvement, Krishna Menon met Addison, Lord President of the Council (in Attlee's absence), and Noel-Baker to urge that British should convey a strong and urgent message to Pakistan regarding use of seconded British officers for illegal purposes in Kashmir. Menon added that a 'Stand Down' should apply only to Pakistan since she was the guilty party.[44]

Noel-Baker countered the Indian demarche in a nine-page minute to Attlee. Side-stepping the legal point raised by Krishna Menon, he argued that 'it would only be open to His Majesty's Government in the United Kingdom to accept this proposal for a unilateral "Stand Down" against Pakistan if they reversed the policy in respect of the "Stand Down" which they have followed and made known to the governments of India and Pakistan from the beginning.' British policy was that:

(i) *the purpose of the 'Stand Down' is to prevent British Officers and men fighting each other and its enforcement would have nothing to do with the rights or wrongs of the disputes between India and Pakistan;*

(ii) *if the 'Stand Down' has to be enforced, it would apply simultaneously to all British personnel in all the Armed Forces of both Dominions.*

Noel-Baker argued that there was no immediate danger of British personnel fighting each other since neither Pakistan nor India employed these personnel in Kashmir. Nor was there an imminent danger of 'formal hostilities' between the two dominions. It would be particularly difficult for Britain to order a 'Stand Down' at a moment when UNCIP had put forward a ceasefire proposal to India and Pakistan. Finally, he pointed to the political results which might flow from a 'Stand Down,' particularly if it applied only to Pakistan. He maintained that 'Pakistan might leave the Commonwealth'; 'the hostility of the Muslim population of the world to the United Kingdom might be increased'; and even that 'it might bring about an internal collapse in Pakistan from the chaos of which the Communists would profit.'[45]

The minute thus reflected the political calculations underlying British policy on Kashmir. Pakistan, unlike India, had declared her intention of remaining in the Commonwealth and seeking close military ties with the West. Britain was reluctant to take any step which might deflect Pakistan from the course she intended to follow. Second, the supposed impact on Muslim opinion in the Middle East weighed heavily in British deliberations. Britain's abandonment of the Palestine mandate and the emergence of the State of Israel had inflamed Arab nationalist sentiments. As a result, British strategic interests in the region had been put in jeopardy. Prone to confuse national with religious sentiment in Asia, British policy-makers drew the conclusion that their Middle Eastern policy demanded a pro-Pakistan stance. Finally, the weakness of Pakistan's domestic structures paradoxically became a source of strength in her foreign policy. Any proposal for taking a firm line against Pakistani misconduct could be easily derailed by the threat of internal collapse and spread of communism.

On 23 August, Attlee responded to Menon's demarche. In a cable to Nehru, he said that 'the question of the presence of Pakistani troops is within the scope of the [UN] Commission's work and I am sure that we must leave any initiative in the matter to the Commission.' As regards the 'Stand Down' arrangement, its purpose was to prevent British personnel from actually taking the field against each other. There was no immediate prospect of 'British personnel getting involved in the fighting. It would, I think, in these circumstances, be a mistake, particularly while arrangements for a Cease Fire are being negotiated, for us to take any precipitate unilateral action.'[46]

XIII
The UN Commission for India and Pakistan

The five-member Commission set up in terms of the Security Council resolution of 21 April consisted of Czechoslovakia (nominated by India); Argentina (nominated by Pakistan); Belgium and Colombia (selected by the Security Council); and the United States (nominated by the President of the Security Council). Though the resolution required it to proceed 'at once' to the Indian subcontinent, the Commission—the United Nations Commission for India and Pakistan (UNCIP), as it later styled itself—was in no great haste to commence its labours. Seven weeks lapsed before it made its first move—to summertime Geneva. There it convened on 15 June, to contemplate the tasks that lay ahead and to familiarise itself with the intricacies of the Kashmir problem.

In the meantime the ground realities in Kashmir had undergone a dramatic transformation. In violation of the 17 January resolution, Pakistan had clandestinely sent in her regular army into the state. As we have seen, both London and Washington were aware of this dangerous development. In Washington, Secretary of State Marshall felt that precipitate action by Pakistan or India prior to the Commission's arrival on the scene might jeopardise the chances of its success. He was concerned that the entry of Pakistani troops into Kashmir would have this effect.[1] The State Department initially thought of drawing Pakistan's (and possibly also India's) attention to the provisions of the Security Council resolution of 17 January but was dissuaded by its British allies from taking this step.[2]

Noel-Baker had regained control over British policy after the temporary setback resulting from the Cabinet's intervention in March–April. He had tried hard at the United Nations to secure a resolution allowing entry of Pakistani troops into Kashmir but had been thwarted by his Cabinet colleagues. Now that Pakistan had gone ahead with the despatch of troops, Noel-Baker made no move to restrain her. Instead, he directed his efforts to saving Pakistan from the diplomatic and military fall-out of her clandestine move. For this purpose, he urged that the UN Commission should proceed urgently to the subcontinent. The imminent clash between the advancing Indian army and the newly-arrived Pakistani forces would inevitably expose Pakistan's violation of the 17 January resolution and the Commission's timely arrival on the scene could avoid 'further recriminations and discussions in N[ew] Y[ork] or elsewhere which might only aggravate the attitude of the two parties.'[3] In Britain's view, the Commission's objectives should be '(a) by their presence to moderate [the] political effects of any such [India–Pakistan] clash and generally to lower the temperature; and (b) to negotiate a ceasefire.'[4] London was particularly anxious that the Commission should be in position before 13 June, the date of Mountbatten's departure from India. In the absence of his restraining influence, London feared that the 'Indians may be looking to [the] last half of June, on [the] assumption that the Commission will not be upon them until July as [a] chance for drastic action in Kashmir or elsewhere.' Hence it objected to the Commission's rendezvous in Geneva, which 'especially at this time of year, is too conducive to leisurely discussion.'[5]

The British failed to persuade the Commission to sacrifice its planned halt in Geneva, where it unhurriedly prepared its rules of procedure and waded through a sea of documents. Members sought protection against the hazards of tropical travel through a comprehensive course of inoculations against typhus, cholera, small-pox, diptheria, plague and yellow fever. After exhausting these preliminaries, the Commission finally left Geneva for Pakistan on 5 July, eleven weeks after the adoption of the Security Council.

In Karachi, the Commission was lodged in the Governor-General's residence but Jinnah himself, terminally ill, was secluded in the distant hill station of Ziarat. A meeting with the Prime Minister, Liaquat Ali Khan, amounted to no more than an exchange of courtesies, with no mention of Kashmir. But when the Commission called on Zafrulla Khan it received—in the words of one of its members—a 'bombshell.'[6]

The Foreign Minister informed the Commission on 9 July that three brigades of the Pakistani army had been operating in Kashmir since May. When asked why the Security Council had not been informed earlier, Zafrulla Khan said that the Commission was daily expected to arrive in Karachi and he had seized the first opportunity to inform them of the development!

To one member of the Commission this disclosure could have caused little surprise. The United States had been aware of the development since May and the American member of the Commission, Ambassador Huddle, had presumably been informed about the move, as well his government's decision to underplay it at the behest of the UK. The Commission decided to refrain from any public reference to the deployment, though members acknowledged to one another that it was a grave and disturbing development.[7]

When the Commission arrived in New Delhi, it received an incisive briefing from Bajpai, the Secretary General in the Ministry of External Affairs. Bajpai highlighted the fact that a great change had occurred in the situation since the adoption of the Security Council resolution: the Indian army was now fighting against the regular armed forces of Pakistan in Jammu and Kashmir. An undeclared war was in progress between the two countries. India attached the 'highest importance to the declaration of Pakistan's guilt and ... to Pakistan being directed to do what, seven months ago, we had asked the Council Pakistan should be asked to do. Until this matter was settled, there could be no question of discussing the details of a plebiscite.' Bajpai pointed out that

> if the future of Jammu & Kashmir was to be determined by the arbitrament of the sword, then, without in any way wishing to utter a threat, or use the language of menace, I should like the Commission, as realists, to recognise that the offer of plebiscite could not remain open. If Pakistan wanted a decision by force and that decision went against Pakistan, it could not invoke the machinery of the United Nations to obtain what it had failed to secure by its chosen weapon of force.[8]

Bajpai left the Commission in no doubt that India would not accept a ceasefire unless it included a condemnation of Pakistan and acknowledged the fact that Pakistan, unlike India, had no legal status in Kashmir. The demand for condemnation was being pressed with increased vigour in view of the Pakistani army's entry into the state. India was not prepared to discuss plebiscite arrangements until these concerns had been suitably addressed. The Commission received an identical message in conversations with Nehru and Ayyangar.

India also pointed out that a plebiscite was not the only means for ascertaining the will of the people. The door should also be left open for other methods. Nehru had come to the conclusion that the conditions necessary for a plebiscite were unlikely to be attained.[9] He therefore favoured a broader reference to the means of ascertaining the views of the people than one confined to plebiscite alone.

Pakistan, likewise, conveyed that she was not prepared to accept an unconditional ceasefire. The conditions she attached to a ceasefire were that India should withdraw her troops simultaneously with Pakistan and that the views of the 'Azad Kashmir Government' should be taken into account. Pakistan moreover expected the Commission to also take up the question of plebiscite arrangements.

The Commission, however, formed the impression that Pakistan was keener on a ceasefire than her words suggested. The impression was reinforced by a letter from Zafrulla Khan, expressing regret that the Commission had not actually made a ceasefire proposal. The Commission saw a connection between this sentiment and developments on the battlefield, where the Indian army had achieved definite progress. '[N]ow that the Indian army was advancing closer and closer to her border, Pakistan might find it very much in her interest to stop fighting, particularly if by the establishment of a ceasefire this advance could be terminated,' observed one of its members.[10]

The Commission informed Pakistan in unambiguous terms that the uninvited movement of her troops into foreign territory was a violation of international law and that it had seriously aggravated the problem. India had valid ground for complaint and the Commission could not but give some expression to this fact in its report.[11]

Having thus prepared the ground, UNCIP presented a finetuned resolution on 13 August. This called for a ceasefire; outlined truce terms; and re-stated the position accepted by both sides that the 'future status of the State of Jammu and Kashmir shall be determined in accordance with the will of the people.' The truce terms required Pakistan to withdraw her forces from the state 'as the presence of troops of Pakistan in the territory of the State of Jammu and Kashmir constitutes a material change in the situation since it was represented by the Government of Pakistan before the Security Council.' India would begin to withdraw the bulk of her forces from the state after the raiders (the tribesmen and other Pakistani nationals) had withdrawn and the Pakistani troops had commenced their withdrawal. Pending acceptance of the conditions for a final settlement, India would maintain, on her side of the line existing at the time of ceasefire, a minimum force to assist in maintenance of law and order. The question of conditions for a 'reference to the will of the people' was left for later consultations between the Commission and the two governments 'upon acceptance of the truce agreement.'

Britain had no representative in the Commission and her ability to influence its work was limited during the period it functioned in the subcontinent. Unlike the Security Council proposals of 21 April, the UNCIP proposals did not reflect a deliberate pro-Pakistan tilt. They were an attempt to balance the interests of India and Pakistan while taking into account the fact that the entry of the Pakistani army into Jammu and Kashmir was a violation of the 17 January resolution.

Ayyangar had complained of the 21 April resolution that it 'put the cart before the horse' by failing to issue a clear call to Pakistan to withdraw the raiders before going into the question of plebiscite arrangements. The UNCIP resolution conceded primacy to a ceasefire based on withdrawal of the invaders. The question of arrangements for a reference to the will of the people was to be taken up later, after both sides had accepted the truce arrangements. Moreover, there was implied criticism of Pakistan in the demand that she withdraw her forces from Jammu and Kashmir since their presence constituted a 'material change in the situation.' This was, of course, no more than a slap on the wrist. The Commission refrained from publicly condemning Pakistan for having violated international law (though it did so in private) because it realised that open condemnation would result in Pakistan's rejecting the proposals.

India asked for clarification of certain aspects of the resolution. She sought confirmation that it recognised that recurrence of aggression in Kashmir must be prevented and that India would have to maintain sufficient forces in the state to meet the threat of external aggression as well as of internal disorder; that the sovereignty of the state extended to its entire territory and that there could be no recognition of the so-called 'Azad Kashmir Government'; and that the Commission did not recognise Pakistan's claim to have any part in a plebiscite, 'should it be decided to seek a solution of the future of the

State by means of a plebiscite.' On receiving satisfactory clarifications on these points, India accepted the resolution on 25 August.

Pakistan wanted the Commission to deal with the question of plebiscite arrangements in the resolution. The Commission, she maintained, should be guided by the terms of the 21 April resolution, which should be interpreted taking into account the explanations offered by its sponsors. She insisted on India's prior acceptance of the plebiscite provisions of the 21 April resolution. She wanted the 'Azad Kashmir Government' to be treated as a separate party to any settlement and to be left in control of the territory it had occupied. She insisted that the 'Azad Kashmir' forces should not be disarmed or disbanded. Pakistan wanted to be placed on a footing of absolute equality with India in connection with the plebiscite and indicated that she would continue to press for the withdrawal of all Indian troops from the state on the grounds that even a minimal Indian presence would be prejudicial to a fair plebiscite. These were among the formidable list of objections raised by Pakistan.

The Commission was prepared to accommodate some of Pakistan's concerns—most notably, by leaving the 'Azad' forces intact—but it could not accept the rest. Pakistan's formal reply, sent on 6 September, contained such far-reaching reservations and qualifications that the Commission interpreted it as tantamount to rejection. While regretting that this response made an immediate ceasefire impossible, the Commission expressed the hope that Pakistan would reconsider her position. The door was thus left open for follow-up action on the 13 August resolution.

XIV
Limited Offensives

The UN Commission left the subcontinent for Geneva on 21 September. Its departure reduced the diplomatic constraints on launching a new military offensive. There was a further positive development from India's point of view. In September the 'police action' to integrate Hyderabad in the Indian Union was successfully completed, releasing troops which now became available for the Kashmir operations. Bucher and his Indian generals reacted in different ways to the new situation.

Bucher's thoughts turned once more to pre-empting an Indian offensive through a ceasefire. He secretly sent a telegram to London, through the UK High Commission channel, urging that the British government should get the United Nations to order a ceasefire. Bucher offered to personally guarantee that India would obey such an order. The Commander-in-Chief informed his Pakistani counterpart, General Gracey, of the initiative in order to point his thinking in the same direction.[1]

Meanwhile, Indian generals in the field were calling for offensive action. Thimayya's view, expressed openly to a member of the UN Commission, was that a military decision could be forced in a matter of weeks if the army were given a free hand. He was openly critical of the government's 'cautious policy.'[2] Cariappa, on his part, presented outline plans in early November for an advance to Mirpur and Muzaffarabad. These were not pursued as Army Headquarters felt that the heavy reinforcements required for the operations would result in weakening Indian defences in East Punjab. Moreover, maintaining additional troops on the Jhangar front would pose major logistical problems. Army Headquarters was of the view that these problems made it impossible to mount a major offensive, at any rate, till the following spring or early summer. Furthermore, if the advance threatened vital strategic points for Pakistan, such as the Mangla headworks, it could lead to a full-scale war with Pakistan, with serious political repercussions and dangers.[3]

In early October, before leaving for London to attend the Commonwealth Prime Ministers' conference, Nehru had asked his Commander-in-Chief to prepare a military appreciation of an Indian offensive to clear Kashmir of Pakistani troops and irregulars. On the Prime Minister's return in November, Bucher submitted an appreciation which concluded that it would not be possible for the Indian forces to successfully clear Kashmir of the invaders during the winter months or even later when weather conditions would improve. The Commander-in-Chief expressed the opinion that, while certain minor offensive operations might be successfully undertaken, from an overall point of view, India was confronted with a military stalemate.

Even before his recommendations were considered in the Indian Cabinet, Bucher informed Nye, the new British High Commissioner about the appreciation he had submitted to the Indian government. General Sir Archibald Nye, who had replaced Sir Terence Shone, was a distinguished soldier who had served as Deputy Chief of the Imperial General Staff during World War II. His appointment as High Commissioner was an inspired choice. The esteem which Nye enjoyed in military circles enabled him to exercise great influence over the British service chiefs in India. Bucher, in particular, readily accepted and even sought his guidance. Nye was to play an important role in shaping military developments during the final stages of the war.

On the basis of the information supplied by Bucher, Nye was able to reassure London that an all-out war was unlikely. 'I think it follows from this [Bucher's appreciation],' he cabled, 'that the possibility of war between the two Dominions breaking out as a result of successful military operations in Kashmir penetrating into Pakistan, is improbable.' Bucher also informed Nye that he had told Sardar Patel that the only effective military step which could be taken to drive the Pakistanis from Kashmir was to attack the bases in Pakistan itself, a course which, he said, could not be contemplated. Bucher claimed that Patel had agreed with this view.[4]

The Defence Committee met on 11 November to decide on military initiatives in Kashmir. As usual, Bucher promptly informed Nye about the outcome. He revealed that the Cabinet had confirmed the general policy of acting on the defensive during the winter months. The on-going operations for a link-up with the Poonch garrison were the only military operations likely to be undertaken. Bucher reported that a proposal made by Cariappa and Mehar Singh to bomb Mirpur and Muzaffarabad had been turned down on military as well as political grounds.[5]

Bucher's version accurately reflected the manner in which he intended to implement the Cabinet decision, but not the decision itself. The Cabinet had, indeed, accepted Bucher's military appreciation that an attack on Mirpur was not immediately feasible since it would have to be preceded by an extensive build-up requiring a great deal of time. The government was also reluctant to precipitate a crisis in relations with Pakistan. The main immediate objectives envisaged by the Cabinet were to regain control of the lines of communication between Srinagar and Leh and to wrest control of the lines of communication linking Naoshera to Poonch. To this extent, Bucher's summary was not inaccurate. But he omitted to mention that it was also the government's objective, in the Poonch–Mirpur sector, to bring the Kotli area under Indian control. This was an important objective since Kotli controlled the approach to Mirpur; an advance upto Kotli would have been a major gain for India and a serious blow for Pakistan. Nehru outlined the Cabinet decision as follows in a letter to Krishna Menon:

I might add that winter prospects of fighting are our clearing up Ladakh valley (which we are in process of doing now), our establishing a safe route to Poonch from the Jammu side (which we are also doing now) and our gradually extending the area under our control in Jammu Province to Kotli and round about. This is not very much but this is about all that we can do in winter conditions. We can perhaps attack Mirpur, but that would be a major operation requiring a great deal of preparation and taking time.... For the present we are avoiding any major operation towards Mirpur partly because that might lead to complications near the Pakistan frontier. We hope, during the winter, to build some more roads and collect materials and supplies for further offensives (emphasis added).[6]

A 'Very Secret Mission'

Pakistan had anticipated an Indian offensive after the departure of the UNCIP mission from the subcontinent, fearing an Indian advance right up to the Jhelum river boundary in the Mirpur area. Such an advance would give India control of the headworks of the Chhamb and Jhelum irrigation system on which Pakistan's agricultural economy was critically dependent and would, moreover, bring India within striking distance of Pakistan's military heartland centred around Rawalpindi.

Pakistan concluded that British assistance was essential in order to meet the threat and that it was time to renew the search for a military understanding. Liaquat Ali Khan decided to urgently explore through a back channel the possibility of a defence pact. The emissary he selected for this purpose was the deputy chief of the Pakistani army, Major-General Cawthorn. Born in Australia, Cawthorn had seen action with the Australian forces in Gallipoli in World War I. He had an intelligence background, having served as the Head of the Middle East Intelligence Centre in Egypt and later as Director of Intelligence in India during World War II.

Cawthorn met Noel-Baker in London on 18 September and told him that he had come on a 'very secret mission' to explore the possibility of beginning staff talks for joint defence arrangements with the UK as soon as possible. He said that Pakistan was greatly alarmed by the world situation and the danger posed by communism. She was resolutely determined to play her part in collective defence against Russian aggression. Cawthorn explained that Liaquat had not yet presented a formal proposal to the Cabinet as he did not wish to do so until he could be sure that UK would respond positively.[7]

From the British point of view, the approach was most welcome but it did raise the difficult question whether a pact should be concluded with Pakistan alone without exhausting the possibility of reaching a similar agreement with India. Noel-Baker arranged for Cawthorn to meet Attlee. The Prime Minister was in favour of accepting Liaquat's proposal, provided India was kept informed. Alexander, Bevin and the Chiefs of Staff were all in agreement with this view and the CRO was instructed to inform Cawthorn orally that a formal proposal from Pakistan would be welcome.[8]

Cawthorn's conversations in London served to enhance the pro-Pakistan tilt in British policy. Liaquat personally followed up in

October, seizing the opportunity provided by the Commonwealth Prime Ministers' Conference. Outwardly, Britain maintained the stance of a neutral conciliator between the warring dominions. Thus, on Attlee's suggestion, Liaquat met with Nehru in the presence of Attlee and Bevin to explore options for a settlement. The talks failed to produce any results and the British role behind the scenes served only to make the Pakistani position more inflexible. Unknown to Nehru, Bevin and Noel-Baker held separate talks with the Pakistani Prime Minister during which they informed the delighted Liaquat that it was time to return the Kashmir question to the Security Council.[9]

This was not all. The Pakistani army received 'hints' and 'assurances' from London on the basis of which it carried out a major redeployment of forces. A brigade of the 7th Division, which was being held in reserve for the defence of West Punjab against a possible Indian attack, was now moved to Palandri, inside Jammu and Kashmir, with the objective of covering Kotli. The move left West Punjab vulnerable to an Indian onslaught. Why was the Pakistani army prepared to accept a risk of this magnitude? The tale is told in the British archives.

On 26 October 1948, the British post in Rawalpindi reported:

The Army command has received two 'tips' of a most important kind, from a source considered absolutely reliable. The first of them is to the effect that there is now a strong likelihood of H.M.G. agreeing to allow British officers to remain with the Pak Forces in the event of Indian aggression against Pakistan. The second suggests that the UNO would be inclined to impose sanctions on the Union if she attacked her neighbour.[10]

This was confirmed by another report from an officer of the Military Wing of the UK High Commission in Karachi, who recorded:

During a conversation with Lt.-Col. Wilson, the C-in-C's Private Secretary, he told me he understood from London assurance had now been given by H.M.G. that an attack by India on West Punjab 'would not be tolerated.' This assurance had been quite definite and in consequence GHQ had felt able to move the reserve Brigade of 7 Div up to PALANDRI to cover the KOTLI ROAD in case the present Indian offensive should prove too much for the Azad Forces.[11]

Cawthorn's secret mission thus yielded important diplomatic and military dividends for Pakistan even though it was to turn out that conditions were not yet ripe for a military pact.

Pakistan's real objective was, of course, to obtain British assistance against India, not to participate in a war against the communist powers. In December, Pakistan conveyed her unqualified acceptance of proposals for Commonwealth defence but she failed to make the expected formal request for staff consultations.[12] In July, 1949, Liaquat sought clarification on two points: first, whether the defence talks would involve the UK and Pakistan exclusively or whether it was intended to also bring in other regional countries (i.e. India); and, second, whether the defence talk would relate only to a 'world war' or also to situations where the security of Pakistan was threatened by a Commonwealth or non-Commonwealth country (i.e. India). The British response was that the talks would initially be confined to the UK and Pakistan, with India and other countries coming in later. On the second point, Britain replied that the talks would be confined to problems relating to a global conflict and to a threat from outside the Commonwealth. Liaquat expressed disappointment with the response and requested reconsideration.[12] It was not until the 1950s that mutually acceptable terms were found for a defence pact between Pakistan and the Western powers. The terms did not cover a conflict with India but this was more than compensated, in Pakistani eyes, by a massive military aid programme which altered the India–Pakistan military balance. Only the United States—not Britain—was in a position to offer military aid on such a scale. But we are digressing from our subject and must now return to the military events of the last quarter of 1948.

The Northern Offensive

India's military plans in November envisaged offensives in both the northern and Jammu sectors. We saw earlier that the seizure of Kargil and Dras by the raiders in the summer posed a threat both to Srinagar and Leh. The objective of the Indian operations in November in the northern sector was to regain control of these positions and to ensure the safety of the lines of communication between Srinagar and Leh.

The ground work for these operations had been laid in the summer by building up an adequate military presence in Leh to protect it from the raiders. When Kargil fell to the invaders on 10 May, the main road to Leh was closed. The only available alternative was the route from Manali, which passed over 250 miles of difficult mountain terrain. With the raiders posing an imminent threat, the Indian airforce came to the rescue of Leh. There was a big question mark over the capacity of old Dakotas, devoid of de-icing equipment, to fly over the Himalayas and land successfully on the improvised airstrip at Leh. The gallant Air Commodore Mehar Singh and Major General Thimayya decided to find the answer by personally making the first attempt themselves. Their safe landing in Leh on 24 May established that troops could be airlifted to Leh. A Gurkha company was flown in on 1 June. In July, troops sent from Manali also arrived in Leh and further requirements were airlifted in August. The immediate threat to Leh was thus removed. It remained to regain control over the land route linking Leh with Srinagar, which ran through Dras and Kargil.

The key to achieving this objective lay in occupying Zoji La, the major pass lying astride the Srinagar–Dras road. The invaders had a strong presence in this area and had beaten off two previous Indian assaults with heavy casualties. An imaginative plan was now devised to employ tanks in the assault on Zoji La. The pass lay at a height of over 16,000 feet and no army in the world had previously used tanks at such altitudes. It could not be predicted with confidence whether the tank engine and lubricating system would function effectively at such heights and low temperature levels. Many of the bridges on the route to Zoji La were not strong enough to support the full weight of a tank, and some stretches of the track as well were unfit for tanks. The first obstacle was overcome by removing the gun turrets from the tanks. The second obstacle was surmounted by the engineers who worked day and night to upgrade the track in time for the operation.

The appearance of tanks at Zoji La on 1 November took the invaders by surprise and resulted in their total collapse. They suffered heavy casualties and the survivors fled the field in panic. The Indian advance continued and on 15 November Dras was freed of the raiders. Fortunately for the army, the weather in late November was exceptionally fair and sunny and the Indians were able to continue their advance till they reoccupied Kargil on 24 November. The northern campaign thus achieved its objectives.

The campaign did not involve an advance to areas which Pakistan considered vital for her security and it does not seem to have aroused particular concern on the part of the British Commanders-in-Chief of the rival armies. Bucher set Gracey's mind at ease by informing him that an advance to Skardu was not contemplated.[13] An incident did occur, however, in what was essentially a side-show in the northern theatre, which caused great anxiety to the British. The event could have led to a serious threat to Pakistani operations in the northern theatre and to the escalation of hostilities into Pakistani territory. The way in which the British service chiefs in India and Pakistan dealt with the incident throws light on the contacts which they maintained with each other in order to contain the hostilities.

On 4 November, a Pakistan air force Dakota on a supply-dropping flight to Gilgit was attacked in the air by the Indian airforce. Grafftey-Smith cabled the CRO as well as his colleague in New Delhi about the incident, adding:

> *I am informed that AOC-in-C, India and Air Commander, Pakistan, have a 'gentleman's agreement' that Pakistan aircraft should not be attacked in the air, though liable to attack on the ground there, and it may well be that this attack was made without former's sanction!*[14]

Grafftey-Smith suggested that, if the attack was indeed unauthorised, a renewed assurance from Air Marshal Elmhirst that the 'gentleman's agreement' would be enforced would be invaluable in restraining the Pakistanis from 'provocative action.'[15]

The 'provocative action' feared by Grafftey-Smith was that Pakistan would decide to provide a fighter escort for supply-dropping aircraft, rather than accept the alternative of suspending the air supply operations for Gilgit. A note on the CRO files in Whitehall brings out the further implications. The apprehension was that if fighters were used to escort Pakistani supply aircraft, India would view this as 'commitment' of the Pakistan Air Force in Kashmir, justifying Indian air attacks on airfields in Pakistan. Moreover, India would call for a 'Stand Down' of British officers on the basis of a 'fallacious' interpretation of the UK government's July statement.[16]

The 4 November attack had been carried out under orders from Air Vice-Marshal Mukerjee, who was officiating for Air Marshal Elmhirst during the latter's absence on tour. Mukerjee informed Perry-Keene, the Pakistan airforce chief, that he had ordered the Indian airforce to shoot down 'any unidentified aircraft' operating over Jammu and Kashmir.

Confronted with a choice between suspending air supplies to Gilgit or providing fighter escorts and thereby risking possible Indian attacks on airbases inside Pakistan, the Pakistani Cabinet decided on 9 November on the latter alternative despite its attendant dangers. Suspension of the supply operation would have jeopardised the entire Pakistani position in the northern theatre because of the importance of the Gilgit base. Gracey and Perry-Keene came straight from the Cabinet meeting to report the development to High Commissioner Grafftey-Smith. The High Commissioner pointed out that the decision would be 'criminally foolish' if it turned out that Elmhirst did not endorse Mukerjee's orders. The army and air chiefs agreed to press this point of view on the Pakistani government and to counsel them to refrain from taking any provocative step until Elmhirst's position became clear. Later in the day, the Secretary-General of the Pakistani government, Mohammad Ali, rang up the British High Commissioner to say that his suggestion had been accepted and Pakistan would hold up the implementation of its decision for some days.[17]

In New Delhi, High Commissioner Nye decided to take matters in hand. On Elmhirst's return to New Delhi, Nye took up the issue with him. Elmhirst stood by his Indian deputy. He denied the existence of a 'gentleman's agreement' between him and Perry-Keene and said that Mukerjee had correctly spelt out the existing instructions of the Indian government. (The dealing official in Whitehall noted in the file: 'Although no agreement may have existed between Perry-Keene and Elmhirst, the fact remains that India did not take any offensive action against these aircraft in the air till a fortnight ago.') However, Perry-Keene readily agreed that the current instructions should be amended and so did Bucher. Nye informed the CRO and Grafftey-Smith in Karachi:

The important point that emerges is what action is now likely to be taken by the Indian Government. I have discussed the matter with both Bucher and Elmhirst and pointed out to them the serious consequences which would ensue if Pakistan provided their supply-dropping aircraft with a fighter escort. They fully appreciated the issues involved. At the next meeting of the Defence Council they propose to raise this question and General Bucher will say that whilst it is true that the supplies dropped from these aircraft are assisting Pakistan military operations, nevertheless

*since these are of a relatively trivial nature he is prepared to rec-
ommend that in future such aircraft should not be attacked and
Elmhirst is prepared to take the same view.*[18]

A few days later, Elmhirst informed the British High Commissioner
that he had had an hour-long discussion on the subject of bombing
operations with Nehru and had finally persuaded him to ignore Pakistani supply-dropping aircraft over Gilgit.[19] Thus, acting in concert,
the British High Commissioners in New Delhi and Karachi and the
British officers in command of the airforces of India and Pakistan had
succeeded in preventing an escalation of the air conflict by reversing
the decisions of the warring states. In the process they had removed
a serious potential threat to the Pakistani operations in the northern
theatre.

The Western Offensive

Before embarking on the relief of Poonch, the Indian army addressed
the question of the availability of additional troops for the operations
in Jammu province. Cariappa felt that a minimum of six battalions
would be required for the operation if the intention was to reinforce
the Poonch garrison by one battalion. Shrinagesh, the Corps Commander, and Atma Singh, the Divisional Commander, both agreed
that this was the absolute minimum but they felt it would be advisable additionally to hold in reserve in the Jammu area a brigade of
four battalions for any contingency that might arise. Cariappa, therefore, proposed to Army Headquarters that, if the Pakistani threat to
East Punjab was not serious, 4 Infantry Division might be moved.
Bucher was not in favour of the proposal pointing to its implications
for the defence of East Punjab. However, he referred the question to
the Defence Committee, which agreed to a maximum of one brigade
being moved.[20]

The Indian advance commenced from Naoshera in mid-October.
The 268 Brigade moved north from Naoshera and took the strong
tactical locality of Pir Badesar on 15 October after routing the enemy
through an artillery assault. Pir Badesar protected Jhangar and could
also be used as the launching point of a threat to Kotli. The enemy
was therefore left guessing whether the move was directed towards
Kotli or Poonch. Next, 5 Brigade, which had been inducted into
Rajouri from Ambala in September, struck north from Rajouri to seize

Pir Kalewa and drive the enemy from the neighbouring hills. Indian forces then turned north-west, freeing Mendhar and its environs. The stage was now set for the link-up with the Poonch garrison, which was effected on 20 November. The primary objective in Jammu province was thus attained.

General Shrinagesh has observed that the key factor in the success of this operation was deception. 'By demonstrating towards Pir Badesar, Kotli and Pir Kalewa, and by carrying out deceptive air drops, we led the enemy to believe that Kotli was our objective and made him disperse his forces. It was only after the operation had been completed that our real intention, which was to link up with Poonch, and not capture Kotli, became known to the enemy.'[21]

This was doubtless a correct assessment of the tactics employed to secure the primary objective in the Poonch–Mirpur sector. But the question remained of implementing the next objective envisaged by the Cabinet—that of 'gradually extending the area under our control in Jammu Province to Kotli and round about.' As we shall see in the next chapter, this objective had far-reaching political implications. Indian commanders were to remain in the dark about the role played by their Commander-in-Chief behind the scenes.

XV
The Last Round

In mid-November, with the Indian army poised to raise the siege of Poonch town, panic spread in Pakistan. Karachi feared that after gaining her objective in Poonch, India would focus her attention on a push right upto the border. This was a prospect which Pakistan believed would have dire implications for her continued existence. The Pakistani government instructed its Commander-in-Chief to prevent such an advance at all costs. General Gracey decided to throw in all available forces, if necessary, including the fledgling Pakistani airforce, in order to prevent an Indian advance upto the Jhelum boundary. High Commissioner Grafftey-Smith informed London:

> Pakistan Commander-in-Chief has reported that he sees no hope of being able to prevent an Indian Army link-up with Poonch and he fears that an all-out effort will be made by India after that to throw the Azad Kashmir and Pakistan forces back on to the Jhelum River. He has been instructed by the Pakistan Government to hold his defensive positions at all costs. The risk is imminent that General Gracey may find it necessary to throw in what further Pakistan armed forces he can collect and to make use of the Pakistan Air Force for offensive purposes.[1]

Her willingness to utilise the fledgling airforce offensively was a measure of Pakistan's desperation. Pakistan had previously refrained from this course because it would inevitably draw a devastating response from the vastly superior R.I.A.F. Moreover, an Indian counter-attack against the airfields in Pakistan would carry the war into the latter's territory, an escalation which could spell disaster for Pakistan. Grafftey-Smith also reported another sign of Pakistan's desperation—plans for a counter-offensive, even though this meant that the West Punjab heartland would be left defenceless.[2]

Pakistan's strategy was to defend her positions across the Jhelum even at the cost of leaving her own national territory virtually defenceless. As we saw earlier, it was a strategic posture which relied heavily on what were believed to be British 'assurances.' This became a cause of anxiety for Grafftey-Smith who felt that it would be disastrous for Pakistan if her moves were based on an incorrect reading of British policy. A full-fledged inter-dominion war would leave Pakistan vulnerable to an Indian attack. If, at the same time, London were to withdraw all British officers in accordance with the 'Stand Down' policy, the effect on Pakistan would be devastating. The High Commissioner therefore sought direct confirmation of Whitehall's position.

I feel it is vital that I should know whether there are any grounds for Pakistan G.H.Q. assumptions and whether there have been any developments on lines suggested in U.K. Government's 'stand-down' policy. If these rumours are totally without foundation and 'stand-down' policy remains unchanged, I shall have to try to find a way of warning Pakistan Government that this is the case.... Pakistan Government have already denuded their defensive front in West Punjab of the key brigade without which they will be in no position to effectively resist Indian attack from East Punjab and they are planning a counter-offensive in Kashmir in reply to present Indian offensive there. Both these moves are almost certainly based on supposed assurance from U.K. Government, and if disaster should overtake them as a result of misplaced confidence in this assurance, effect on relations between Pakistan and U.K. would be incalculable.[3]

Grafftey-Smith now provided an indication of the identities of the recipient as well as the source of the 'hints' and 'assurances.' These were received, he said, by Major-General Cawthorn from a 'member of the Cabinet.'[4]

The High Commissioner had raised an awkward question. As is common in such cases, the source of the 'hints' and 'informal assurances' had omitted to bring his initiative on the official record. The obvious suspect was Noel-Baker. It was to him that Cawthorn had conveyed Liaquat's proposal for an alliance. Noel-Baker had led the UK delegation in the discussions over Kashmir in the Security Council. As Commonwealth Secretary, he had a major say in interpreting the 'Stand Down' order. It is difficult to think of any other minister who might be inclined to anticipate Cabinet decisions and offer informal assurances concerning a 'Stand Down' or about British policy on Kashmir at the United Nations.

The Commonwealth Relations Office replied with a well-formulated evasion. 'We still cannot trace [the] basis for these rumours and believe them to be quite unfounded,' cabled Patrick, the Deputy Secretary. 'It is difficult to pursue the matter without knowing which Minister is alleged to have spoken to Cawthorn.' And, since it was a simple matter for Grafftey-Smith to ascertain this from Cawthorn, Patrick cautioned, 'But we appreciate the difficulty of obtaining this'![5] There is nothing on file to indicate that Patrick had consulted his minister, Noel-Baker.

A Warning

Even as officials engaged in this exchange of cables, the British government at the highest level signalled the position it would take in the event of a major Indian offensive. On 17 November, Liaquat sent a desperate telegram to Attlee appealing for support in the Security Council for a ceasefire call.

Now clear that Indian Army and Air Force have actually started major offensive on both Mirpur–Poonch and Dras fronts. Object of former undoubtedly to secure all territory up to Jhelum River including whole of Poonch and face U.N. with fait accompli. Quite clear that Azad forces with present defensive support by minimum of Pakistan Regular Forces cannot hope to hold up advance in Mirpur–Poonch. Unless Security Council can be induced to order unconditional ceasefire immediately, Pakistan will be forced to stage counter-offensive with all resources including armour and air to stop this Indian offensive.[6]

Attlee sent an immediate reply. 'I am taking action to do anything I can to secure the halting of any offensive that may be taking place,' he responded. 'I hope that you will not precipitate any action on your part until these measures have been tried out.'[7] Simultaneously, Attlee sought an assurance from Nehru that India did not intend to launch an all-out offensive. His message read:

> I am informed that a communication is being made to the Security Council alleging that Indian Army and Air Force operating in Kashmir have been considerably reinforced and that Indian Forces have started an all-out offensive in the State.
>
> I sincerely trust you will be able to assure me that this is not the fact. Remembering the assurances from yourself and the Prime Minister of Pakistan when you were in London, I am sure that neither of you would wish to settle the fate of Kashmir by military force.[8]

The exchange of messages left no doubt regarding the position the UK would take in the Security Council and elsewhere if India were to try driving out Pakistan's forces from Jammu province. Nehru was furious and his anger showed in his reply to Attlee.

> This message has surprised me. We have had no protest yet from U.K. Government about Pakistan armies functioning in Kashmir and being continually reinforced and carrying on offensive operations.... We have also not had any expression of opinion of United Kingdom Government on our acceptance of Kashmir Commission's ceasefire resolution and Pakistan's rejection of it. But now Pakistan objects and that objection is apparently supported by United Kingdom Government.
>
> We have no desire to settle any question by military force, but if our territory is invaded as it has been invaded in Kashmir, it is our intention to resist to the utmost of our capacity.... There has been no major offensive and there is no question of an all-out offensive in the State....
>
> It will be observed Pakistan complaint is without foundation and we have deliberately avoided major offensive. I should like to make it clear however that presence of Pakistan troops on Indian Union territory is a continuing irritation and we cannot possibly agree to their staying there....
>
> It is a matter of deep regret to my Government that these hostile forces are controlled and led by British officers who are thus participating in invasion of the territory of the Indian Dominion.[9]

The Indian Prime Minister thus registered a protest against Britain's pro-Pakistan stance. He defended India's right to expel Pakistani forces from her territory in Kashmir, while rejecting Liaquat's charge of an all-out Indian offensive. He offered no assurances concerning limited operations.

Nye called on him in order to probe his intentions and reported: 'He[Nehru] did not say categorically that they had no intention of carrying out further operations, but he implied quite clearly that if anything more was undertaken during the winter it should be of a minor nature.' Nye added the further assurance that he knew from 'unimpeachable sources' that India had no plans in existence for any large-scale offensive.[10]

Around this time, the UK again took recourse to delaying military supplies urgently required by India. In mid-December, Nehru complained to Krishna Menon about British prevarication and instructed him to seek a clear answer as to whether the promised supplies would be sent. If not, Nehru intended to 'make other arrangements'[11]—presumably to explore the possibility of sourcing defence requirements from the United States. In 1948, India possessed only a rudimentary defence industry and her dependence on the UK for spares and equipment was almost total.

Bucher's Role

Bucher now set himself a twofold task: to restrict Indian offensive action to the extent possible and to reassure the Pakistani army about India's intentions. Spurred on by Nye, he lost no opportunity to impress upon the Indian government the limitations of its army and the need to adopt a strictly defensive posture. The cable traffic from the UK High Commission provides glimpses of the *modus operandi*. Thus, Nye reported on 22 November that he was 'arranging to be fed into' Nehru from professional sources that the morale of Indian troops in Kashmir had begun to deteriorate. 'I hope by making these various representations to Nehru that it will be possible to bring home to him that there is no military solution to this [Kashmir] problem.'[12] The same day, Bucher wrote to Nehru on the indicated lines, adding for good measure that the army was very short of transport and vehicle spares as well as certain types of ammunition and that there was no prospect of new supplies in the near future.[13] These representations generally served to reinforce the restraint reflected in

Indian operational plans. Nehru's thinking was conditioned also by the prospects of a ceasefire emerging from the labours of the UN Commission. Responding to Bucher, the Prime Minister wrote that 'Muzaffarabad and Mirpur are out of our reach at present for many months and I cannot say just yet what line in regard to them might be. But Kotli is of somewhat different category. It is conceivable that we might consider it desirable to go towards Kotli. But not yet or in the near future.'[14] Thus the government kept open its options on Kotli, though the objective was not treated as urgent.

Bucher attended an inter-dominion conference of Defence Secretaries and Officers in Karachi on 26 and 27 November and took the opportunity to hold private discussions with the Pakistani Commander-in-Chief, General Gracey, and Chief of Staff, General McCay. Grafftey-Smith cabled that Bucher had assured McCay that:

> there would be no (repeat no) attack on Irpur [sic. Mirpur?] or any staged (repeat staged) attack on Kotli or Bhimbar ... [Bucher] had indeed promised to send him [McCay] a personal signal should Indian Government 'double-cross' him over this. Most strict orders had been given that towns (he mentioned Domel and Muzaffarabad) were not (repeat not) to be bombed. After much difficulty he had succeeded in getting one R.I.A.F. squadron withdrawn from Jammu.[15]

Bucher had considerable success in reassuring Gracey. In Grafftey-Smith's words:

> ... it is clear that confidential exchanges between him [General Gracey] and General Bucher during recent defence discussions here have usefully cleared the air and very considerably relieved tension, at least on top level. But situation in Poonch area remains precarious because of risk that Indian commanders on the spot may edge forward here and there in search of better position with dangerously provocative effect on morale of Azad Kashmir and Pakarmy.
> 2. Both C-in-Cs were agreed on essential necessity of localising effect of Indian advance on Poonch, and Gracey has no doubt of Bucher's good intentions in this respect. He is less sure whether General Cariappa is firmly under Bucher's control, and is very apprehensive of forward action (militarily unexceptionable)

by local commanders in sense suggested above. He insists that
any suggestion of an Indian advance towards Kolti [sic, Kotli?],
Palundri and Mirpur would be fatal and would involve instant
counter offensive by Pakistan forces.[16]

Thus Bucher was able to calm Gracey's fears of an all-out Indian
drive to the Jhelum river but the Pakistani army remained uncertain
about more limited actions on the part of India. Bucher's dedication
to curbing Indian initiatives was not in doubt; the question was
whether he would succeed in restraining Indian generals from launching forward actions which were 'militarily unexceptionable.' Bucher
'frankly admitted to General Gracey that he cannot control Cariappa.'[17]
Regarding Kotli, Gracey noted that Bucher offered a qualified assurance—that there would be no 'staged' attack on Kotli. Bucher's offer
to alert Pakistan in case the Indian government tried to 'double-cross'
him was deeply appreciated. (Did Bucher chose his words for their
delicious irony?) There was no mention of any reciprocal assurance
sought by Bucher and it is clear that Gracey, on his part, volunteered
no assurance. It continued to be Pakistan's policy to retaliate with a
counter-offensive if there were to 'any suggestion of an Indian advance'
towards Kotli. As High Commissioner Grafftey-Smith reported: 'Gracey
considers that the Indian forces are in a highly vulnerable position
and that a Pakistan brigade shelling the Indian C. of C. [sic, L. of C.?]
between Akhnur and Naoshera would cause havoc.'[18]

It was a high risk strategy. Since the Indian army in Kashmir was
critically dependent on the single road running through this area to
the valley, a strong reaction was to be expected to a Pakistani attack
at this point. One can only speculate that military planners in Pakistan were confident that India had no plans for carrying the war into
Pakistan (as was indeed the case) and, furthermore, that India would
be restrained from launching such an attack by the UK and the Security Council.

Operation Venus

To return to the battlefront, in early December the Indian army
launched some local initiatives in the Poonch–Mendhar area. Indian
forces took the Salhotri ridge, where Pakistan had earlier established
a forward headquarters. By 15 December, the Indian army dominated the main road from Mendhar to Kotli. These actions were in full

conformity with the government's decisions as summarised in Nehru's message to Krishna Menon. As Gracey had feared, Bucher had not succeeded in preventing his generals from taking militarily unexceptionable forward actions. Though these were only local actions, they triggered off Pakistani fears about a major Indian offensive. After the action at the Salhotri ridge, Liaquat sent a telegram to Attlee (on 8 December) alleging that 'Indian forces are making preparations for a further offensive in the near future with the probable object of capturing Kotli.' He warned: 'Unless ... India immediately orders her commanders to restrict their dispositions and activities to the minimum areas essential for the protection of the above [Rajouri–Poonch and Srinagar–Leh] route I shall be compelled to order active counter-measures.' He called for an urgent Security Council decision to send military observers to the state and sought Attlee's assistance to 'avert the tragedy that is looming ahead.'[19]

At the time of Liaquat's appeal, Pakistan's military dispositions were described by the UK High Commission in Karachi, as follows:

For the first time Pakistan forces ... are so placed that they can deliver a blow ... against Indian lines of communication in Kashmir, splitting Indian Army and endangering the safety of a large part of it.

Any such counteroffensive would, of course, entail major clash between two Dominion armies which could hardly fail to extend beyond Kashmir.[20]

The planned counter-offensive, codenamed 'Operation Venus'* envisaged a major artillery attack on the vital Indian line of communications in the Naoshera area, particularly the bridge at Beri Pattan. Akhnur, an even more vulnerable position on account of its proximity to the border, was initially considered for the target area but it was realised that a successful Indian counter-attack here would inevitably carry the war into Pakistan territory. Beri Pattan had the advantage of being situated at a slightly greater distance from the border. The idea apparently was to create a 'running sore' where Pakistan could turn on the pressure at will in order to divert India's forces from advancing in other sectors. The beleaguered Poonch garrison had served this

---

* The name was inspired by Victorian pornography, not classical mythology. *Venus in India* was the title of a lubricious novel set in another Naoshera—the cantonment in North West Frontier Province.

purpose at an earlier stage but Pakistan lost this advantage when the Indian army succeeded in establishing control of the lines of communication between Rajouri and Poonch. The Beri Pattan area was viewed as a substitute.[21]

On 12 and 13 December, the Indian airforce bombed the Pakistani position at Palak, which lay behind Kotli in the direction of Mirpur. This was a minor operation intended to destroy the military stores and ammunition dump in Palak. The Pakistani army, however, viewed the action as a breach of the assurance which they believed was given by Bucher that no attack would be launched in this area.

Pakistan responded on 14 December by launching 'Operation Venus.' The Naoshera–Beri Pattan area was subjected to heavy shelling from 5'5 inch medium guns, 25 pounders and also 75 mm shells from medium tanks. The strategically important bridge at Beri Pattan was badly damaged.

The threat at this vital point aroused strong feelings in India. The general feeling in Army Headquarters was that the only satisfactory response would be to drive the Pakistani forces in the area back across the border.[22] Prime Minister Nehru, in a message to Attlee, hinted at a possible counter-attack across the Pakistani border. 'In view of Pakistan Army's offensive against our Army in Indian Union territory,' he cabled, 'we consider ourselves free to take any appropriate action to check this *wherever necessary*'[23] (emphasis added).

In later years Bucher was to claim that his initial reaction to the Pakistani attack was to assemble armoured units and send them into Pakistan.[24] If so, he quickly composed himself, regaining sight of his primary responsibility as a British officer to prevent a full-scale inter-dominion war. Advised by High Commissioner Nye, the Commander-in-Chief restrained his generals.

According to Nye, Bucher 'admitted' to him on 17 December that he found that an Indian battalion in the Mendhar area had 'moved much further west than was necessary to occupy objectives ordered' and that he had 'issued instructions to Cariappa that this battalion is to be withdrawn east at once.'[25] It is possible though that Bucher somewhat exaggerated the categorical nature of his instructions in order to satisfy Nye. He gave a slightly different account to the High Commissioner's Military Adviser. To the latter, Bucher revealed that 'one or two Indian battalions advanced further west than intended in the Mendhar area' and that 'he had ordered Lt. Gen. Cariappa and Lt. Gen. Shrinagesh that these battalions were on no account to be allowed to advance further west and that if possible they should withdraw to positions further east.'[26] It is clear in any case that the burden of the Commander-in-Chief's instructions were to halt and pull-back the Indian advance.

Questioned by Nye about the Palak incident, Bucher said that his assurance to Gracey related only to action by land forces in the area, not the airforce. The bombing attack, he said, was carried out under the authority of Air Marshal Elmhirst. 'It was of course a very foolish, unnecessary and provocative action,' observed Nye, 'and I have made my views very clear to all concerned in Delhi.'[27] In other words, the High Commissioner had pulled up the chief of the R.I.A.F.!

On the same day, despite the strong feelings in India that she was the aggrieved party, Bucher took the initiative to call the Pakistan Army Chief of Staff on the telephone in order to propose cessation of hostilities in the Naoshera area. In Nye's words:

I have done and will continue to do everything in my power to restrain people on this side from doing anything foolish. In taking these measures, I have found Bucher extraordinarily cooperative.... He has taken the initiative in telephoning and sending signals to either General Gracey or to his C.O.S.... Bucher talked to the C.O.S. Pakistan yesterday evening on the telephone, told him of the action taken by the Pakistan troops, impressed on him the seriousness of the situation which would result and C.O.S. promised that he would give categorical orders for the firing of arty etc. to cease.[28]

The understanding between the British officers leading the two armies was spelt out in more specific terms in a telegram from High Commissioner Grafftey-Smith. General Gracey, he reported, 'assured me that, unless India started a counter-attack against Pakistan gun positions, no further action would be taken.'[29]

Whitehall commended the actions of the rival Commanders-in-Chief. In identical cables addressed to Nye and Grafftey-Smith, Noel-Baker pronounced:

We welcome Gracey's assurances ... that unless Indians counter attack Pakistan gun positions there will be no further action by Pakistan and we note helpful attitude of Bucher ... in restraining Indian commanders of air and land forces....

You and Grafftey-Smith/Nye are the best judges whether there is anything further, and if so what, that can be done to help to

188 ♦ War and Diplomacy in Kashmir: 1947–48

*make an understanding between the two Commanders-in-Chief
stronger and perhaps more extensive.*[30]

Thus the guns fell silent on the Naoshera front, averting the possibility of a full-scale Indo–Pakistan war.

The 'Stand Down' Instructions—A Final Twist

The last round of the war provided proof that Pakistan's faith in the informal assurances it had received from London were not misplaced. 'Operation Venus' carried a serious risk of precipitating an all-out war. Yet the British government made no effort to hold back Pakistan, a result which it could easily have achieved by threatening to implement the 'Stand Down' order. Unlike India, Pakistan remained critically dependent on the services of British officers to man her seniormost posts.[31] A British officer, Major-General Loftus Tottenham, was in charge of 'Operation Venus' and he was assisted by other compatriots holding senior positions in the Pakistani forces. British officers were thus responsible for both planning and executing the Naoshera attack.

Nehru protested in the strongest terms against the role of these British officers. 'We take the strongest exception,' he cabled Attlee, 'to this carefully planned operation of Pakistan and more especially to the part that British officers have taken in it.' He demanded that these British officers be withdrawn from Pakistan. 'The Government of India, as is well known, desire to maintain close and friendly relations with the United Kingdom. It is not in keeping with such relations that British officers should be actively engaged in hostilities against the Indian Union.'[32]

He received no satisfaction from the UK Premier. Attlee reminded Nehru that the 'purpose of our Stand Down arrangements is to prevent British officers and men actively taking the field against one another.... I do not think it would be right for us to withdraw British officers from one side except in pursuance of some decision of the Security Council.[33]

The UK government had deftly changed the rules of the game to render the 'Stand Down' order meaningless. The few remaining British officers in the Indian forces served at the highest level and there was no question of their personally 'taking the field.' This was very far from the interpretation given to the decision in October 1947 (when it had been employed to thwart Jinnah's order to the Pakistani army) or December 1947 (when General Russel was obliged to hand in his papers simply because he had toured Kashmir). British ministers, however, came to Pakistan's rescue by re-defining the ban to permit every form of participation except actually 'taking the field.' The name-less cabinet minister who had proferred advance 'hints' and 'informal assurances' to Cawthorn had known what he was talking about.

Attlee bent the rules in favour of Pakistan even though he was fully aware that there was no basis for Liaquat's charge against India. Nye had informed Whitehall in the most categorical terms that the Indian army had prepared no plans for seizing Kotli.[34] Thus in reply to the Pakistani Prime Minister's telegram, Attlee had stated:

> *I must tell you that I myself accept the assurance of the Govern-ment of India that it is not their intention to set in motion in major attack such as you fear....*
>
> *... I therefore beg you to do nothing which might precipitate an extension of the military operations.*[35]

Yet Attlee chose to acquiesce in the Pakistani offensive despite the risk he knew it entailed of a major escalation. Why did the British authorities take this position? A 'draft note' for Attlee prepared in the CRO provides a clue to Noel-Baker's line of argument. The draft note, produced specifically in connection with Nehru's protest, lists a number of 'relevant points' supplementing those mentioned in Attlee's earlier letter of 23 August. It argued that the 'enforcement [of the Stand Down decision] might drive Pakistan to desperate courses.' She 'might leave the Commonwealth.' Moreover, if she suffered a serious reverse, 'an internal collapse in Pakistan might result, pro-ducing chaos from which the communists would profit.' Finally, the 'hostility of the Muslim population of the world to the United King-dom might be increased.'[36] Thus the document suggests that the CRO once again fell back on its time-tested strategy of stoking fears that a military defeat would lead to internal chaos in Pakistan, with consequent communist gains; that a desperate Pakistan might quit the Commonwealth and turn to the Soviet Union; and that by anta-gonising Pakistan, Britain would undermine her own interests in the Middle East. In 1947–48 Pakistan was able to reap a rich diplomatic harvest from her perceived political and military fragility.

The events of December once more turned Nehru's thoughts in the direction of a possible counter-offensive in Pakistan territory. 'There is always a possibility,' he wrote to Bucher at the end of the month, 'that if Pakistan is foolish enough to indulge in any attack on us, we shall counter it even by crossing Pakistan territory towards Wazirabad or Sialkot. Whether we do so or not, it will be for us to determine at the time. But we must be in a position to do so, if necessity arises.[37] He had pointed out this imperative requirement one year ago but had been foiled by Mountbatten and the British service chiefs. The result had been a long drawn and inconclusive war at the end of which Pakistan, confident that India would not counter-attack across the Punjab border, felt it could afford to leave its heartland without adequate defences in order to mount a threat to India at a vital choke point. The strategic solution envisioned by Nehru as early as in December 1947 could not be implemented in practice so long as a British general held the post of Commander-in-Chief.

XVI
Ceasefire

The ceasefire and truce terms set out in the UNCIP resolution of 13 August called for the withdrawal of all Pakistani troops from Kashmir and involved at least mild censure of Pakistan's decision to send her army into the state. The proposals were accepted by India but rejected by Pakistan. Karachi's rejection of the ceasefire terms opened the way to an intensification of the military conflict—a prospect which aroused deep apprehension in Pakistan. Thus Pakistan was unable to accept the UNCIP proposals as well as unprepared for the consequences of rejecting them. Liaquat sought to resolve the dilemma by turning to Britain for assistance. He pinned his hopes on an unconditional ceasefire imposed by the Security Council. This would not only restrain India from launching a military offensive but would also obviate the necessity of accepting the UNCIP resolution. Liaquat expected Britain to take the lead in the Security Council.

Unconditional Ceasefire?

As we saw in Chapter 14, Pakistan's offer of a military pact elicited from London not only operationally valuable 'hints' and 'assurances' but also an offer to return the Kashmir question to the Security Council. British views on the latter question were elaborated at a ministerial meeting held by Attlee in early November. The ministers reached two important conclusions. First, they concluded that, in view of the 'increasingly dangerous' situation in Kashmir, the Security Council should demand an immediate and unconditional ceasefire. The ministers believed that a 'firm recommendation' by the Security Council would be accepted by both parties since 'it was clear that the General Staff of neither army wished for open war and would cooperate in applying the ceasefire arrangements.' The second conclusion was that the 'best hope for securing a final settlement ... lay in the appointment of a mediator of international reputation who could negotiate with the two governments on the spot.' Since this was at variance with both the Security Council resolution of 21 April as well as the UNCIP process, it would be politic to 'introduce the mediator under the guise of the Plebiscite Administrator already provided for in the Resolution of April 21,' broadening his mandate to give him 'general discretion to mediate and to adjust ... the detailed arrangements for the plebiscite.' The British hoped that an American statesman—they suggested General Eisenhower—would play the role of mediator.[1]

The British move was intended to derail the UNCIP process. The UNCIP truce terms called for the withdrawal of all Pakistani troops from Kashmir; in contrast, an unconditional ceasefire would permit Pakistan to retain her forces in the state. A 'mediator'—whom the British hoped to influence—would elaborate plebiscite arrangements already rejected by India. The plan would halt the Indian military advance and impose political terms favourable to Pakistan and repugnant to India.

What led the British to entertain the notion that a 'firm recommendation' of an unconditional ceasefire would be accepted by India? The answer lies in the reference British ministers made to the attitude of India's 'General Staff,' i.e., her Commander-in-Chief. General Bucher, it will be recalled, had urged Whitehall in September to impose a ceasefire in view of India's planned advance. He had even offered to 'guarantee' India's compliance, revealing a boldness of judgement that he had scrupulously avoided in his military planning. The British move to impose an unconditional ceasefire on India thus originated with the proposal mooted by India's own Commander-in-Chief!

The British move ran into an unexpected problem. It was based on the assumption that American cooperation would be readily available, as in the past, in order to secure broad support in the Security Council. The assumption proved to be ill-founded. Huddle's prominent role in the UNCIP had given the Americans an independent perspective on the Kashmir issue and they were less willing than in the past to defer to British claims of expertise on South Asia. For the

Americans, Huddle's role created a sense of involvement in the UNCIP process. The UNCIP had resumed its labours in Paris, where the UN General Assembly was in session. After the adoption of the 13 August resolution setting out acceptable ceasefire and truce terms, India indicated her willingness to discuss—though only in general terms—the arrangements for a plebiscite or an alternative method of ascertaining the wishes of the people of Jammu and Kashmir. This enabled the UNCIP to accomodate one of Pakistan's concerns. The UNCIP was therefore engaged in formulating a supplementary resolution setting out its recommendations on a plebiscite.

On 10 November, Cadogan, Britain's Permanent Representative at the UN, called on Secretary of State Marshall (who was in Paris for the General Assembly session) and presented to him the latest British proposals. Cadogan emphasised the danger of an incident which might precipitate a full-scale war between India and Pakistan. He asserted that London had reason to believe that an immediate and unconditional ceasefire order would be welcomed 'on a high political level' in both India and Pakistan. Marshall shrewdly inquired whether the interest in a ceasefire in the two countries originated with the British officers serving in the Indian and Pakistani armies. This threw the British team into confusion. Cadogan said he believed that high political leaders in both countries wanted a ceasefire but Curson, the CRO official accompanying him, stated more accurately that a ceasefire would be easier to administer because of the presence of British officers in each army.[2]

Washington's response was conveyed to Cadogan on 13 November. The Americans saw no necessity for an immediate ceasefire order since extensive military operations were not expected in the immediate future. Furthermore, a simple ceasefire order would imply sanctioning the presence of Pakistani troops in Jammu and Kashmir. This would not only be inconsistent with the previous approach of the Security Council and the UNCIP but would also be highly unacceptable to India.[3]

The British thus failed to win American support for their plan to impose an unconditional ceasefire, circumventing the UNCIP. This development was not known to Liaquat when he sounded the alarm bell on 17 November in his telegram to Attlee. Liaquat's appeal for intervention reflected genuine apprehension about an Indian offensive but it was also a tactical move on the diplomatic chess board. The Pakistani Prime Minister addressed a similar appeal to the UN

Security Council, alleging that India intended to face the United Nations with a military *fait accompli* and that unless the Security Council took immediate steps to halt the Indian offensive, Pakistan would have no option but to undertake a counter-offensive with all available resources in an attempt to prevent the Indian army from overrunning the Poonch and Mirpur areas. In keeping with the strategy he had recently concerted with Bevin and Noel-Baker, Liaquat hoped that his allegation of an all-out Indian offensive and his appeal for an immediate and unconditional ceasefire would trigger off action by the Security Council. He was unaware that the plan had suffered a setback in the informal Anglo-American discussions over the past few days.

Liaquat instructed his Foreign Minister to transmit his appeal to the Security Council 'at once.'[4] The astute Zafrulla, however, realised that an undisguised attempt to bypass the UNCIP would alienate it. After careful consideration, he formally delivered the Prime Minister's message to the UNCIP on 19 November, with the request that it be transmitted to the Security Council and that the UNCIP might take such urgent action as it deemed appropriate.[5]

The UNCIP was in favour of deferring a Security Council debate lest it jeopardise its own efforts to arrive at an agreement on plebiscite terms to supplement its 13 August resolution on ceasefire and truce arrangements.[6] By mid-November, an indication had already been received from Pakistan that she was willing to abandon her previous insistence on a coalition government in Kashmir.[7] The UNCIP was optimistic about the prospects of a peaceful settlement provided its work was not interrupted. On 20 November the UNCIP handed over to India and Pakistan draft plebiscite suggestions as a basis of negotiations.

Loy Henderson, who had succeeded Grady as the US Ambassador in New Delhi, informed the State Department that the assessment of his Military Attaché, which coincided with information furnished to the embassy by General Bucher, was that Pakistan was exaggerating the importance of local actions being carried out by the Indian army. Henderson's opinion was that 'it would be unfortunate to press for [a] ceasefire order on [the] assumption [that] India is planning a general offensive in [the] immediate future.'[8] The advice received from Huddle and Henderson strengthened Washington's conviction about the inappropriateness of an unconditional ceasefire imposed by the Security Council.

On 20 November, Cadogan requested the US delegation to support a move to convene an urgent meeting of the Security Council. He proposed that the same six countries which had sponsored the 21 April resolution, together with the current President of the Security Council (Argentina) should now move a resolution calling for an immediate and unconditional ceasefire. Cadogan furnished a summary of High Commissioner Grafftey-Smith's cable of 19 November, drawing particular attention to the passage claiming that if India was not restrained, Pakistan would in despair experience a 'nationwide revulsion of feeling favourable to Russia.' Marshall was unimpressed and Cadogan was informed that the difficulties involved in an immediate ceasefire remained substantial in the absence of an over-all political settlement and in light of India's claim to Jammu and Kashmir.[9] John Foster Dulles, the US delegate at the United Nations, complained to Washington that the 'present UK approach [to the] Kashmir problem appears extremely pro G[overnment] o[f] P[akistan] as against [the] middle ground which we have sought to follow,' urging that the United States should not depart from its neutral path in seeking common ground with the British.[10]

UNCIP Proposals

The UNCIP met on 22 November to consider what action it should take on the Pakistani complaint. It decided to seek India's observations on Zafrulla's letter 'as a matter of urgency' and to address similar appeals to both India and Pakistan 'to refrain from any action which might aggravate the military and political situation and thus endanger the negotiations' being concluded by the UNCIP. The UNCIP also transmitted Zafrulla's letter to the President of the Security Council, together with a summary of the letters it had addressed to India and Pakistan.

Britain reluctantly agreed to go along with the American proposal that the Security Council should confine itself at this stage to endorsing the UNCIP actions and requesting the latter to submit a progress report and further recommendations. The British still planned to seek an unconditional ceasefire if the UNCIP failed to report progress very quickly. In this respect, their position continued to diverge from the American position but there was agreement at least on the first step. Thus, when the Security Council met on 25 November, the US and UK delegates took a similar line in support of the UNCIP and this found strong support among other members.[11] For the first time, Britain and the United States had found common ground on the latter's terms.

Thus by the last week of November, Britain had to abandon the attempt to marginalise the UNCIP process through an unconditional ceasefire imposed by the Security Council. She now threw her weight behind the UNCIP's search for a speedy resolution, pinning her hopes on the early appointment of an American Plebiscite Administrator authorised to work out the important details of the plebiscite arrangements.[12]

Mention may be made here of a development which helped stimulate British support for an early UNCIP success. On 5 December, the Government of India announced that. General Cariappa would take over as Commander-in-Chief of the army in succession to General Bucher. Nye spelt out the implications of this decision in a top secret cable to London.

> The major consideration is the effect this appointment may have on the Indian Government's Kashmir policy. Bucher has not only been ready to receive advice, he has consistently sought it and his influence, which has been considerable, has undoubtedly been an accomodating one. He has consistently opposed all proposals likely to widen the existing breach between the two Dominions and has done so with some success.
>
> ... I think it unlikely he [Cariappa] will seek my advice.... Our influence in military circles will therefore diminish and disappear altogether.
>
> In brief, his appointment makes the finding of a political solution to the Kashmir problem even more urgent.[13]

The UNCIP finalised its supplementary proposals on 11 December. These proposals reaffirmed the earlier UNCIP resolution and provided for a plebiscite after the ceasefire and truce terms of the 13 August resolution had been implemented. They also envisaged the appointment of a Plebiscite Administrator by the Jammu and Kashmir Government to be nominated by the UN Secretary General; the determination of the final disposition of Indian and state armed forces by the Commission and the Plebiscite Administrator, in consultation with the Government of India and with due regard to the security of the state and freedom of the plebiscite; and the determination by the Commission and the Plebiscite Administrator of the disposal of troops in the territory vacated by the tribesmen and other Pakistani nationals, in consultation with the local authorities. Pakistan's concerns were accommodated to the extent that the proposals dealt with plebiscite terms. Indian concerns were met to the extent that the plebiscite terms were only outlined in very general terms and in the exclusion of any suggestion for reconstituting the state government or for subordinating it to a UN authority.

Pakistan's expectations had been raised to great heights by Noel-Baker's manoeuvres in the Security Council culminating in the 21 April resolution. The UNCIP resolution of 13 August was a major setback to her ambitions and she sought to marginalise its significance by returning the Kashmir issue to the Security Council. These hopes faded with the failure of the Anglo-Pakistan move to obtain an unconditional ceasefire imposed by the Security Council. Pakistan was left with no option but to seek the most favourable interpretation it could get of the UNCIP terms. The only other alternative was to prolong a war in which India would have the upper hand in the final analysis.

For India too the options were limited. A quick and decisive military solution required an incursion into Pakistani territory. Nehru's efforts to draw up plans for such an operation had been thwarted by Mountbatten and the Commander-in-Chief at the end of 1947. More recently, in 1948 October, Nehru had asked Bucher to prepare an appreciation of an operation to rid Kashmir of the invader but had been advised that the objective was unattainable, assuming that the war was not to be carried into Pakistani territory. The Commander-in-Chief maintained that a military stalemate was unavoidable except for some limited offensive operations. Nehru therefore came to believe that 'while gradual success would come to us, no quick or effective decision was likely. We might carry on the war in Kashmir itself, for a considerable time, gaining some successes and advancing our fronts, but this would be a long drawn-out affair, and would not put an end to the conflict or the problem.'[14] Moreover, 'there was always the question of what foreign powers might do either in interfering or in aiding Pakistan in other ways.'[15] Attlee's messages and British moves in the Security Council provided ample grounds for concern.

The choice before India in 1948 December was between carrying on a desultory war or accepting a ceasefire which met India's minimum terms. In these circumstances India, like Pakistan, sought to obtain the best possible terms by seeking favourable clarifications and interpretations of the UNCIP proposals. This diplomatic exercise proceeded side by side with military operations in December.

India's initial reaction to the UNCIP proposals was cool. She made it clear that the process of rejection of Commission proposals by Pakistan and the adoption of a responsible attitude by India could not continue indefinitely and that there was a limit to India's spirit of conciliation. India received assurances from the UNCIP on some important questions. For New Delhi, the 13 August resolution was of primary importance since it implicitly recognised the legal basis of India's presence in Kashmir, in contrast to that of Pakistan. The UNCIP agreed with India's view that she could not be bound by the agreement if Pakistan failed to fully implement her obligations under the 13 August resolution. New Delhi was also assured that there would be large-scale disarming of the 'Azad Kashmir' forces. In response to India's request for an assurance that methods other than plebiscite were not being ruled out, the UNCIP stated that the possibility of a plebiscite should first be explored but, if the Plebiscite Administrator were to find the method impracticable, other methods could be considered for ascertaining the wishes of the people of Jammu and Kashmir. Pakistan, in turn, was assured that a Plebiscite Administrator would be appointed at an early date, though it was made clear to her that discussion of the details of the plebiscite arrangements would commence only after the truce agreement had been signed and the UNCIP was satisfied about progress in implementation of the 13 August resolution.

In light of the assurances offered by the UNCIP, India accepted the supplementary proposals on 23 December and Pakistan followed two days later. India viewed the supplementary proposals as amounting only to a general statement of principles, leaving details of the plebiscite to be discussed after Parts I and II of the 13 August resolution had been implemented. Pakistan, on the other hand, maintained that the implementation of the plebiscite arrangements would proceed simultaneously with the implementation of the earlier resolution, inasmuch as the appointment of the Plebiscite Administrator was not contingent on prior fulfilment of Parts I and II of the 13 August resolution.

Thus by 25 December, the UNCIP's mediatory efforts had resulted in an agreement between India and Pakistan. The promulgation of a ceasefire in terms of the agreement was now only a matter of time. However, the events of the past fortnight had shown how relatively minor moves on the battle front could lead to sudden escalation. Wishing to avoid possible complications, High Commissioner Nye suggested to Air Marshal Elmhirst, who at the time was the Chairman of the Chiefs of Staff Committee, that India should take the initiative in proposing that a ceasefire take effect immediately, in anticipation of the formal adoption of the UNCIP resolution. The service chiefs agreed to make a recommendation to Nehru.[16] On 30 December, the Prime Minister authorised General Bucher to convey a ceasefire proposal to General Gracey in Pakistan.

The ceasefire came into effect one minute before midnight of 1 January, 1949.

XVII
Conclusion

In August 1947 India and Pakistan emerged as independent states but they had yet to gain full control over that essential instrument of sovereignty, the armed forces. In both countries the armed forces were led by British officers. In India, moreover, a British naval officer, Lord Mountbatten, presided over the Defence Committee of the Cabinet. It was quite natural and proper that these British officers owed their primary loyalty to their King rather than to the South Asian governments in whose service they were employed. British policy shaped the military advice they gave to their respective governments, as well as the manner in which they carried out—or failed to carry out— government directives.

Mountbatten's role has been much misunderstood in Pakistan as well as India. Mountbatten was in some ways a friend of India but he was in no sense a foe of Pakistan. The Governor-General's affection for India never interfered with his pursuit of the British interest. He rendered a great service to Britain—and, incidentally, also to Pakistan—by restraining Indian military initiatives on more than one critical occassion. He made sure that India did not extend operations upto the Pakistan border in the Poonch and Mirpur districts, going to the extent of sabotaging his government's plans for creating a *cordon sanitaire* along the border by aerial action. He foiled his government's instructions for preparing contingency plans for a counterstrike across the Pakistani border, while prevailing upon Nehru to take the Kashmir issue to the UN. Contrary to popular belief, he achieved his ends mainly by exercising his official powers, not by influencing Nehru's thinking behind the scenes. The fact that India's first Governor-General was not a mere constitutional figurehead has gone almost unnoticed. Mountbatten's appointment as Chairman of the Cabinet's Defence Committee invested him with very real executive authority in an area of vital importance to the state. By securing this appointment, Mountbatten manoeuvered himself into a position from where he could directly influence government policy, where possible, or undermine it, where necessary.

When India and Pakistan gained independence, secret orders were issued to senior British military officers in both countries to 'Stand Down' in the unprecedented event of an imminent inter-dominion war. Thus when tension arose over Junagadh, Mountbatten and the Commander-in-Chief, General Lockhart, did their best to restrain India from taking recourse to military action. Mountbatten took the position that Junagadh had become Pakistani territory by virtue of the Nawab's accession, even though the accession was clearly indefensible on moral grounds. In September, apprehending a clash with the Nawab, the service chiefs addressed a joint letter to the Defence Minister urging a negotiated settlement and declaring their inability to participate in any way in operations which were likely to precipitate an inter-dominion war. Ministers reacted sharply to this 'invasion of the political domain' and the offending letter was withdrawn. The service chiefs, however, restated their position with greater circumspection and the 'Stand Down' instructions remained in place.

At the inception of the Kashmir crisis in October, the position adopted by Mountbatten and the British generals was essentially a mirror image of their position on Junagadh. Accession was the touchstone of their policy. Military intervention in a princely state, or even military aid to its ruler, was viewed as legitimate only if the state had already acceded to the dominion concerned and thus become part of its territory. The danger of an inter-dominion war would not arise if both countries could be made to respect this principle. Thus, in early October, General Lockhart refrained on Auchinleck's advice from implementing the Indian government's order to send military supplies to the Maharaja. Likewise, he decided not to share with his government the indications he had received from Messervy and Cunningham about the movement of armed Pakistani tribesmen towards Kashmir.

When news of the threat to Srinagar finally reached the Indian government, Mountbatten insisted that military intervention was impermissible in the absence of accession. It was only after he had been accomodated on the question of accession that he agreed to an air-lift. Even at this stage, the Governor-General and the service chiefs sought to dissuade the government by emphasising the military risks and difficulties of the operation. The problems were indeed real but innovative solutions were required and these were suggested not by the Commander-in-Chief but by the Prime Minister himself. It must be said to the credit of the service chiefs, however, that once the government had decided on the airborne operation, it was carried out with exemplary efficiency.

The final act in the first stage of the conflict was General Gracey's refusal to carry out Jinnah's order to send the regular Pakistani army into Kashmir. Gracey acted in conformity with the 'Stand Down' instructions and Field Marshal Auchinleck, the Supreme Commander for India and Pakistan, flew to Lahore to inform Jinnah that all British officers would be withdrawn if the Pakistani army was sent into territory which now belonged to the Indian Union by virtue of the Maharaja's accession.

Thus in the first week of the conflict, British policy was largely elaborated by the men on the spot—Mountbatten, Auchinleck and the British generals commanding the forces of India and Pakistan. Their actions conformed to the 'Stand Down' instructions and the legal implications of accession. In Kashmir as in Junagadh, they sought to avert an inter-dominion war by strictly respecting the legal consequences of an act of accession.

By the begining of November, British policy entered a new phase. The initiative passed from the men on the spot to the mandarins in Whitehall. Britain began to move away from a position based on legality and impartiality to a policy based on immediate political and strategic considerations. Though London congratulated Auchinleck and Gracey on their initiative, it soon had second thoughts. British political and strategic interests dictated a tilt in favour of Pakistan. The Foreign Office feared that antagonising Pakistan might 'align the whole of Islam against us', jeopardising British interests in the Middle East. Pakistan was a potential ally and her proximity to the Gulf gave her great geopolitical importance. Finally, Britain feared that Pakistan's very survival would be challenged if India were to gain control over the entire territory of Jammu and Kashmir. An Indian presence along the borders of the princely state with Pakistan would encourage seperatist forces in Pakistan's North West Frontier Province, bring the Mangla irrigation headworks under Indian control, and place the Indian army within striking distance of Pakistan's military heartland centred around Rawalpindi.

Britain therefore fell in with the Pakistani line that the raiders could not be persuaded to leave Kashmir until a satisfactory agreement had been reached on the state's future. The prime mover of the policy shift, Noel-Baker, also realised that the 'Stand Down' instructions placed Pakistan at a disadvantage because of her heavy dependence on the services of British officers. The instructions were therefore amended to allow maximum latitude in interpretation. The full significance of the amendment was to be revealed in stages as the conflict developed in 1948.

Mountbatten played a dual role in this new phase of British policy. In the first place, he assumed the role of a mediator between India and Pakistan. This must be the only case in the annals of diplomacy where the holder of the highest office in a country has attempted mediation between that country and another! Though he was personally unconvinced about Jinnah's inability to call off the raiders, Mountbatten adhered loyally to the new line taken by London and made it a feature of his mediatory initiative. Second, he left no stone unturned to dissuade or thwart the Indian government from extending military operations right upto Jammu and Kashmir's border with Pakistan. Joining hands with the Commander-in-Chief, he strongly opposed operations in the western areas of Mirpur and Poonch. In collusion with Lockhart, he effectively sabotaged plans for air operations against the raiders along the border.

By mid-December, Mountbatten's mediatory exercise had failed, despite concessions on the part of India. Nor did Lockhart's military plans hold out any prospect of an early solution. The Commander-in-Chief ruled out the possibility of expelling the raiders before the next spring. Nehru therefore came to the conclusion that a radically different military approach was required. He envisaged a strike across the border against the invader's bases and lines of communication in Pakistan. 'From a military point of view, this would be the most effective step,' he wrote, pointing out that this was the only approach that offered a speedy solution.

Mountbatten threw his full weight against the proposal in the Defence Committee. He pressed for a reference to the UN which, he said disingenuously, would promptly direct Pakistan to withdraw the raiders. The Committee agreed, as a compromise, to proceed on both lines simultaneously. A reference would be made to the UN in a last attempt to obtain a peaceful settlement, even though the Prime Minister expected it to be a fruitless exercise. At the same time, the service chiefs were instructed to draw up contingency plans for a military strike against the raiders in their bases in Pakistan.

In collusion with the service chiefs, Mountbatten ensured that nothing came of the government's decision for preparations to be made for a cross-border operation. Meanwhile, he alerted Attlee about India's intentions, passing on full details of his exchanges with Nehru, through the UK High Commissioner. Mountbatten was able to vindicate his boast that his presence in India as Governor-General was the 'best insurance' against a full-scale inter-dominion war.

Upto the end of 1947 Britain was the only overseas power with a significant involvement in the Kashmir conflict. Referral to the UN fully internationalised the issue. From New Year's Day of 1948 events in Kashmir unfolded against a more complex international background. Britain remained the prime overseas player but other powers—in particular, the United States—also contributed to influencing developments.

At the end of December Britain's first priority was to dissuade India from launching a counter-strike across the border and from thereby precipitating a full-scale war with Pakistan. Attlee warned Nehru that such a move would invite UN censure. At London's request, the US chargé d'affaires in New Delhi made a pointed enquiry about India's policy and Nehru had to assure him that he had no intention of causing the situation to deteriorate further. Even though India asserted her right to launch a counter-attack across Pakistani territory, she accepted the British-inspired Security Council resolution of 17 January urging the two countries to refrain from any step which might aggrevate the situation and to immediately inform the Council about any material change in the situation. At this stage Mountbatten was able to persuade Nehru that there was no current need to pursue the question of an operation across the Pakistan border. Since secrecy and surprise were absent, international intervention had preempted exercise of the option.

Under British inspiration, the Security Council next turned its attention to the question of a ceasefire linked with arrangements for a plebiscite, brushing aside the question of Pakistan's involvement in the invasion. Noel-Baker skilfully orchestrated the positions adopted by the Western powers and persuaded the United States to seemingly take the lead. For reasons of alliance solidarity, the United States was prepared to offer the maximum possible support to Britain but it demurred when Noel-Baker advanced proposals involving the unqualified acceptance of Pakistan's demands and the outright rejection of Indian views. His proposals would have placed Kashmir under effective UN control, pending a plebiscite, and permitted induction of Pakistani troops into the state with a status similar to that of the Indian army.

In 1948, US officials were prepared to recognise the fact that Jammu and Kashmir legally belonged to India. This became clear in Anglo-American discussions in February, even though US officials refrained from publicly breaking ranks with their British ally. US officials told their British colleagues that they were disturbed by the implications of a Security Council resolution recommending the use of foreign (Pakistani) troops in Kashmir. When the British side asserted that Kashmir was a 'territory in dispute', the Americans disagreed, stating that they 'found it difficult to deny the legal validity of Kashmir's accession to India'. Secretary of State Marshall expressed 'grave doubts' about the plan which, he pointed out, excluded the possibility of a compromise solution acceptable to India.

Noel-Baker's initiatives were also questioned by leading members of the British Cabinet. He had far exceeded his instructions in extending unqualified support to Pakistan. Attlee had approved a pro-Pakistan tilt in general terms but not the detailed and totally one-sided proposals advocated in New York by Noel-Baker. The minister had acted on his own initiative without waiting for Cabinet approval. Attlee summoned him to London for a policy review and Noel-Baker was given new instructions which diverged widely from the line he had been pursuing in New York. It was not easy, however, to rein in Noel-Baker. Attlee had to rebuke him for straying from his brief but the minister pleaded that he could not change course totally at this late stage without losing all credibility. The outcome was a Security Council resolution which did not go as far as Noel-Baker's original draft but which, nevertheless, remained unacceptable to India.

While Noel-Baker was trying in the UN to obtain a ceasefire on the basis of inducting Pakistani troops into Jammu and Kashmir, India's Commander-in-Chief, General Bucher, was engaged in a parallel venture behind the back of his government. Bucher sought a private understanding with his counterpart in Pakistan, General Gracey, to observe an informal truce on the basis of his turning a blind eye to induction of Pakistani regulars into specified areas of Jammu and Kashmir. The intention presumably was to pave the way for a cease-fire on the terms envisaged by the British delegation at the UN. The Commander-in-Chief's schemes came to nought when Gracey, not realising the delicacy of Bucher's position, set out proposals in an official telegram. The Indian government at once rejected the proposals and instructed General Bucher to desist from entering into unauthorised negotiations.

In early May, with the spring offensive approaching, Mountbatten asked Bucher to instill in the government the notion that India was 'militarily impotent' in order to reduce the risk of an all-out war after his departure from India in June. The Commander-in-Chief obliged by advising the government that the army was in no position to expel the invaders from the Poonch and Mirpur areas or even from Muzaffarabad. His assessment contrasted sharply with that offered by his counterpart to the Pakistani government. General Gracey was convinced that the raiders stood no chance of holding out against a full-fledged Indian offensive. Gracey advised Karachi that India's spring offensive could not be halted unless the Pakistani army moved into Kashmir, operating behind a screen of irregulars.

Gracey's move could not have taken Bucher by surprise since the two generals had discussed deployment of Pakistani troops in Kashmir during their abortive truce talks in March. Yet Bucher took no step to warn his government or to send additional troops to Kashmir. On the contrary, after the spring offensive had been launched, he made every effort to delay confirming the presence of Pakistani regulars in the state. In Whitehall, this was attributed to his prior knowledge of Pakistani intentions.

The evidence also suggests that Noel-Baker—without consulting the Cabinet—gave the nod for the Pakistani move into Kashmir. Gracey stated categorically that London was aware of the plan. In October Gracey had refused to obey Jinnah's order to march into Kashmir; yet a few months later he advocated a similar move. His behaviour is inexplicable unless he had reason to believe that London had cleared the move. Noel-Baker's complicity is suggested by his conduct in dissuading Alexander from bringing up the question of applying the 'Stand Down' instructions as well as by his subsequent interpretation of these instructions in Pakistan's favour.

By sending in her regular forces, Pakistan blunted the Indian offensive in May–June. The UNCIP's arrival in the subcontinent in July also imposed a diplomatic constraint on the level of military activity. In other respects, however, the Commission's arrival produced favourable results from India's point of view. Since the UNCIP had no British member, London had no direct say in its proceedings. The Commission was therefore able to formulate a set of balanced recommendations calling for a truce on the basis of the withdrawal of all Pakistani forces, regulars and irregulars, from Kashmir and retention of minimal Indian forces for maintaining law and order in areas under Indian control. The question of conditions for a reference to the will of the people was left for later consultations.

The UNCIP's departure in September reduced the political constraints on a new military offensive. Indian generals in the field called for vigorous measures. Nehru instructed the Commander-in-Chief in early October to prepare a military appreciation of an offensive to drive out the invaders from Jammu and Kashmir. Anxious to thwart such moves, Bucher sent a secret message to London urging that a ceasefire be imposed through the Security Council. In response to the Prime Minister's instructions, the Commander-in-Chief advised the government that the army was in a position to undertake only some minor operations and that, from an overall point of view, a military stalemate was unavoidable. In light of this assessment, the Indian government approved a limited plan of operations. The Commander-in-Chief immediately reported the details to the new British High Commissioner, General Sir Archibald Nye, who had replaced Mountbatten as Bucher's guide and mentor.

Unwilling to accept the UNCIP truce terms and unprepared to face an Indian onslaught, Pakistan sought an escape through high diplomacy. Liaquat Ali Khan sent the deputy chief of the army, General Cawthorn, on a top secret mission to London with a proposal for a military alliance. Though the proposal did not see immediate fruition, it created a very favourable impression in London and inspired British ministers to fresh exertions on behalf of Pakistan. Britain launched a new initiative to impose an unconditional ceasefire through the Security Council—a proposal mooted earlier by General Bucher. Had it succeeded, the iniative would have made it unnecessary for Pakistan to accept the UNCIP proposals and simultaneously removed the threat of an Indian offensive. Secret assurances were also given to Pakistan by a British minister that, in the event of an Indian incursion into Pakistan, the Security Council would impose sanctions against India and that London would not ask British officers in Pakistan to 'Stand Down'. On the basis of these secret assurances, Pakistan decided to take the risk of denuding her defences in West Punjab in order to reinforce her positions in the Poonch–Mirpur sector, where she feared an Indian offensive.

The Anglo-Pakistani attempt to derail the work of the UNCIP by returning the Kashmir issue to the Security Council ran into unexpected resistance. The United States had an active representative in the UNCIP and had developed a commitment to its approach. Washington was not inclined to abort the Commission's work at a time when it held out promise of early results. London was obliged to suspend its efforts to take the issue back to the Security Council. Thus, in the last quarter of 1948, the war in Kashmir proceeded in parallel with the UNCIP's efforts at securing a truce agreement.

The British archives throw a fascinating light on the ways in which the British generals and diplomats in India and Pakistan coordinated their moves to contain the war and ensure that an Indian advance stopped well short of the Pakistani border. India's Commander-in-Chief, General Bucher, kept his colleagues in Pakistan informed about his military plans, giving them an assurance that he would not advance beyond specified positions. He even offered to send a secret signal to his counterpart in Rawalpindi in case the Indian government 'double-crossed' him by changing his plans! Bucher's assurances were gratefully received but they did not fully remove Pakistan's apprehensions. The generals in Pakistan did not question Bucher's intentions but they doubted his ability to restrain his Indian subordinates—Cariappa, in particular—from launching militarily unexceptionable forward actions.

Indeed, this turned out to be crux of the matter. Thus, in early November, during Air Marshal Elmhirst's absence from headquarters, Air Vice-Marshal Mukerjee ordered the Indian airforce to attack a Pakistani airforce Dakota on a supply-dropping flight to Gilgit. The Pakistani airforce chief, Perry-Keene, believed that he had a 'gentleman's agreement' with Elmhirst which exempted his supply flights from interception in the air. Whatever the truth about the existence of an agreement, it was a fact that no such interception had occurred previously. In view of the importance of Gilgit as an operational base, the new development was viewed as a major threat to Pakistani positions in the northern theatre and the Pakistani Cabinet decided to provide fighter escorts for the supply flights. This aroused British fears that Indian might be provoked to attack airfields in Pakistan, thus widening the conflict beyond the borders of Kashmir. On Grafftey-Smith's advice, Gracey and Perry-Keene persuaded the Cabinet to hold their hand until Elmhirst's position could be clarified. In New Delhi, at Nye's behest, Elmhirst persuaded Nehru that the supply flights could be ignored as they were of trivial importance from a military point of view.

In December, as Gracey had feared, Bucher was unable to prevent Indian commanders from taking forward actions in the Kotli area. The Indian army occupied the Salhotri ridge, dominating the main road from Mendhar to Kotli. Moreover, the Indian airforce bombed the Pakistani position at Palak, behind Kotli. Gracey maintained that the attack on Palak violated Bucher's assurance. Though these were local actions, Pakistan reacted with alarm, launching a heavy artillery attack on the vital Beri Pattan bridge on the Naoshera road. Indian generals wanted to respond by driving back the Pakistanis across the border and Nehru informed Attlee that India considered herself free to take appropriate action 'wherever necessary'. However, the situation was quickly brought under control by British diplomats and generals in the subcontinent. Advised by High Commissioner Nye, Bucher instructed Cariappa and Shrinagesh to pull back Indian forces in the Mendhar area. Questioned by Nye about the Palak incident, the Commander-in-Chief explained that his assurance to Gracey only covered actions by the army, not the airforce. The High Commissioner pulled up Elmhirst for not stopping a 'foolish, unnecessary and provocative action'. Finally, Bucher telephoned the Pakistani Chief of Staff and arranged to halt the artillery attack, on the understanding that India would not launch a counter-attack against the Pakistani gun positions. London commended the two Commanders-in-Chief for their roles in ending what proved to be the last major clash in the war.

Since the end of October, Nehru's thinking had increasingly turned towards a ceasefire. He had been foiled in his attempt to prepare contingency plans for a counter-attack across the Pakistani border and this no longer appeared to be a feasible option in view of the part played by the Security Council. General Bucher ruled out the possibility of a speedy military decision. On the other hand, the UNCIP proposals held out the prospect of a ceasefire which met India's minimum political terms. As for Pakistan, the only alternative she had to acceptance of the UNCIP proposals was a long drawn out conflict in which India would inevitably have the upper hand. Thus by the last week of December the UNCIP succeeded in laying the basis of a ceasefire agreement. For High Commissioner Nye the only cloud in the horizon was Bucher's impending retirement and the appointment of General Cariappa as the first Indian Commander-in-Chief. At Nye's instance, Bucher approached Nehru with a suggestion for an immediate ceasefire in anticipation of the formal adoption of the UNCIP resolution. With the Prime Minister's approval, Bucher conveyed the offer to Gracey, who promptly accepted on behalf of Pakistan. Thus ended the first Indo–Pakistan war.

In the last days of the war Nehru once again drew the Commander-in-Chief's attention to the importance of being prepared to launch a counter-attack across the border in case of need. He had urged such preparations a year earlier but had been foiled by Mountbatten. In wars in the third world, secrecy, surprise and speed are essential *political* requirements for a decisive campaign. In the absence of these factors, an offensive runs the risk of being aborted by external intervention in the shape of a Security Council resolution or simply by a warning from one or more of the great powers. Unless a benign superpower is prepared to hold the ring—by exercising its veto against a Security Council resolution or deterring intervention by other powers—secrecy, surprise and speed are of fundamental importance from a diplomatic as well as military point of view. These conditions were unattainable in a situation where Britons presided over the Defence Committee as well as all the three services. It was only after the Indianisation of the military leadership that contingency planning could be undertaken for a counter-attack across the Pakistani border. Thus in August 1952, Nehru was in a position to inform parliament that 'any further aggression or attack or military operations in regard to Kashmir, if such takes place by the other side, that would mean all-out war not in Kashmir only, but elsewhere too'. This was the policy implemented in 1965.

Postscript

Biographical Notes

ABDULLAH, SHEIKH MOHAMMED (1905–82). 'Sher-e-Kashmir' (Lion of Kashmir). Established National Conference, Jammu and Kashmir State, 1938. Prime Minister of Jammu and Kashmir (1948–53). Detained for several years following dismissal from office in 1953. Chief Minister of Jammu and Kashmir (1975–82).

ADDISON, (VISCOUNT) CHRISTOPHER (1869–1951). Professor of Anatomy, Universities of Cambridge and London. Minister of Munitions (1916–17). Minister of Health (1919–21). Minister of Agriculture and Fisheries (1930–31). Secretary of State for Commonwealth Relations (1945–47). Lord Privy Seal (1947–51).

ALEXANDER OF HILLSBOROUGH, (EARL), ALBERT VICTOR (1885–1965). First Lord of the Admiralty (1929–31, 1940–45 and 1945–46). Member of Cabinet Delegation to India, 1946. Minister of Defence (1947–50).

ALI, CHAUDHRI MOHAMMAD (1905–80). Member of Indian Audit and Accounts Service. Secretary-General, Government of Pakistan (1947–51). Finance Minister (1951–55). Prime Minister (1955–56).

AUCHINLECK, FIELD MARSHAL (SIR) CLAUDE JOHN EYRE, DSO (1884–1981). Commissioned, Indian Army, 1903. Deputy Chief of General Staff, Army Headquarters, India (1936–38). Commander-in-Chief, Middle East (1941–42). War Member of Viceroy's Executive Council (1943–46). Field Marshal, 1946. Supreme Commander in India and Pakistan, 1947.

BAJPAI, (SIR) GIRJA SHANKAR (1891–1954). Entered Indian Civil Service, 1914. Agent-General in USA (1941–47). Secretary-General, Ministry of External Affairs, India (1947–52). Governor of Bombay (1952–54).

BEVIN, ERNEST (1881–1951). General Secretary of the Transport and General Workers' Union (1919–40). Minister of Labour and National Service (1940–45). Secretary of State for Foreign Affairs (1945–51).

BUCHER, GENERAL (SIR) ROY, MC (1895–1980). Major-General in charge of Administration, Southern Army, India (1942–45). GOC Bengal and Assam Area (1946–January 1947). Chief of Staff, AHQ, Indian Army (August–December 1947). Commander-in-Chief, Indian Army (1948–49). Officer on Special Duty, Defence Ministry, India (1949).

CADOGAN, (SIR) ALEXANDER (1884–1968). Career diplomat. British Ambassador to China (1935–36). Deputy Under-Secretary of State, Foreign Office (1936–37). Permanent Under Secretary of State for Foreign Affairs (1938–46). UK Permanent Representative at UN (1946–50).

CARIAPPA, LIEUTENANT GENERAL (LATER FIELD MARSHAL) K.M. (1899–1993). Commissioned, 1919, in first batch of Indian officers to be given the King's Commission. Served in Iraq, Syria and Iran (1941–42). Imperial Defence College, London (1946–47). Promoted Major–General, July 1947. Deputy Chief of General Staff (August–November 1947). Lieutenant-General, GOC-in-C, Eastern Command (November 1947–January 1948). GOC-in-C, Delhi and East Punjab (later Western) Command (January 1948–January 1949). General, Commander-in-Chief Indian Army (1949–53). High Commissioner in Australia (1953–56). Appointed Field Marshal, 1986.

CARTER, (SIR) ARCHIBALD (1887–1958). Private Secretary to the Secretary of State for India (1924–27). Assistant Under-Secretary of State for India, 1936. Permanent Secretary of the Admiralty (1936–40). Permanent Under Secretary of State for India, 1947. Joint Permanent Under-Secretary for Commonwealth Relations, 1948.

CAWTHORN, MAJOR-GENERAL (SIR) WALTER JOSEPH (1896–1970). Born and educated in Australia. Head of Middle East Intelligence Centre (1939–41). Director of Intelligence, India Command (1941–45). Appointed Deputy Chief of Staff, GHQ, Pakistan Army (1948–51). Retired 1951. Director, Joint Intelligence Bureau, Department of Defence, Australia (1952–54). Australian High Commissioner in Pakistan (1954–58). Australian High Commissioner in Canada (1959–60).

CRIPPS, (SIR) RICHARD STAFFORD (1889–1952). Solicitor-General (1930–31). Ambassador to USSR (1940–42). Lord Privy Seal and Leader of the House of Commons, 1942. Minister of Aircraft Production (1942–45). Chancellor of the Exchequer (1947–50). President of the Fabian Society, 1951.

ELMHIRST, AIR VICE-MARSHAL (LATER HONY. AIR MARSHAL) (SIR) THOMAS WALKER (1895–1981). Deputy Director, Intelligence, UK Air Ministry and Air Cdre HQ, Fighter Command (during Battle of Britain, 1940). Served in North Africa and Europe in World War II. Commander-in-Chief, Indian Air Force (1947–50). Hony. Air Marshal, IAF, 1950.

GHULAM MOHAMMED (1895–1956). Member of Indian Audit and Accounts Service. Finance Minister, Hyderabad State (1942–46). Director of Tatas (1946–47). Finance Minister of Pakistan (1947–51). Governor-General of Pakistan (1951–55).

GORDON-WALKER, (LORD) PATRICK (1907–80). History Tutor, Christ Church (1931–40). BBC (1940–45). Parliamentary Under Secretary of State, CRO (1947–50).

Secretary of State for Commonwealth Relations (1950–51). Secretary of State for Foreign Affairs (1964–65). Secretary of State for Education and Science (1967–68).

GRACEY, GENERAL (SIR) DOUGLAS, MC & bar (1894–1964). Son of an ICS officer, he was commissioned in the Indian Army in 1914. Served in Middle East and South East Asia theatres in World War II. Officiating GOC-in-C, Northern Command, India, 1946. Chief of Staff, Pakistan Army (1947–48). Commander-in-Chief, Pakistan Army (1948–51).

GRAFFTEY-SMITH, (SIR) LAWRENCE (1892–1989). Joined Levant Consular Service, 1914. Consul-General, Albania (1939–40). Consul-General, Antananarivo, 1943. Minister to Saudi Arabia (1945–47). UK High Commissioner in Pakistan (1947–51).

ISMAY, GENERAL (LORD), HASTINGS LIONEL, DSO (1887–1965). Joined 21st Cavalry (Frontier Force), 1907. Military Secretary to Viceroy (1931–33). Secretary, Committee of Imperial Defence, UK, 1938. Chief of Staff to Minister of Defence (Winston Churchill) and Deputy Secretary (Military) to War Cabinet (1940–45). Chief of Staff to Mountbatten (March–November 1947). Secretary of State for Commonwealth Relations (1951–52). Secretary-General of NATO (1952–57).

LIAQUAT ALI KHAN, (NAWABZADA) (1895–1951). U.P. landlord, lawyer and Muslim League leader. General Secretary, All-India Muslim League (1936–47). Finance Minister in the Interim Government (1946). Prime Minister of Pakistan (1947–51). Assassinated in Rawalpindi on 16 October, 1951.

LOCKHART, GENERAL (SIR) ROB (1893–1981). Commissioned, Indian Army, 1913. Military Secretary, India Office, London (1941–43). Deputy Chief of General Staff, India (1944–45). Commander-in-Chief, Indian Army (August–December 1947). Retired 1948.

MAHAJAN, MEHR CHAND (1889–1967). Judge, Lahore High Court, 1943. Member, Punjab Boundary Commission, 1947. Judge, East Punjab High Court, 1947. Prime Minister, Jammu and Kashmir State (1947–48). Judge, Federal Court (1948–53). Chief Justice of India, 1954.

McCAY, MAJOR-GENERAL (LATER HONY. LT. GENERAL) (SIR) ROSS, DSO (1895–1969). Born and educated in Australia. Deputy Military Secretary, India (1940–41). Brigadier, General Staff, India Office (1941–43). Military Secretary, India, 1946. Commander, Peshawar Area, 1947. Chief of Staff, Pakistan Army, 1948. Chief Military Adviser, Pakistan (1951–53).

MENON, V.K. KRISHNA (1896–1974). Secretary, India League, London (1929–47). Borough Councillor for St. Pancras, London (1934–47). Indian High Commissioner in UK (1947–52). Delegate, UN General Assembly (1952–62). Minister without Portfolio (1956–57). Minister for Defence (1957–62).

MENON, V.P. (1894–1966). Reforms Commissioner (1942–47). Secretary Ministry of States (1947–51). Governor of Orissa, 1951. Founder member of the Swatantra Party.

MUKERJEE, AIR VICE-MARSHAL (LATER AIR MARSHAL) SUBROTO (1911–60). Commander, RIAF Station, Kalat, August 1943. Director of Training, Air Headquarters, 1946. Deputy Chief of Air Staff, 1951. Chief of Staff, IAF (1954–60).

NOEL-BAKER, (LORD), PHILIP (1889–1992). Professor of International Relations, University of London, (1924–29). Parliamentary Secretary, Ministry of War Transport (1942–45). Minister of State, Foreign Office (1945–46). Secretary of State for Air (1946–47). Secretary of State for Commonwealth Relations (1947–50). Minister of Fuel and Power (1950–51). Author of *The Arms Race: A Programme for World Disarmament*, 1958. Nobel Peace Prize, 1959.

NYE, LIEUTENANT-GENERAL (SIR) ARCHIBALD, MC (1895–1967). Enlisted in Ranks, British Army, 1914. Appointed 2nd Lt., 1915. General Staff Officer, War Office, London (1931–32 and 1936–37). Commander, Naoshera Brigade, 1939. Vice-Chief of the Imperial General Staff (1941–46). Governor of Madras (1946–48). UK High Commissioner in India (1948–52). UK High Commissioner in Canada (1952–56).

PATEL, (SARDAR) VALLABHBHAI (1875–1950). Barrister. President of Gujarat Provincial Congress Committee, 1921. Organised Bardoli peasant movement, 1928. President of Congress, 1931. Chairman, Congress Parliamentary Board, 1935. Member of the Interim Government (1946–47). Deputy Prime Minister and Minister for Home, States and Information and Broadcasting (1947–50).

PERRY-KEENE, AIR VICE-MARSHAL ALLAN (1898–1987). Director of Ground Training and Training Plans, UK Air Ministry (1943–45). Air Officer-in-charge, Administration, Air Headquarters, India, 1946. Air Commander, Royal Pakistan Air Force (1947–49).

PETHICK-LAWRENCE, (LORD), FREDERICK WILLIAM (1875–1961). Labour politician and prolific writer on mathematics, economics and politics; co-author of a book on Mahatma Gandhi. Financial Secretary to the Treasury (1929–31). Secretary of State for India and Burma (1945–47).

SCOONES, GENERAL (SIR) GEOFFREY ALLEN PERCIVAL, MC (1893–1975). Director of Military Operations and Intelligence, India (1941–42). GOC 4 Corps, Burma (1942–44). GOC-in-C, Central Command, India (1945–46). Principal Staff Officer, CRO (1947–53). UK High Commissioner in New Zealand (1953–57).

SHONE, (SIR) TERENCE ALLEN (1894–1965). Career diplomat. British Minister, Cairo, 1940. Minister to Syria and Lebanon (1944–46). UK High Commissioner in India (1946–48). Deputy Permanent Representative at the UN, 1948.

SINGH, (SARDAR) BALDEV (1901–61). Minister of Development, Punjab Government (1942–46). Member for Defence, Interim Government, 1946. Defence Minister (1947–52).

SINGH, LIEUTENANT-GENERAL, KALWANT (1905–66). Instructor, Staff College, Quetta (1941–43). Served in Burma and Thailand, 1945. Director of Military Training (August–November 1947). Commander, J&K Division (November 1947–January 1948). Commander J&K Force (January–May 1948). Chief of General Staff (1948–50). Corps Commander (1950–55).

THIMAYYA, MAJOR-GENERAL (LATER GENERAL) K.S. (1906–65). Commissioned, 1926. Kashmir (1947–50). Chairman, Neutral Nations Repatriation Commission for Korea (1953–54). Chief of Army Staff (1957–61). Died in air crash while commanding UN peace-keeping force in Cyprus, 1965.

WAVELL, FIELD MARSHAL (EARL), ARCHIBALD, MC (1883–1950). Commissioned, British Army, 1901. GOC-in-C, Southern Command (1938–39). Commander-in-Chief, Middle East (1939–41). Commander-in-Chief, India (1941–43). Viceroy and Governor-General (1943–47).

ZAFRULLA KHAN, (SIR) MUHAMMAD (1893–1985). Barrister. President, All-India Muslim League, 1931. Member, Viceroy's Executive Council (1935–41). Judge, Federal Court (1942–47). Foreign Minister of Pakistan (1947–54). Pakistan's Permanent Representative at UN (1961–64). President, UN General Assembly, 1962.

Endnotes

1. Introduction

1. Wavell to Pethick-Lawrence, 13 July 1946, forwarding paper No. C-in-C. Sectt./37/82 prepared by the Chiefs of Staff (India) Committee. Mansergh, N., Lumby, E.W.R. and Moon, E.P. (eds), *The Transfer of Power, 1942–47*, 1970–83, Vol. VIII, item 26, London: HMSO.
2. Ibid., item 254.
3. Monteath (Permanent Under-Secretary, India Office) to Machtig (Dominion Office), 8 November 1946. Mansergh et al., *Transfer of Power*, Vol. IX, item 17.
4. Minutes of the Cabinet India and Burma Committee meeting on 13 March 1946. Ibid., item 529.
5. Attlee to Mountbatten, 18 March 1947. Mansergh et al., *Transfer of Power*, Vol. VIII, item 543.
6. Monteath to Major General Hollis (Secretary, Chiefs of Staff Committee), 31 October 1946. Ibid., item 537.
7. Sargeant to Monteath, 7 December 1946. Mansergh et al., *Transfer of Power*, Vol. IX, item 173.
8. Note on Pethick-Lawrence's briefing to Dominion High Commissioners, 9 January 1947. Ibid., item 268.
9. Mountbatten's interview with Nehru, 24 March 1947. Mansergh et al., *Transfer of Power*, Vol. X, item 11.
10. Mountbatten's Interview with Liaquat Ali Khan, 11 April 1947., Ibid., item 126.
11. Viceroy's Personal Report dated 17 April 1947. Ibid., item 165.
12. Mountbatten's interview with Jinnah, 26 April and Viceroy's Personal Report dated 1 May 1947. Ibid., items 229 and 276.
13. Viceroy's Staff Meeting, 1 May 1947. Ibid., item 272.

14. British policy-makers regularly underestimated the new forces of secular nationalism in Asia, preferring to interpret events in terms of the supposed interests of diverse religious groupings. Events soon demonstrated the ignorance of this approach. For instance, Iran was among the countries which accorded early recognition to the State of Israel.
15. Minutes of Chiefs of Staff Committee Meeting on 12 May 1947. Mansergh et al., *Transfer of Power*, Vol. X, item 416.
16. Draft Memorandum from the Chiefs of Staff to the Ministry of Defence. Mansergh et al., *Transfer of Power*, Vol. XI, item 554.
17. See ibid., item 506 and Mansergh et al., *Transfer of Power*, Vol. XII, item 166.
18. Nehru's Interview with Lt. Gen. Sir A. Smith (C.G.S. and Deputy C-in-C), 13 July 1947. Ibid., item 88.
19. Nehru to Mountbatten, 11 July 1947. Ibid., item 69.
20. Mountbatten's Interview with Auchinleck, 15 July 1947. Ibid., item 113; also, M.N. Das, *Partition and Independence of India*, New Delhi: Vision Books, 1982, p. 180.
21. Minutes of the Meeting of the Provisional Joint Defence Council on 28 July 1947. Mansergh et al., *Transfer of Power*, Vol. XII, item 276.
22. Auchinleck to UK Chiefs of Staff, 28 October 1947, File L/WS/1/1138, India Office Records, London.

II. Junagadh—A Curtain Raiser

1. Menon, V.P., *The Story of the Integration of the Indian States*, Orient Longman, 1956, p. 127.
2. He conveyed this view to Liaquat Ali Khan. See his report to the King, cited in Hodson, H.V. *The Great Divide*, Hutchinson of London, 1969, p. 436.
3. Ismay's Memorandum to Mountbatten, 17 September 1947. *Mountbatten Papers* (micro-film). Roll 10, File 90-A, Nehru Memorial Library, New Delhi.
4. Menon, *Story of Integration*, p. 130.
5. Mountbatten's Report to the King, cited in Hodson, *Great Divide*, pp. 430–31. See also undated, unsigned draft in *Mountbatten Papers*. Roll 10, File 90-A, Nehru Memorial Library, New Delhi.
6. Cabinet decisions, 17 September 1947. *Mountbatten Papers*. Roll 10, File 90-A, Nehru Memorial Library, New Delhi.
7. The echo of Ismay's advice can be heard clearly in these words.
8. Cited in Hodson, *Great Divide*.
9. Record of the Governor-General's meeting with the Prime Minister, Deputy Prime Minister, etc. on 22 September 1947. *Mountbatten Papers*. Roll 10, File 90-A, Nehru Memorial Library, New Delhi. See also Menon, *Story of Integration*, pp. 136–37.
10. Joint letter to the Defence Minister, dated 27 September 1947. *Mountbatten Papers*. Roll 10, File 90-A, Nehru Memorial Library, New Delhi. Partly cited also in Hodson, *Great Divide*, pp. 432–33.

11. Nehru to Mountbatten, 28 September 1947. *Mountbatten Papers*. Roll 10, File 90-A, Nehru Memorial Library, New Delhi.

12. Lockhart to Nehru, 29 September 1947. *Mountbatten Papers*. Roll 10, File 90-A, Nehru Memorial Library, New Delhi.

13. The Supreme Commander presided over the division of military assets between India and Pakistan. He also exercised administrative control over British officers serving in the armed forces of India and Pakistan. In the latter capacity he was responsible for implementing the 'Stand Down' instructions. Auchinleck, the last Commander-in-Chief of the pre-independence Indian army, assumed the post of Supreme Commander for India and Pakistan on 15 August 1947.

14. Cited in Noel-Baker's minute to Attlee, 20 August 1948. (This minute includes an outline of developments concerning the Stand Down instructions.) File PREM 8/800, Public Records Office, London.

15. Record of Mountbatten's interview with Patel, 3 October 1947. Collins, L. and Lapierre, D., *Mountbatten and Independent India*, New Delhi: Vikas, 1985. p. 99.

16. Proceedings of the Defence Committee of the Indian Cabinet, 15 October 1947. *Mountbatten Papers*. File MSS Eur F200/246, India Office Records, London.

17. Hodson, *Great Divide*, p. 433.

18. Record of Mountbatten's meeting with Nehru, Patel and Ayyangar on 27 September; and Mountbatten's note on Junagadh dated 29 September 1947. *Mountbatten Papers*, Roll 90-A, Nehru Memorial Library, New Delhi.

19. Nehru's Note on Junagadh, 29 September 1947. *Mountbatten Papers*. Roll 90-A, Nehru Memorial Library, New Delhi.

20. Hodson, *Great Divide*, pp. 434–35.

21. Ibid., pp. 435–36.

22. Menon, *Story of Integration*, p. 140.

23. Liaquat Ali Khan to Nehru, 5 October (received 6 October) 1947. *Mountbatten Papers*. Roll 10. File 90-B, Nehru Memorial Library, New Delhi. Menon, *Story of Integration*, pp. 140–41.

24. Cited in Hodson, *Great Divide*, p. 437.

25. Extracts from minutes of the meeting of the Defence Committee on 30 October 1947. *Mountbatten Papers*. Roll 10, File 90-C, Nehru Memorial Library, New Delhi.

26. Cited in Menon, *Story of Integration*, pp. 142–43.

27. Ibid.

28. Hodson, *Great Divide*, p. 437.

29. Minutes of the Commonwealth Affairs Committee meeting on 13 October 1947. File CAB 134/54, Public Records Office, London.

30. Noel-Baker's minute to Attlee, 20 August 1948, outlining developments conveying the 'Stand Down' instructions. File PREM 8/800, Public Records Office, London.

III. Crisis in Kashmir

1. Jha, Prem Shankar, *Kashmir 1947*, Delhi: Oxford University Press, 1996 is a recent account drawing on the British archives.
2. Cited in M. Brecher, *The Struggle in Kashmir*, 1953, p. 4.
3. Cited in Sisir Gupta, *Kashmir: A Study of Indo-Pakistan Relations*, Bombay: Asia Publishing House, 1966. p. 62.
4. See Jha, *Kashmir 1947*, pp. 44–46.
5. Nehru to Patel, 27 September 1947. Durga Das (ed.), *Sardar Patel's Correspondence*, Ahmedabad: Navjivan Publishing House, 1971, Vol. 1, pp. 45–46. Also, *Selected Works of Jawaharlal Nehru*, Vol. 4, second series, New Delhi: Jawaharlal Nehru Memorial Fund, p. 263.
6. Patel to Maharaja of Kashmir, 3 July 1947, in Durga Das, *Correspondence*, pp. 32–33.
7. Patel to Mahajan, 21 October 1947, in ibid., p. 62.
8. Nehru to Mahajan, 21 October 1947. *Selected Works*, Vol. 4, p. 274.
9. Khan, Akbar, *Raiders in Kashmir—Story of the Kashmir War (1947–48)*, Karachi: Pak Publishers, 1970.
10. In the BBC programme (produced and directed by John Das), Shaukat Hayat Khan was asked the question: 'Did Jinnah actually say to you "invade Kashmir"?' Hayat Khan replied: 'Of course; no one could move, not a leaf could move, in those days without Jinnah's blessings.'
11. Grafftey-Smith to Noel-Baker, 9 October 1947. File L/PS/13/1845 b, India Office Records, London.

IV. The Defence of Srinagar

1. Batra to Patel, 3 October 1947. Durga Das, *Correspondence*, p. 48.
2. Patel to Baldev Singh, 7 October 1947, ibid., p. 57.
3. Minutes of the Defence Committee, 25 October, 1947. *Mountbatten Papers*. File MSS Eur F200/246, India Office Records, London.
4. *Mountbatten Papers*. File MSS Eur F200/246, India Office Records, London.
5. Campbell-Johnson A., *Mission with Mountbatten*, London: Robert Hale, 1951. Diary entry for 28 October 1947.
6. Nehru wanted the airforce to bomb the bridges at Muzaffarabad and Domel but was advised that this was not technically possible, given the types of aircraft available with the RIAF. He gave up the idea only after this assessment was confirmed by the senior-most Indian Air Force officer, Air Commodore Mukerjee (Nehru to Atal, 27 October 1947, *Selected works*, Vol. 4, p. 284).
7. Menon, *Story of Integration*, p. 379.
8. Note jointly signed by the Chiefs of the Indian Defence Services. Cited in ibid., p. 383.
9. Ibid., pp. 379–80.
10. The account of the meeting is based on the Minutes of the Defence Committee, 26 October, 1947. *Mountbatten Papers*, File MSS Eur F 200/246, India Office Records, London.

11. This was a surprising assessment considering the haste with which Menon himself had had to depart from Srinagar. He later wrote about the events of 25 October that the raiders were only a 'day or two' away from Srinagar. But Menon's assessment in the Committee served a good cause!
12. Hodson, *Great Divide*, p. 452.
13. Mountbatten to Patel, 27 October 1947. Durga Das, *Correspondence*, p. 68.
14. *Selected Works*, Vol. 4, p. 284.
15. Auchinleck to (UK) Chiefs of Staff, 28 October 1947, File L/P&S/13/1845b, India Office Records, London.
16. In August 1947 there were only fifty-six senior Pakistani officers ranked from Colonel to Major-General. Some 500 British officers served in the Pakistan army. (See Cloughley, Brian, *A History of the Pakistan Army*, 2nd edition, Karachi: Oxford University Press, p.2).
17. Hodson, *Great Divide*, p. 507.
18. For Lockhart's own account, see Major General Palit, D.K., *Major General A.A. Rudra*, New Delhi: Reliance Publishing House, 1997, pp. 328–30.
19. See *Selected Works*, Vol. 7, p. 284 and footnote and pp. 520–21 and footnote. See also Hodson, *Great Divide*, p. 446 (footnote) for a differing account.

V. Reactions in London

1. Nehru to Attlee, 25 October 1947, in *Selected Works*, Vol. 4, pp. 274–75.
2. Attlee to Nehru, 26 October 1947. File L/P&S/13/1845b, India Office Records, London.
3. Attlee to Liaquat Ali Khan, 20 October 1947. File L/P&S/13/1845b, India Office Records, London.
4. Nehru to Attlee, 27/28 October 1947, in *Selected Works*, Vol. 4, pp. 286–88a.
5. Nehru to Liaquat Ali Khan, 28 October 1947, in ibid., pp. 288a–89.
6. Attlee to Liaquat Ali Khan, 27 October 1947. File L/P&S/1845b, India Office Records, London.
7. Attlee to Nehru, 29/30 October 1947. File L/P&S/1845b, India Office Records, London. Also, see Jha, *Kashmir 1947*, p. 97.
8. Nehru to Attlee, 1 November 1947, in *Selected Works*, Vol. 4, pp. 302–04.
9. Noel Baker's handwritten note to Attlee on Nehru's telegram of 1 November, 1947. File L/P&S/1845b, India Office Records, London.
10. Alexander to Auchinleck (in reply to the latter's telegram dated 28 October 1947), File L/P&S/1845b, India Office Records, London.
11. Grafftey-Smith to CRO, 29 October 1947. File L/P&S/1845b, India Office Records, London.
12. Auchinleck to UK Chiefs of Staff, 30 October 1947. File L/P&S/1845b, India Office Records, London.
13. Ismay to Noel-Baker, 31 October 1947. File L/P&S/1845b, India Office Records, London.

14. Shone to Noel-Baker, 31 October 1947. File L/P&S/1845b, India Office Records, London.
15. Noel-Baker to Ismay, 'Private & Personal' telegram (through UKHC(I) 31 October 1947. File L/P&S/1845b, India Office Records, London.
16. 'Memorandum of Developments in Kashmir upto 31st October 1947', File L/P&S/1845b, India Office Records, London.
17. Attlee to Liaquat Ali Khan, 31 October 1947. File L/P&S/1845b, India Office Records, London.
18. This was suggested in the original draft telegram to Ismay, which was not issued as it failed to secure Attlee's approval. The draft is in File L/P&S/1845b, India Office Records, London.
19. Alexander to Auchinleck, 6 November 1947. File L/P&S/1845b, India Office Records, London.

VI. Jammu Province

1. Ministry of Defence, Government of India, *Operations in Jammu & Kashmir 1947–48*, New Delhi: GOI, 1987, p. 48.
2. Minutes of the Defence Committee meeting on 4 November 1947, as quoted in Mountbatten's letter to Nehru, dated 25 December 1947. Text of letter in telegram dated 28 December 1947 from Shone to CRO. File WS 17135, India Office Records, London.
3. Minutes of the Defence Committee meeting on 4 November 1947. *Mountbatten Papers.* File MSS Eur F 200/246, India Office Records, London.
4. Minutes of the Defence Committee meeting on 14 November 1947. *Mountbatten Papers.* File MSS Eur F 200/246, India Office Records, London.
5. GOI, *Operations*, pp. 51–52.
6. Nehru, J. *Letters to Chief Ministers 1947–64*, New Delhi: Jawaharlal Nehru Memorial Fund, 1985, Vol. 1, pp. 13–14.
7. GOI, *Operations*, pp. 52–54.
8. Ibid.
9. Telegram from UK High Commissioner in New Delhi to CRO, dated 28 October 1947. The telegram conveyed the text of Mountbatten's letter to Nehru, dated 25 December 1947. File L/WS/1/1139, India Office Records, London.
10. Nehru to Mountbatten, 26 December 1947, in *Selected Works*, Vol. 4, p. 400.

VII. The Governor-General as Mediator

1. Auchinleck to UK Chiefs of Staff, 28 October 1947. File L/P&S/13/1845b, India Office Records, London.
2. Campbell-Johnson, *Mission with Mountbatten*, pp. 226–27.
3. Nehru to Mahajan, 31 October 1947. *Selected Works*, Vol. 4, p. 293.
4. Nehru to Mahajan, 31 October 1947. Ibid., p. 294.

5. Mountbatten to Nehru, 2 November 1947 and enclosed note on conversation with Jinnah and Liaquat. In Durga Das, *Correspondence*, pp. 71–81.
6. Ibid.
7. Ibid.
8. Durga Das, *Correspondence*.
9. CRO to Grafftey-Smith, 6 November 1947. File L/P&S/13/1845b, India Office Records, London.
10. *Jawaharlal Nehru's Speeches*, Vol. 1, 2nd edition, New Delhi: Publications Division, Government of India, 1958, pp. 160–61.
11. Attlee to Nehru, 3 November 1947. File, L/P&S/13/1845b, India Office Records, London.
12. Liaquat Ali Khan to Attlee, 4 November 1947. File L/P&S/13/1845b, India Office Records, London.
13. File L/P&S/13/1845b, India Office Records, London.
14. Attlee to Liaquat Ali Khan, 6 November 1947. File L/P&S/13/1845b, India Office Records, London.
15. Letter dated 2 November 1947. Nehru, *Letters to Chief Ministers*, p. 9.
16. Mountbatten's note on his meeting with the Prime Ministers of India and Pakistan on 26 November. Collins and Lapierre, *Mountbatten*, pp. 218–21.
17. Mountbatten's note on his meeting with the Prime Ministers of India and Pakistan on November 27. Ibid., pp. 221–22.
18. Campbell-Johnson, *Mission with Mountbatten*, pp. 251–52. Hodson, *Great Divide*, pp. 461–62.
19. Mountbatten's note on his meeting with the Prime Ministers of India and Pakistan on 28 November 1947. Collins and Lapierre, *Mountbatten*, pp. 226–27.
20. Nehru to the Maharaja of Kashmir, 1 December 1947. *Selected Works*, Vol. 4, pp. 349–53.
21. Nehru to Liaquat Ali Khan, 3 December 1947. Ibid., p. 358.
22. Nehru to Maharaja of Kashmir, 3 December 1947. Ibid., p. 356.
23. The account which follows is based on the record of the meeting on 8–9 December 1947 (text in Collins and Lapierre, *Mountbatten*, pp. 230–41) and Mountbatten's own Report to the King (cited in Hodson, *Great Divide*, pp. 464–65).
24. Mountbatten reported to the King: 'Eventually, after trying every means I knew to find common ground between the two parties, I realised that the deadlock was complete, and that the only way out now was to bring in some third party in some capacity or other. For this purpose, I suggested that the United Nations Organisation should be called upon.' (cited in ibid., p. 465).

VIII. Military Plans

1. Nehru to Hiralal Atal, 27 October 1947. *Selected Works*, Vol. 4, pp. 283–84.
2. GOI, *Operations*, p. 65.

3. These concerns were reflected in the Joint Planning Staff paper on the overall military situation in India, dated 27 November 1947. See ibid., pp. 68–70.
4. Ibid., pp. 68–71.
5. Ibid., p. 65.
6. Minutes of the Defence Committee meeting on 28 November 1947. *Mountbatten Papers*. File MSS Eur F 200/246, India Office Records, London.
7. GOI, *Operations*, pp. 72–75.
8. Minutes of the Defence Committee meeting on 3 December 1947. *Mountbatten Papers*. File MSS Eur F 200/246, India Office Records, London.
9. GOI, *Operations*, p. 76.
10. Record of the Governor-General's interview with Mr. V.P. Menon and General Lockhart, 3 December 1947, in Collins and Lapierre, *Mountbatten*, p. 229. See also Hudson, *Great Divide*, p. 463. V.P. Menon's presence in the discussion with Lockhart reflected the overlapping loyalties of this remarkable civil servant who had made himself indispensable to both Mountbatten and Patel.
11. GOI, *Operations*, pp. 78–79.
12. Ibid., pp. 76–77.
13. Minutes of the meeting of the Defence Cornmittee, 5 Dec. 1947. *Mountbatten Papers*. File MSS Eur F 200/2461, India Office Records, London.
14. GOI, *Operations*, pp. 79–80.
15. Ibid., pp. 81–82.
16. Ibid., pp. 83–85.

IX. Counter-Attack or UN Appeal?

1. Nehru to Sheikh Abdullah, 4 November 1947. *Selected Works*, Vol. 4, p. 319.
2. Nehru's note on Kashmir dated 19 December 1947. Ibid., pp. 375–78.
3. Mountbatten to Nehru, 25 December 1947 (copy forwarded by Shone to CRO on 28 December 1947). File L/WS/1/1139, India Office Records, London.
4. Whitehall advised its High Commissioner in India on 29 December: 'If in fact war breaks out and the stand down order has to be issued, H.M.G. in the United Kingdom will of course have to consider whether they ought not to advise the King that it was no longer appropriate for a United Kingdom national to continue to hold the post of Governor-General of India.' File L/WS/1/1140, India Office Records, London.
5. Minutes of the Defence Committee's meeting on 20 December 1947. Mountbatten Papers. File MSS Eur F 200/246, India Office Records, London. According to the minutes of the Defence Committee's meeting on 20 December, the Committee 'directed the Chiefs of Staff to prepare a paper, on the assumption that the U.N.O. had given such a directive, setting out our plans for military operations to evict the raiders from their bases in Pakistan'. This failed to reflect accurately the sense of the Prime Minister's instructions. Nehru's letter of 26 December to Mountbatten, and his instructions to Bucher, contain no qualifying reference to an assumed UN directive. The minutes

appear to have been given a slant favoured by Mountbatten, the Committee's Chairman.

6. Nehru to Bucher, 26 December 1947. *Selected Works*, Vol. 4, p. 398.
7. Nehru's letters to Maharaja of Kashmir, 23 and 25 December 1947. Ibid., pp. 392–94.
8. Nehru to Liaquat Ali Khan, 22 December 1947. Ibid., pp. 391–92.
9. Nehru to Maharaja of Kashmir, 25 December 1947. Ibid., pp. 393–94.
10. The Commonwealth Relations Office anticipated that in the event of war breaking out, India would immediately demand the withdrawal of all British officers from the Pakistani army in order to cripple her adversary. This was conveyed to the US chargé d'affaires in London by Sir Paul Patrick of the CRO on 29 December. Patrick added that Britain would withdraw British officers from both armies as quickly as possible. Chargé d'affaires in UK to Secretary of State, 29 December 1947. *Foreign Relations of the United States*, Vol. 3, US Department of State, Washington D.C.: Government Printing Office, 1947, pp. 186–87.
11. Nehru to Patel, 29 December 1947. *Selected Works*, Vol. 4, pp. 411–12.
12. Mountbatten to Nehru, 25 December 1947 (copy forwarded by Shone to CRO through telegram dated 28 December 1947). File L/WS/1/1139, India Office Records, London.
13. Nehru to Mountbatten, 26 December 1947. *Selected Works*, Vol. 4, pp. 399–403.
14. Shone to CRO, two telegrams both dated 28 and telegram dated 29 December 1947. File L/WS/1/1139, India Office Records, London.
15. File L/WS/1/1139, India Office Records, London.
16. Shone to CRO, 28 December 1947. (This is a third cable of the same date.) File L/WS/1/1139, India Office Records, London.
17. Shone to CRO, 28 December 1947. (This is a fourth cable of the same date.). File L/WS/1/1139, India Office Records, London.
18. Nehru to Attlee, 28 December 1947. *Selected Works*, Vol. 4, pp. 406–7.
19. Attlee to Nehru, 29 December 1947. File L/WS/1/1140, India Office Records, London.
20. Chargé d'affaires in UK to Secretary of State, 29 December 1947. *Foreign Relations*, Vol. 3, pp. 186–87.
21. Chargé d'affaires in India to Secretary of State, 4 January 1948. *Foreign Relations*, 1948, Vol. 5, p. 270.
22. Shone to CRO, 30 December 1947. File L/WS/1/1140, India Office Records, London.
23. Text in Appadorai, A. *Selected Documents on India's Foreign Policy and Relations 1947–1972*, Vol. 1, Delhi: Oxford University Press, 1982.
24. Nehru to Baldev Singh, 24 January 1948. *Selected Works*, Vol. 5, p. 200.
25. Chargé d'affaires in India to Secretary of State, 2 January 1948. *Foreign Relations*, 1948, Vol. 5, p. 267.
26. Shone to CRO, 28 December 1947. (This is the same cable to which reference has been made at note 17 above.)

X. The Security Council

1. Noel-Baker to Shone, 27 December 1947. File L/WS/1/1139, India Office Records, London.
2. Ibid.
3. Sargent's minute to PM dated 6 January 1948. File FO 800/470, Public Records Office, London.
4. Kirkpatrick's minute to PM dated 13 January 1948 and Attlee's noting thereon of the same date. File FO 800/470, Public Records Office, London.
5. CRO to UK Delegation, New York, 3 January 1948. File L/WS/1/1140, India Office Records, London.
6. Secretary, Chiefs of Staff Committee to CRO. Letter No. COS 36/9/1/8 dated 9 January 1948. File L/WS/1/1148, India Office Records, London.
7. CRO to UKHC, New Delhi and Karachi, 15 January 1948. File L/WS/1/1140, India Office Records, London.
8. Attlee to Noel-Baker, 10 January 1948. File L/WS/1/1148, India Office Records, London.
9. Memorandum of Conversation between Noel-Baker and Lovett, 10 January 1948. *Foreign Relations*, Vol. 5, Pt. I, pp. 276–78. The discussion took place before Noel-Baker had received the comments of the Chiefs of Staff. Hence the reference to an 'international' force.
10. Secretary of State (Marshall) to US Representative (Austin) at UN, 14 January 1948. Ibid. pp. 280–82.
11. The source of this and further quotations in this chapter, where not specifically indicated otherwise, is Gupta, *Kashmir*, Chapter 7.
12. Austin to Marshall, 16 January 1948. *Foreign Relations*, Vol. 5, Pt. I, p. 283.
13. Austin to Marshall, 21 January 1948, and 28 January 1948. *Foreign Relations*, Vol. 5, Pt. I, pp. 285–86 & 291–94.
14. Nehru to Ayyangar, 23 January 1948. *Selected Works*, Vol. 5, p. 199.
15. Noel-Baker's speech and his reference to US position, SCOR, 240th meeting. See also Gupta, *Kashmir*, Chapter 7.
16. Memorandum on 'Private Discussions in New York of Detailed Plans for Settlement of Dispute', appended to Minutes of CAC meeting on 5 March, 1948. File CAB/134/55, Public Records Office, London.
17. Nehru to Ayyangar, 3 February 1948. *Selected Works*, Vol. 5, pp. 205–7.
18. Marshall to Austin, 20 February 1948. *Foreign Relations*, Vol. 5, Pt. I, pp. 301–2.
19. The US delegation made it clear to their British colleagues that this was the farthest they were prepared to go to accommodate the latter. Memorandum of Conversation, 27 February 1948. *Foreign Relations*, Pt. 1, pp. 306–7.
20. Marshall to the US Embassy in India, 25 February 1948. Ibid., pp. 304–6.
21. Memorandum of Conversation, 27 February 1948. Ibid., pp. 306–7.
22. Marshall to Austin, 20 February 1948. Ibid., p. 302.
23. Minute by F.K. Roberts (Foreign Office) to Dening (Foreign Office, 3 March 1948. File F800/470, Public Records Office, London.

24. Gordon-Walker to Carter, 1 February 1948. File L/WS/1/1148, India Office Records, London.
25. Nehru to Krishna Menon, 16 February 1948. Also Nehru to Vijayalakshmi Pandit, same date. *Selected Works*, Vol. 5, pp. 218–24. Nehru's initial reaction was reported by Gordon-Walker on 30 January 1948 (see *ibid.*, pp. 203–4)
26. Nehru to Atlee, 8 February 1948. Ibid., p. 211
27. Mountbatten to Attlee, 8 February 1948. File L/WS/1/1140, India Office Records, London.
28. Gordon-Walker's messages to Noel-Baker dated 21 and 22 February 1948. File L/WS/1/1140, India Office Records, London.
29. Minutes of CAC meeting on 27 February 1948. File CAB/134/55, Public Records Office, London.
30. Minutes of CAC meeting on 1 March 1948. File CAB/134/55, Public Records Office, London.
31. The Commonwealth Affairs Committee referred only to the 'Poonch area'. Draftsmen in the Commonwealth Relations Office expanded this to include Mirpur and even Muzaffarabad. The inclusion of Muzaffarabad was particularly significant since it would have the effect of denying India full control of the Jhelum valley.
32. File CAB/134/55, Public Records Office, London.
33. Minutes of CAC meeting on 5 March 1948. File CAB/134/55, Public Records Office, London.
34. File CAB/134/55, Public Records Office, London.
35. Foreign Office to UK delegation in New York, 6 March 1948. File L/WS/1/1151, India Office Records, London.
36. Marshall to Austin, 22 March 1948. *Foreign Relations*, Vol. 5, Pt. I, pp. 313–14.
37. Iengar, the Indian Foreign Secretary, lodged a complaint on this account with the UK High Commissioner. Shone to CRO, telegram No. 800 dated 31 March 1948. File L/WS/1/1141, India Office Records, London.
38. Nehru to Ayyangar, 1 April 1948. *Selected Works*, Vol. 5, p. 264.
39. Nehru to Ayyangar, 6 April 1948. Ibid. pp. 271–72.
40. Attlee to Noel-Baker, 1 April 1948. File FO 800/470, Public Records Office, London.
41. Noel-Baker to Attlee, 2 April 1948. FO 800/470, Public Records Office, London.
42. Attlee to Noel-Baker, 4 April 1948. FO 800/470, Public Records Office, London.
43. Noel-Baker to Attlee, 6 April 1948. FO 800/470, Public Records Office, London.
44. Attlee to Noel-Baker, 8 April 1948. FO 800/470, Public Records Office, London.

XI. A Private Initiative

1. Palit, *Major General Rudra*, pp. 328–30.
2. Report by the Military Advisor to the UK High Commissioner in New Delhi, dated 4 September 1948. File L/WS/1/1187, India Office Records, London.

3. Nehru to Krishna Menon, 20 February 1948. *Selected Works*, Vol. 5, p. 222.
4. Nye to CRO, 6 December 1948. File L/WS/1/1217, India Office Records, London.
5. UK HC, New Delhi to CRO, 16 February 1948. File L/WS/1/1141, India Office Records, London.
6. Nehru to Krishna Menon, 20 February 1948. *Selected Works*, Vol. 5, pp. 221–23.
7. GOI, *Operations*, pp. 96–101.
8. Record of the Governor-General's interview with Mr. V.P. Menon and General Lockhart on December 3, 1947. Collins and Lapierre, *Mountbatten*, p. 148.
9. Khanduri, Brigadier C.B., *Field Marshal Cariappa—His Life and Times*, New Delhi: Lancer, 1995, pp. 165–66.
10. Grafftey-Smith to CRO, repeated to Shone. Top Secret telegram No. 294, dated 26 March 1948. File L/WS/1/1141, India Office Records.
11. Shone to CRO, repeated to Grafftey-Smith. Top Secret telegram No. 770, dated 28 March 1948. File L/WS/1/1141, India Office Records, London.
12. Shone to CRO, 3 April 1948. File L/WS/1/1141, India Office Records, London.
13. File L/WS/1/1141, India Office Records, London.
14. Grafftey-Smith to CRO, 1 April 1948. File L/WS/1/1141, India Office Records, London.
15. CRO to UK High Commissioners in India and Pakistan, 30 March, 1948. File L/WS/1/1141, India Office Records, London.

XII. The Spring Offensive

1. Mountbatten was thinking of Hyderabad. He had just discovered that the Government of India had asked for plans to be drawn up for possible military action in Hyderabad.
2. Record of Governor-General's interview with General Gracey on May 2, 1948 in Collins and Lapierre, *Mountbatten*, pp. 292–94.
3. D.O. No. 6/C-in-C dated 5 May 1948. *Mountbatten Papers*. File 11B (microfilm), Nehru Memorial Library, New Delhi.
4. Campbell-Johnson, *Mission with Mountbatten*, pp. 322–23 and 325.
5. Minutes of the Defence Committee meeting on 13 May 1948, Mountbatten Papers, File MSS Eur F 200/246, India Office Records, London.
6. Shone to CRO, 14 May 1948. File L/WS/1/1142, India Office Records, London.
7. Communication from the Pakistani Commander-in-Chief to the Government of Pakistan, 20 April, 1948. Text in Hasan, K. Sarwar, (ed.), *The Kashmir Question*, Karachi: Pakistani Institute of International Affairs, 1966.
8. Referred to in UK High Commission, Karachi, to CRO, 6 May 1948. File L/WS/1/1142, India Office Records, London.
9. Shone to CRO, 4 May 1948. File L/WS/1/1142, India Office Records, London.
10. Grafftey-Smith, to CRO, 10 May 1948. File L/WS/1/1142, India Office Records, London.

11. US Ambassador in Pakistan to the Secretary of State, Washington, telegram dated 8 May 1948. *Foreign Relations*, Vol. 5, Pt. 1, pp. 340–41.
12. Note No. 15555 on '*Overall Appreciation of the Commitments of the Indian Army*,' dated 9 June 1948. *Mountbatten Papers*. File No. 12 (micro-film), Nehru Memorial Library, New Delhi.
13. Cabinet Secretariat (Military Wing), note No. DCC(48)/5 dated 11 June 1948. Mountbatten Papers. File No. 12 (Micro-film), Nehru Memorial Library, New Delhi.
14. GOI, *Operations*, p. 251.
15. Shone, to CRO. Telegram No. 2247 dated 12 July 1948. File L/WS/1/1142, India Office Records, London.
16. Symon to CRO, 26 July 1948. Repeated to UKHC, Karachi. File L/WS/1/1143, India Office Records, London.
17. File L/WS/1/1143, India Office Records, London.
18. Acting UK High Commissioner, Karachi, to CRO, 28 July 1948. Repeated to UK HC, New Delhi. File L/WS/1/1143, India Office Records, London.
19. Acting UK High Commissioner, Karachi, to CRO, 30 July 1948. Repeated UK HC, New Delhi. File L/WS/1/1143, India Office Records, London.
20. Sen, Lt. Gen. L.P., 1969, *Slender was the Thread—Kashmir Confrontation 1947–48*, Orient Longman, pp. 242–43.
21. Ibid., p. 239.
22. Letter dated 20 May 1948. Nehru, *Letters to Chief Ministers*.
23. UK High Commission, New Delhi, to CRO, 7 June 1948. File L/WS/1/1142, India Office Records, London.
24. UK High Commission, New Delhi, to CRO. Telegram No. 1804, MILSIT, 9 June 1948. File L/WS/1/1142, India Office Records, London.
25. UK High Commission, New Delhi, to CRO, 19 May 1948. File L/WS/1/1142, India Office Records, London.
26. Shone to CRO, 11 June 1948. File L/WS/1/1142, India Office Records, London.
27. General Scoones' note dated 1 June and Noel-Baker's minute dated 2 June 1948. File L/WS/1/1142, India Office Records, London.
28. Shone to CRO, telegram No. 2519 dated 28 July 1948. File L/WS/1/1143, India Office Records, London.
29. CRO to Grafftey-Smith, 5 May 1948. File L/WS/1/1143, India Office Records, London.
30. Note dated 29 July. File L/WS/1/1143, India Office Records, London.
31. Grafftey-Smith to CRO, 10 May 1948. File L/WS/1/1142, India Office Records, London.
32. The letter mentions that Nehru had denounced the Pakistani move as 'improper' and 'full of dangers' in a public speech on 6 June. Noel-Baker hints that the delay in India's reaction resulted from the nature of Bucher's conversations with his Pakistani counterpart in Kashmir.
33. Noel-Baker to Alexander, 15 June 1948. File L/WS/1/1142, India Office Records, London.

34. Grafftey-Smith to CRO, telegram No. 735 dated 8 July 1948. File L/WS/1/1142, India Office Records, London.
35. Grafftey-Smith to CRO, telegram No. 763 dated 15 July 1948, File L/WS/1/1143, India Office Records, London.
36. CRO to Grafftey-Smith, telegrams (2) dated 16 July 1948. File L/WS/1/1143, India Office Records, London.
37. Grafftey-Smith to CRO, 17 July 1948. File L/WS/1/1143, India Office Records, London.
38. CRO to Shone, telegrams dated 20 July, 26 July and 31 July 1948, respectively; Shone to CRO, 22 July 1948 and Symon to CRO 26 July 1948. File L/WS/1/1143, India Office Records, London.
39. Foreign Office to UK embassy in Washington, 12 July 1948. File L/WS/1/1153, India Office Records, London.
40. Attlee to Liaquat Ali Khan, 14 July 1948. File L/WS/1/1143, India Office Records, London.
41. Liaquat Ali Khan to Attlee, 20 July 1948. File L/WS/1/1143, India Office Records, London.
42. Attlee to Liaquat Ali Khan, 23 July 1948, cited in Noel-Baker's minute to Attlee dated 20 August 1948. File PREM 8/800, CRO.
43. Noel-Baker to UK High Commissioners in New Delhi and Karachi, 5 August 1948. File L/WS/1/1143, India Office Records, London.
44. Noel-Baker to UK High Commissioners in New Delhi and Karachi, 9 August 1948. File L/WS/1/1143, India Office Records, London.
45. Noel-Baker's minute to Attlee, 20 August, 1948. File PREM 8/800, CRO.
46. Attlee to Nehru, 23 August 1948. File L/WS/1143, India Office Records, London.

XIII. The UN Commission for India and Pakistan

1. Secretary of State to US Embassy in Pakistan, 12 May 1948. *Foreign Relations*, 5 Pt. II, pp. 341–42.
2. Lord Inverchapel (British Ambassador in Washington) to Foreign Office, 10 May and 12 May, 1948. File L/WS/1/1152, India Office Records, London.
3. Foreign Office to British Embassy Washington, 27 May 1948. File L/WS/1/1152, India Office Records, London.
4. Foreign Office to British Embassy, Washington. Telegram No. 6088 dated 5 June 1948. File L/WS/1/1152, India Office Records, London.
5. Foreign Office to British Embassy, Washington. Telegram No. 6106 dated 5 June 1948. File L/WS/1/1152, India Office Records, London.
6. Korbel, Josef *Danger in Kashmir*, New Jersey: Princeton University Press, p. 121.
7. Ibid.
8. Korbel, *Danger in Kashmir*, p. 124.
9. Nehru to Sheikh Abdullah, 25 August 1952. *Selected Works*, Vol. 19.
10. Korbel, *Danger in Kashmir*, p. 134.
11. Ibid., p. 140.

XIV. Limited Offensives

1. Brigadier Walker, UK High Commission, Karachi, to Major-General Rodman, DMO, War Office, London, letter No. 1039/MA dated 24 September 1948. File L/WS/1/1187 (WS 17169 Pt. I), India Office Records, London. This important document also reveals that, in the early days of the Kashmir conflict, General Gracey had informed Nazimuddin, then Chief Minister of East Pakistan, that the battle for East Pakistan would have to be fought in West Punjab!

2. Acting UK High Commissioner, Karachi, to CRO, 22 September 1948. File L/WS/1/1144, India Office Records, London.

3. GOI, *Operations*, pp. 276–77.

4. Nye to CRO (repeated UKHC, Karachi), 5 November 1948. File L/WS/1/1144, India Office Records, London.

5. Nye to CRO (repeated UKHC, Karachi), 12 November 1948. File L/WS/1/1144, India Office Records, London.

6. Nehru to V.K. Krishna Menon, 18 November 1948. *Selected Works*, Vol. 8, p. 46.

7. Noel-Baker's record of his conversation with Cawthorn, 18 September 1948. File PREM 8/997, Public Relations Office, London.

8. 'L.N.H.' to Cumming-Bruce, 26 September 1948. Also, extract from Minutes of C.O.S. (48) 136th Meeting, 24 September 1948. File PREM 8/997, Public Relations Office, London.

9. Liaquat Ali Khan to Attlee, 11 November 1948. File L/WS/1/1144, India Office Records, London.

10. A.H. Reed, Rawalpindi to S.J.L. Olver, Karachi. Letter dated 26 October 1948. File L/WS/1/1188 (WS 17169/II), India Office Relations, London.

11. Captain Mc Cullough's report on his tour to Rawalpindi. Forwarded by Brigadier Walker, UK High Commission, Karachi, to Major-General Rodman, War Office, London. Letter dated 30 October 1948. File L/WS/1/1188 (WS 17169/II), India Office Records, London.

12. Liaquat Ali Khan to Noel-Baker, 3 July 1949; Addison to Liaquat Ali Khan, 12 August 1949; and Liaquat Ali Khan to Noel-Baker, 11 November 1949. File PREM 8/997, Public Relations Office, London.

13. Grafftey-Smith to CRO, 29 November 1948. File L/WS/1/1144, India Office Records, London.

14. Grafftey-Smith to CRO (repeated UKHC, New Delhi). Telegram dated 4 November 1948. File L/WS/1/1144, India Office Records, London.

15. Grafftey-Smith CRO (repeated UKHC, New Delhi). Telegram dated 5 November 1948. File L/WS/1/1144, India Office Records, London.

16. Note recorded by 'B.G.S.' dated 20 November 1948. File L/WS/1/1144, India Office Records, London.

17. Grafftey-Smith to Laithwaite, CRO. Letter dated 6 December 1948. File L/WS/1/1145, India Office Records, London.

18. Nye to CRO (repeated UKHC, Karachi), 19 November 1948, File L/WS/1/1144, India Office Records, London.
19. Nye to CRO, 24 November 1948. File L/WS/1/1144, India Office Records, London.
20. GOI, *Operations*, p. 256.
21. Quoted in ibid., p. 264.

XV. The Last Round

1. Grafftey-Smith to CRO. Telegram No. 1395 dated 18 November 1948. File L/WS/1/1144, India Office Records, London.
2. Grafftey-Smith to CRO. Telegram No. 1396 dated 18 November 1948. File L/WS/1/1144, India Office Records, London.
3. File L/WS/1/1144, India Office Records, London.
4. File L/WS/1/1144, India Office Records, London.
5. CRO to UKHC(P), telegram dated 20 November 1948. File L/WS/1/1144, India Office Records, London.
6. Message conveyed in UKHC(P) to CRO, telegram dated 17 November 1948. File L/WS/1/1144, India Office Records, London.
7. Attlee to Liaquat Ali Khan, 18 November 1948. File L/WS/1/1144, India Office Records, London.
8. Attlee's message is quoted in Nehru's letter of 18 November, 1948, to Krishna Menon. *Selected Works*, Vol. 8, p. 47.
9. File L/WS/1/1144, India Office Records, London. Date not available. See also Nehru to G.S. Bajpai, 23 November 1948. *Selected Works*, Vol. 8, pp. 51–52.
10. Nye to CRO. Telegram No. 4018 dated 19 November 1948. File L/WS/1/1144, India Office Records, London.
11. Nehru to Krishna Menon, 18 December 1948. *Selected Works*, Vol. 8, p. 77.
12. Nye to CRO, 22 November 1948. File L/WS/1/1144, India Office Records, London.
13. Nye to CRO, 26 November 1948. File L/WS/1/1144, India Office Records, London.
14. Nehru to Bucher, 24 November 1948. *Selected Works*, Vol. 8, p. 87.
15. Grafftey-Smith to CRO, 27 November 1948. File L/WS/1/1144, India Office Records, London.
Bucher had succeeded in persuading the Indian government that the aircraft were not needed. '[We] are withdrawing part of our Air Force from Kashmir simply because there is no present use for it there', Nehru informed Bajpai on November 24. *Selected Works*, Vol. 18, p. 57.
16. Grafftey-Smith to CRO. Telegram No. 1461 dated 29 November 1948. File L/WS/1/1144, India Office Records, London.
17. Brig. Walker, Karachi, to Major General Rodman, D.M.O. Letter No. 1039/MA dated 20 November 1948. File L/WS/1/1188, India Office Records, London.

18. Grafftey-Smith to CRO. Telegram No. 1461 dated 29 November 1948. File L/WS/1/1144, India Office Records, London.
19. Conveyed through UKHC(P) telegram to CRO, 8 December 1948. File L/WS/1/1145, India Office Records, London.
20. UK High Commission, Karachi, Opdom No. 47 for 3–9 December 1948. File L/WS/1/1599, India Office Records, London.
21. Birdwood, Lord, *Two Nations and Kashmir,* London: Robert Hale, 1956, p. 72.
22. Nye to CRO, 18 December 1948. File L/WS/1/1145, India Office Records, London.
23. Message to C.R. Attlee, 20 December 1948. *Selected Works,* Vol. 9, p. 204.
24. Birdwood, *Two Nations,* p. 73.
25. Nye to CRO, repeated UKHC(P). Telegram dated 17 December 1948. File L/WS/1/1145, India Office Records, London.
26. UKHC(I) to CRO, Telegram No. 4346 dated 18 December 1948. File L/WS/1/1145, India Office Records, London.
27. Nye to CRO, repeated UKHC(P), Karachi. Telegram dated 22 December 1948. File L/WS/1/1145, India Office Records, London.
28. Nye to CRO, 18 December 1948. File L/WS/1/1145, India Office Records, London.
29. Grafftey-Smith to CRO, 19 December 1948. File L/WS/1/1145, India Office Records, London.
30. Noel-Baker to Nye/Grafftey-Smith, 20 December 1948. File L/WS/1/1145, India Office Records, London.
31. According to British records, in December 1948, some 440 British officers served in executive positions in the Pakistani army. In the Indian army, only three British officers held executive posts, while 227 were employed as advisers. (Extract from Record of the COS Committee Meeting on 20 November 1948. File L/WS/1/1153, India Office Records, London).
32. Nehru's message to Attlee dated 20 December 1948. *Selected Works,* Vol. 9. pp. 203–4.
33. Attlee to Nehru, 23 December 1948. File L/WS/1/1145, India Office Records, London.
34. Nye to CRO, 9 December 1948. File L/WS/1/1145, India Office Records, London.
35. Text of Attlee's message to Liaquat Ali Khan in telegram from CRO to UKHC(P) dated 15 December 1948. File L/WS/1/1145, India Office Records, London.
36. Unsigned note at p. 90. File L/WS/1/1145, India Office Records, London.
37. Nehru to Bucher, 29 December 1948. *Selected Works,* Vol. 9, p. 210.

XVI. Ceasefire

1. Foreign Office to UK Embassy in Washington, 9 November 1948. File L/WS/1/1153, India Office Records, London.

2. Memorandum of Conversation by Secretary of State, 10 November 1948. *Foreign Relations*, 5, Pt. 1, pp. 445–46.
3. Lovett to US delegation, 11 November 1948 and Marshall to Lovett, 13 November 1948. Ibid., pp. 448–50.
4. Liaquat Ali Khan to Zafrulla Khan, telegram No. 4526 dated 17 November 1948, as re-transmitted in telegram No. 460 dated 19 November 1948 from UK delegation to Foreign Office. File L/WS/1/1153, India Office Records, London.
5. Huddle to Secretary of State, 20 November 1948. *Foreign Relations*, Vol. 5, Pt. 1, pp. 454–55.
6. Ibid.
7. Acting Secretary of State (Lovett) to US delegation, 19 November 1948. Ibid., p. 452.
8. Henderson to Marshall, 20 November 1948. Ibid., pp. 453–54.
9. Marshall to the Acting Secretary of State (Lovett), 20 November 1948. Ibid., pp. 455–56.
10. Dulles to Marshall, 23 November 1948. *Foreign Relations*, 5, Pt. 1, pp. 459–60. Dulles became the Acting Chairman of the US delegation in Paris on Marshall's departure for Washington 21 November. Since he was later to gain notoriety for his description of non-alignment as 'immoral', some Indian readers might be bemused by his sympathetic stand in 1948, which contrasted sharply with the British position. It must not be forgotten that in 1948, Britain—not the United States—had primary 'responsibility' for Middle East defence. When the United States took over the task of organising defence pacts for the Middle East in the early 1950s, the American and British roles in the subcontinent were also reversed, with the former taking the lead in pressing for a pro-Pakistan policy.
11. Dulles to the Secretary of State, 26 November 1948. *Foreign Relations*, p. 463.
12. On 22 March, 1949, the UN Secretary-General, in consultation with the governments of India and Pakistan, appointed Admiral Chester Nimitz of the US Navy as the Plebiscite Administrator. General Eisenhower was not available.
13. Nye to CRO, 6 December 1948. File L/WS/1/1217, India Office Records, London.
14. Nehru to Sheikh Abdullah, 25 August 1952. *Selected Works*, Vol. 19, pp. 322–25.
15. Ibid.
16. Nye to CRO, 29 December 1948. File L/WS/1/1145, India Office Records, London.

Index

About the Author

C. Dasgupta had a distinguished career in the Indian Foreign Service. He served as India's Ambassador to China (1993–96) and the European Union (1996–2000). Apart from international relations, his interests include modern history and global environmental issues. This is his first book.